Distance in our blood

Distance in our blood

Marc Rogatschnig

Dear Sandra! Al
All our relationships
define our journeys;
I hope you enjoy it,
Love Marc

First edition 2016

ISBN 978-0-620-70712-1
eISBN 978-0-620-70713-8

Published by Author using Reach Publishers' services,
P O Box 1384, Wandsbeck, South Africa, 3631

Printed and bound by Novus Print Solutions

Edited by Bronwen Brickerton for Reach Publishers

Website: www.reachpublishers.co.za
E-mail: reach@webstorm.co.za

Reach
PUBLISHERS

Cover designed by Shaune Rogatschnig

To my wife Shaune for the hand and heart that eventually healed me.

To my mother for raising me to be the man I am today.

For my children, Bailey and Payton, that you may be inspired to live fully.

For my brother who helped me to value family roots.

And to my father, who unwittingly gave me the gift of myself. He was a man I wanted to love, needed love from, but struggled to like.

Contents

The End, Almost

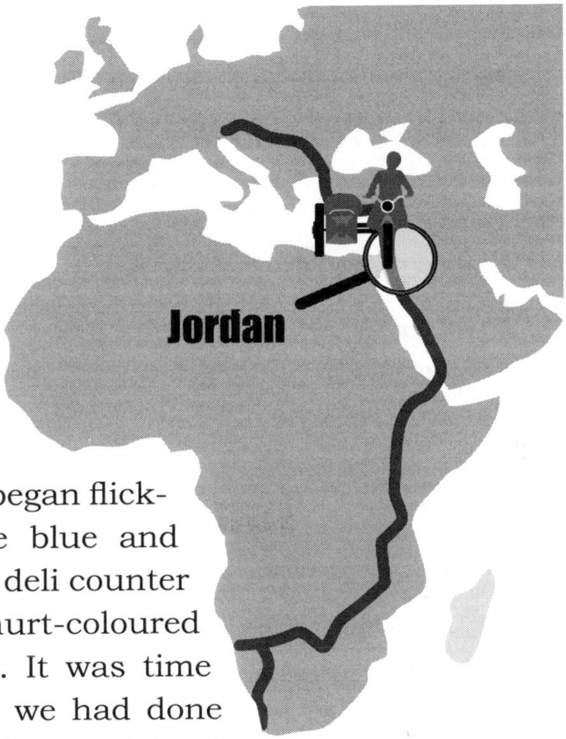

Fluorescent lights began flickering to life. The blue and white tiles behind the deli counter lost their cool, yoghurt-coloured modesty in the glare. It was time to go again, just like we had done each of the 12 days since arriving in Jordan. We finished our spicy falafels as we exited onto the freshly-wet pavement, and walked up the winding track back to our hotel. The Amman skies were a patchwork splatter of pink and blue. The white haze had promised clouds all afternoon. As the sun beamed a last ray across the horizon, it lifted those faint puffs of vapour from their nondescript form, and released delicate plumes of cumulus that floated across the sky like pink lanterns. It was a peaceful night. The fir trees stood still and stark against the white-walled homes, like vinyl stickers perfectly cut to shape. The light made everything look manicured and fake, as if made from factory-moulded plastic. The cars, the light posts, they all looked two dimensional, more like in a painting than reality. Twilight can be magical in that way, giving permission for reality to momentarily shift in shape. Looking at those trees I was reminded that, even in the desert towns of the Middle East, it must rain sometimes. *That must be special*, I thought.

Back at our room, we headed out to the balcony to watch the world go to sleep beneath the star-filled sky. It remained quiet, but our height and the buffer of cloud made all and any sound richer and fuller as it bounced around us. We could hear TVs, children playing, people walking in the streets below, doors closing, dogs barking and the last of the bird songs. I almost began to feel like I was on holiday, as if we were truly relaxed, escapees of our anguish and frustration. That thought began to calm my underlying anxiety about the next chapter of our trip across the Red Sea to Africa.

'Police! Police! Open this door!' ordered a deep male voice, 'Open it right now!'

We were startled but unmoved. It was more the fact he was speaking in English that pricked my ears to attention.

'Police! Open! Now!' came the voice again, more forceful than before. Closer too.

'Is that coming from our door, Papa?' I asked.

'I don't think so,' shrugged my dad, leaning over the railing and peeping into the apartments below.

'But they are speaking in English?'

'Umm true, but it's none of our business, it really isn't.'

'I'll go and have a look down the passage to see what is going on.'

We both turned and I walked back into the room. I leaned towards the door and held my finger to my lips.

'Open this door! This is the police!' bellowed another voice, more agitated than the first. 'This is your *final* warning, and we *will* push your door open.'

'They are definitely very near to us…' I paused and shuffled closer, 'I think they are behind this door in fact.'

I could hear movement and scuffling, even the odd whisper. There was one person speaking, but he was clearly not alone.

'Maybe it's the room across the corridor,' said Papa.

I wanted to have a look and twisted the key to release the bolt. Suddenly, as if spring-loaded, our door was forced open and a small army of men stormed in. They were heavily armed, with greyish berets and black uniforms. The silver of their belt buckles and lapel stars competed with the iron muzzles for our attention. They swept their guns across our chests and shoved us forcefully away from them. We instinctively retreated back to the veranda door, but stopped short of exiting the room. Two men with pistols checked the bathroom and shook their heads at the leader standing his ground. His gun was pointing straight at me when he raised his eyes away from the sight of his rifle.

'You come with us,' he ordered calmly, 'you are under arrest, *yala!*'

'Can we help you? What is wrong?' asked Papa. 'This must be a mistake? What is going on?'

'I tell you already; you are under arrest and *must* come with us right now. Right now, and no more questions!' stamped the leader.

'Arrest? But for what? You have the wrong people,' Papa began to sound dangerously argumentative. I couldn't take my eyes off the barrel that was boring my chest. 'This is a misunderstanding, our names are ...'

'Silence!' the leader commanded and stepped forward. He glared at us and pushed his rifle forward with vigour. Each syllable was punctuated by a stab of his weapon, 'No more questions mister. You are Mr Hans Ro...Rogush.'

'Rogatschnig,' I said out of habit.

'You are a very sick man mister and you *must* now come

with us.'

It all happened so quickly. Throughout the arrest, none of them wanted to touch or get close to us. They used a baton to prod and push us around, like cattle driven to the stables. They were nervous and belligerent, a combination of emotions that rattled me every time a cold firearm touched my skin. It took my breath away.

Night had fallen and it was pitch black in the van. They handcuffed us with old-style shackles to a central pillar that was bolted to the roof and the floor. Only the two of us sat in the back. There was an unmistakably stale human smell, which made our noses sting. The only way we could sit was opposite each other, on hard, bowed, wooden benches that bounced with every movement. We were forced to lean forward and rest our palms on the pole. It was painfully uncomfortable.

They drove at high speed through the streets of Amman. No sirens blared, but they were in a hurry. I focused my attention on a small mesh window about the size of a postcard behind my dad's head. I tried to identify landmarks along the way. I was hoping to keep my bearings so we at least knew where we were headed, but it was too dark and I was lost after the third turn.

'If we crash, we will die a painful death,' said Papa.

'*Shit* this is all crazy, what the hell is going on?'

'They must have the wrong people, they must have a reason.'

'But for what? We've done nothing.'

We were both launched off our seats as the driver clipped a pavement.

'If we crash, we will definitely be killed … crushed … burned,' he despaired, 'to be tied like this in a crash? *Shit* man, what the hell is going on!'

For the first time that evening my dad broke his calm,

elder disposition and showed anger. And helplessness. I tried to douse the image of us rolling in the back of the pickup as we were engulfed by flames. I couldn't ignore the fact of no probable escape. Through the small window I saw white light cast over the landscape, there was more sand than anything else. I couldn't make out if they were street lights or large spotlights. Or even stadium lights, they were that bright. I could then see a long row of palm trees on our left, and then a winding road which guided our driver through the gates of a large multistorey building. It had all the grandeur of an official structure. It was the central police station of Jordan, the headquarters. I felt a chill run down my body. As the central police station, the rows of concrete barriers and barbed wire gave it away. Those places, in third world countries, were not always places of safety.

The men who opened the back of the vehicle were again visibly uncomfortable being close to us. They gestured and barked orders. One brave soul actually touched my hands as he unlocked the cuffs. He recoiled like a cobra when he felt my warm skin. We were led into a long entrance room with a heavy, dark-varnished wooden counter. They snatched our passports from us and we were separated, my dad to the one end of the waiting area and I to the other. It felt like we were continents adrift.

They started with me. It was an interrogation. A barrage of questions followed: 'What were we doing in Jordan?'; 'Where were we going next?'; 'Who had we befriended?'; 'Who had we spent time with?'; 'Did we have any friends who were Jordanians?'; 'Did we live with any Jordanians?'; 'How had we ended up there?'; 'And what was the purpose of our visit?' It was relentless and haphazard and their broken English made it cumbersome too.

They tried to piece together a trail of the places and

people we had interacted with, but I could see they didn't believe me. They couldn't grasp the idea of the motorbikes and kept asking if they could see them. The more I explained they had been shipped to Africa, the more they couldn't understand. The suspicion on both sides escalated. I began to seethe.

'Why ship them, why not drive them?' They kept asking.

The bikes became a focal point of their wariness. They were trying to crack us to reveal something we were doing that might be underhanded, illegal, illicit, and maybe even immoral. The more answers I gave, the more agitated they became. It was difficult to explain we hadn't chosen Amman as a destination, but were forced to be there due to the bikes. They didn't believe that either. A few of them kept shuttling between the two conversations, whispering into the interrogator's ears. They then started booking me, filling out an official charge sheet. After 45 minutes, they discovered I was the wrong Rogatschnig. They asked me more than five times what my first names were. I looked into my lap, trying to hide my contempt. I wanted to laugh at them. It felt like a victory; that I had wasted their time was probably the only recourse we had at that point. Little things when one feels shamed and powerless.

We still didn't know officially why we were there, and part of me hung onto a belief we would be released that night. That it was all a mistake, or a precaution, or just not happening. A large clock hung above a filing cabinet behind the counter. It was close to midnight by the time the official paperwork had been done. Throughout the ordeal, we were the only people there.

'Come with us now,' beckoned an elderly officer from behind the counter. He slowly began to unlock a thick, vault-like door.

'What's happening?' I asked my dad, knowing he wouldn't have an answer. 'Are we staying here?'

I had thought we might leave via the front door, but we were herded through the back. We walked over a landing between two buildings and entered the next windowless structure through a narrow metal door. There were holding cells lining both sides of a dank and dreary corridor. We unexpectedly took a sharp right turn at the entrance and proceeded up a spiralling staircase which led to another door. Behind that door was a cell, with bars across the small windows. The entire room was covered with small blue and white tiles. It was shiny, clean and cold, like an abattoir, or our falafel deli. In the centre was another shackling pole and a bright fluorescent light was caged to the roof.

'You are under arrest Mr Hans,' blurted the police officer through his stately moustache. 'You will be deported tomorrow.'

They dumped my dad on the floor and threw his small bag in behind him. They pushed him, and one of his knees gave way. He hit the tiles and sprawled into the corner of the room. My handler dug his knee into my thigh to stop my attempt to help him. There was no bed, no toilet, and no tap. Just blinding whiteness.

'In my country, all the people with this sickness, we send them to camps in the desert,' continued the officer. 'You are lucky to not be going there, those are very bad places.'

I was prevented from saying a proper goodbye. I could only straighten my fist momentarily. They blocked the door and then pushed me back down the stairs. The last thing I saw was him, crumpled in the corner, and then slip as he tried to get a grip against the tiles. I just wanted to hug him. I needed to touch him.

'Marc, if they send me away,' he called as the dented cell door was closing, 'I will try to get them to send me to Ethiopia and not Austria, come and ...'

The cell door slammed shut and I almost tripped off the lip of the first step. I heard my dad's muffled voice but couldn't make out what he was saying. Then it went silent and I was ordered to leave. My protestations were ignored. My body went numb and I was bullied away.

Reality dawned on me as I climbed back into the police van to return to the hotel. Alone. That was not what I had signed up for. Granted, for me the trip had originally been about unbridled adventure. It was about doing what almost every boy dreamed of: crossing continents on steel horses. It was about randomly rolling down the maps of Europe, the Middle East and Africa, like a drop of water turning and stopping on its way down a misted window pane. Adventure had no specific definition for me when we had started out. I imagined near misses, long curious searches, and encounters with intriguing people and customs. It all became real when the law turned against us.

For my dad, it was always about being contrary and about proving this trip of epic proportions was possible. It was also a convenient way to celebrate the turn of the Millennium, the year 2000. The probable failure and toils of travel were stacked against us, but we would also be the first to have done it on those motorbikes, at least that is what we believed. It was that ambition that seemed to literally drive my dad across the world.

From the day we left middle Europe, so much adventure had already become a norm. It had faded into the realm of the expected. All that changed that night. The trip inevitably became more about my father and me and, in the end, it became all about me, alone in my journey.

Nothing could have prepared me for what happened that night in Amman, or indeed the way it all ended at the very southern tip of Africa.

The Invitation

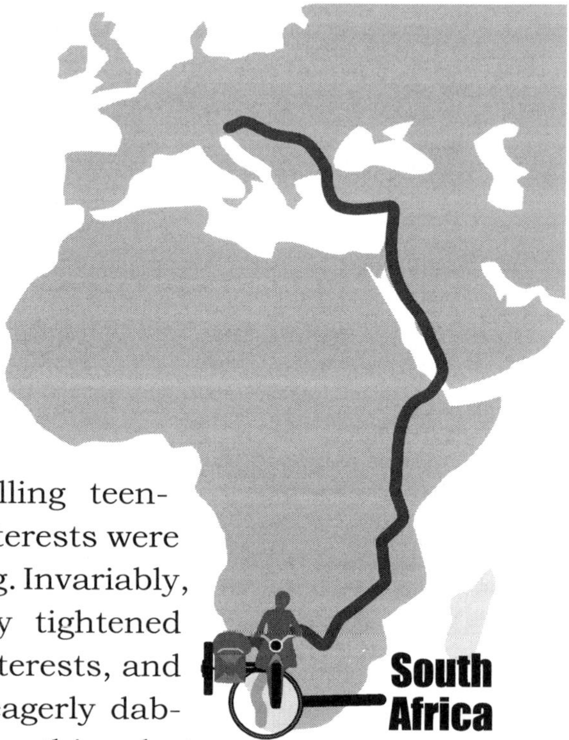

During my spiralling teenage years, my interests were numerous and fleeting. Invariably, boredom prematurely tightened the noose on these interests, and I would move on. I eagerly dabbled in pretty much anything, but stuck to very little for any meaningful amount of time. There were spells when it was all sports, then politics, languages, and outliers such as ancient history and cheese making. There was even a peculiar interest in thick, syrupy varieties of alcohol. The latter being more as a budding connoisseur of liqueur than the shelf-wrecking escapades of a truant youth. I admit that was a fine line to dance at times.

Despite all these diverse hobbies, I had never nurtured an interest in travel. The simple explanation is we weren't a family that travelled. We roamed within a tight radius of Cape Town, and rarely scaled the mountains that circled the city. But in late high school a friend and I made a typically adolescent pact. We promised each other to spend a year in Europe after we graduated. I never believed it would actually happen, but sure enough, in 1994, as autumn malted, I tentatively stumbled and backpacked across the western hemisphere for eleven exhilarating months. In between bully beef and tent pegs, overnight train rides and free-loading sofa stints, I unearthed more than a passing curiosity for travel. I was intoxicated by the freedom.

I was so addicted to road tripping that, in 1995, at the end of my first year of university, I went to the bank with an elaborate story which pivoted on a blatant lie. I convinced them my errant father had reneged on his commitment to pay the last instalment of my university fees, and that threatened to block me from passing that year. It was loaded with equal parts sob and charm. Astonishingly, the bank believed me. I immediately drew the cash and, with three friends, bought a 25-year-old Series 2 Land Rover. We laboured out of Cape Town on the last day of our exams and spent three months bouncing around southern Africa. It was pure bliss and an adventure replete with knuckle-whitening danger and blistered, sun-soaked skin. It altered my view of possibility and delivered my emerging manhood. I became particularly obsessed with travel in Africa. Year after year, I headed off while the ink on my exam papers was still drying and consequently missed all three of my university graduations. Travel adventure surged through my veins. It left a stubborn mark on who I was and what I valued. There was no doubt, pushing beyond and into new terrain would remain an inevitable, lifelong chase.

The timeline of my young adult life is defined according to the trips I notched up; Europe/US '94, Africa South '96, Namibia/Botswana '97. The list went on. Strangely however, I don't recall the exact date of a significant, late summer evening. We had prepared a light meal with the last rays of sun peeking through our windows before it slipped behind Table Mountain. It was just my brother, my mother and I at the table when the phone rang, which it didn't often do. But that raised no particular interest or alarm in any of us.

My brother was closest and answered the call. The surprise in his voice hushed our conversation instantly.

'Hi Papa,' he said with boyish exuberance, 'Wow, nice to hear from you! How are you?'

It was my dad. He called maybe twice a year, usually on our birthdays, sometimes at Christmas, and on occasion at New Year. That day was a random day, with no particular significance. Something was up.

I leaned closer to the phone and watched my brother as he listened for about a minute. He stood there patiently deciphering the broken English on the other end of the line. His eyebrows rose and fell in a random sequence. He smiled, then grimaced, and eventually shook his head. His eyes were wide when he handed me the phone.

'You have to listen to this. He wants to ask you too.'

'Hi Papa,' I said tentatively. As always, when talking to him, I was nervous.

He cut straight to it, without pleasantries.

'I was just asking your brother the same thing,' his strong Germanic accent crackled over the line. 'Do you want to come from Austria to Cape Town with me? I have found a motorbike from the Ukraine and I want to drive it down Africa.'

Thud! That was how the invitation landed in the deepest parts of my brain. It jolted me and was so startling all I could focus on was the smell of burning onion. I squinted into the last golden rays that slipped between the trees. My brother was staring at me with anticipation; my bewildered mom's jaw dropped ever lower. The sizzle of the scorched pan was the only background noise to my racing thoughts. I didn't know what to say.

'So what do you think?' he asked, after a short silence. 'You want to come on a trip with me? It's a motorbike with a sidecar and if we do it, I think we will be the first to have ever done it on these bikes down Africa.'

'Wow,' was all I could say.

'I was thinking maybe you do Austria to Nairobi and Daniel does the rest to Cape Town. You have travelled so much in southern Africa, so maybe you can do the northern hemisphere. You know what I mean?'

'When are you thinking of doing this?' I asked, trying to find my bearings within more details.

'Well, we will do it next year for the Millennium. The year 2000. We will aim to be in Cape Town for New Year's Eve.'

'When do you want to leave?'

'At the end of winter. The European winter. So you will need to come in April, maybe March, which is not long from now.'

'Do you want an answer now, or can I think about it?'

'Sure, think about it. Talk to Daniel and call me back, okay?'

'Right, thanks. Otherwise, are you well?' I asked, sensing he was about to hang up.

'Yes, all good. Say hi to your mom. Bye.'

The end. I dropped the phone into its cradle. I noticed how the call had already activated my fertile imagination. I felt myself come alive with the possibilities. My face swelled with a smile I could not resist.

'So?' said my mom, holding a wooden spoon and knife in her hands. 'What did he say?'

'I'm definitely not doing it,' said Daniel, with his typically resolute firmness. 'Bugger that, I'm not doing any trip with Papa; no flipping way.'

'What are you guys talking about?' pressed my mom.

'He wants us to drive down Africa with him ... on motorbikes,' said Daniel, swatting the invitation away with a dismissive flick of his wrists. 'I have to study anyway, the timing is wrong for me.'

'*Geez* man, really? I don't understand. You'll do Kenya to Cape Town and I'll do the northern section,' I said, trying to work out what he was resisting. 'It's the trip of a lifetime! Are you sure?'

With every passing second I felt a bristling excitement. My imagination danced with images and connections to dreams I never knew I had. I was both in the conversation and already well on my way down the continent.

'No, it's not that for me. I am not prepared to travel anywhere with that man. I don't think we would handle it. I think it would break us both,' Daniel's voice was calm.

I felt my initial excitement waning and reviewed my assumptions to check what I might have missed. I thought I understood the call as no more than a clear invitation. It was a chance to join my dad on a trip across a number of continents, over many months, and for free. It came at a time I actually had time, when I had no plans.

'Look, think about it. This is still like five months away from actually happening. If you change your mind, that's cool,' I said, trying to keep the door open.

'I won't change my mind, Marc. I won't do it. I can't do it. You can let him know tonight, if you want.' He had made his choice and slammed the door on the offer.

I must admit, a part of me was pleased I might not have to share that adventure. I didn't want to show it, but I was thrilled at the prospect of doing it all the way and having a crack at making history too. And that was that. I was going to do the entire trip.

Daniel's choice was true to character. He had always managed to avoid the romanticism and delusional hope of a spontaneous reunion that would bring our dad back into our lives. I, on the other hand, had held onto the fantasy, and most probably craved it. Ironically, Daniel's stance made his relationship with my dad more real and robust. It was the opposite of the tissue-paper bond I felt I had. My dad knew what he had with Daniel; he understood the boundaries and the open caution. I was in a different realm. The links to my dad were charged with hope and impossible expectation. I was envious of Daniel's clarity and neatly-cropped limits. He seemed so independent of him. I certainly wasn't, even though being the elder son had given me a longer period of time to work it through. I still had an enduring and volatile need to be acknowledged and praised by my dad.

I wasn't sure what drove my unrestrained interest in that invitation. Part of me believed it offered the prospect of rekindling a broken relationship. The other part fist-pumped the air with a more egotistical agenda; to be that guy who made it, in khakis and boots, across the wild continent on a motorbike.

The Starting Line

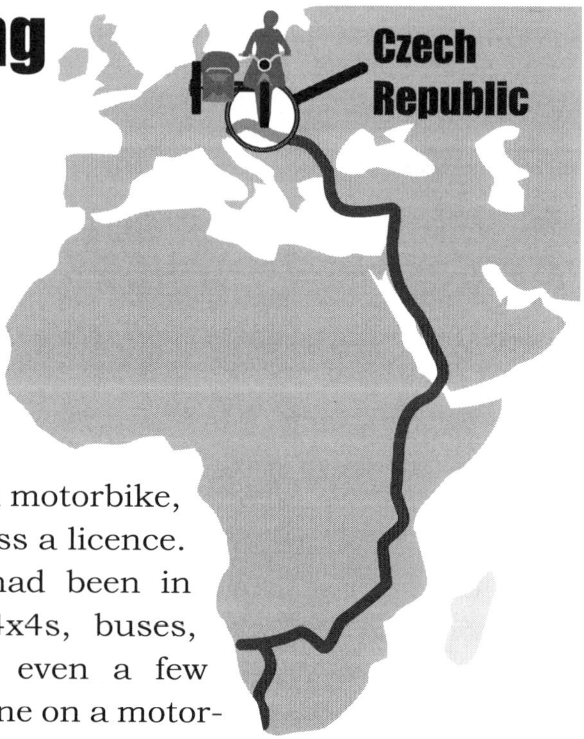

I had never ridden a motorbike, neither did I possess a licence. All my prior trips had been in enclosed vehicles: 4x4s, buses, planes, trains, and even a few boats. So to do this one on a motorbike would be a novelty; spice in the recipe of the trip. That two-wheel option tipped the appeal of the invitation towards *impossible to decline*, which was exactly what I suspect my dad had hoped.

I quickly found a bike – a big, black Kawasaki – and practiced with a friend who drove a 50cc Yamaha. I passed at my first attempt in a rural village not far from Cape Town. I should have failed, but small-town folk are forgiving and nice. The ease with which it all fell together created a bank of expectations the rest of the trip might be just as straightforward. In fact, the good fortune continued unopposed. I discovered all costs were indeed for my dad's account and the bike was a gift for keeps. All I had to do was get myself to Europe. There was none of the tough, sponsorship-grovelling reality that many trans-Africa travellers faced. As the support ramped up, the length and the details of the trip became irrelevant. At times it felt rather like a package holiday. I was allowed, and even encouraged to remain focused on the adventure, the continental epic, and the simple coolness of the whole thing. I thought very little about my dad as my travel partner, about the distance between us, and about the breach we were attempting to cross. Reality was suspended somewhere between places and plans, denial and busyness.

I left Cape Town in March 1999, travelling to Austria via London, Germany and the Czech Republic. I was 23 years old. My short European tour was designed to visit two old friends. The first I had met in 1994 while backpacking. The second was a childhood buddy who knew me better than most. We called him Gor. Curiously, we'd never considered 'Greg' to be the right diminutive. 'Gor' suited him, the way an umbrella suits a sandy beach. He was unassuming, gentle and kind. Soft in both features and nature, and he was loved by many. Gor was bright-eyed, mischievous and full of life. He taught me to love surfing and the deep caverns of a barrelling wave. The sea, his art and people made him the happiest. He always made me smile, and he was the best of my friends.

While I had been preparing for the trip, Gor, a gifted artist, had earned a dream scholarship to study animation in Prague. Nineteen ninety-nine was a big, open-ended year for both of us. I remember feeling both excited and nervous at the prospect of our reunion.

As the bus pulled in to the stop, I peered out the window. Gor should've been there, as promised. I didn't spot him, but quickly gathered my gear and shuffled along the emptying aisle. My first impression of the place was depressing. The ashen sky matched the grey cement. Weeds had grown like juvenile forests between the cracks in the pavement. Each green stem sheltered and snagged litter and debris.

Gor suddenly appeared in front of me. He was pale, gaunt and stiff. It looked like his skeleton had been locked and frozen into an upright pose. His eyes seemed smaller and without lustre, and he battled to smile. He had wilted. It was a troubling start. We greeted, hugged and walked in silence to his hostel. The air was abrasive and stung my nostrils; the smells were foreign and each step was heavier and slower than the last.

When we eventually reached his building, Gor hurried us through the cracked, glass door. It looked more like a Soviet-era barracks than an apartment block. A gruff female voice barked at us as we entered. Her face twisted with venom as she pushed the buzzer on the security gate to let us through.

'Now they know me, they hate me,' whispered Gor, cowering under the woman's glare.

I didn't know what he meant and was baffled by the idea of anyone hating him. No one even mildly disliked him. Every pulse of excitement I had about seeing him was vacuumed from my veins. I could feel myself sinking to match his mood.

We shuffled through the gate and ambled down a long, dank corridor. I could not have walked any slower.

'My room is this way,' he said, pointing down a staircase.

I looked down the steps where a single bulb buzzed in the landing. It barely illuminated the bottom steps.

'Down there?' I was horrified. 'Really?'

Gor ignored me. At the bottom of the flight we turned into an even longer, mustier passage. There were small, shoebox-sized windows high in the walls. Some of them let natural light through, others were blocked by earth or grass or litter. One of the panes near the end of the passage was broken, and I saw a shoe shuffling against the edge of the frame outside. We were below ground level. I smelled cigarette smoke and a black pair of leather boots. We quietly passed by, as if in hiding.

'There are my showers,' he said, as he pushed open a door that led into a green, tiled room. Each wall had three taps and there was a big drain in the centre. It was hard to see at first, but there were small holes in the tiles about head high above each tap. Just holes that oozed slimy drool.

'And the water is never hot,' he added, 'even in winter, and it gets flipping freezing here. Anyway…'

He became as speechless as I was. Each word required too much effort and explanation. So we said nothing to each other. The very last door was Gor's room. It had a bed tightly squeezed between its walls. The bright light was exposed and hung from a wire that swung in the middle of the concrete ceiling.

'This is where I live. It's not much, I am so sorry, but its home for me right now.'

'You officially live below the ground? That's a first, hey?' I quipped, with as much spark as I could muster.

'Yes, it's the only room down here, and it's mine,' he said, with no attempt to join my banter.

We sat on the bed for what felt like an hour, but was probably no more than a few minutes. I couldn't take it anymore; it was so degrading and deeply depressing. The walls caved in on me and the darkness strangled me with claustrophobia.

'Come, let's go for a walk, let's go for lunch,' I blurted.

'I am sorry, but I can't,' said Gregor, looking away. He stared at his shoes tucked under him. 'I have no money at all. I only have enough to get to college and back. The bursary pays for this room and the food. That is it.'

'No, sorry, what I mean is, I will pay for lunch,' I said, sensitive to his flushed cheeks. He squirmed with embarrassment. There was shame there too. I could see it, even though he tried so hard to hide it.

'What is this place, Gregor?' I asked as we walked towards the stairwell. 'Was this a jail? It really feels like a prison.'

'*Ya*, this is where I have to stay.'

'But can't you move, even to another room?'

'No! No, that is not possible!'

'But what's going on here? Why are they doing this to you? Do your parents know?' I peppered him with questions, my sense of injustice beginning to bubble out.

'It's because I have a Russian surname,' he said in resignation. 'And I can't change that; I have no way to escape it. They hate the Russians and they think I am one. They really hate them.'

'But it's just your surname. You are really no more Russian than I am!'

'Well, here they have long memories and they are even more hectic and racist than back home.'

At first I thought he hadn't tried hard enough but the further we walked, the more I empathised. He was condemned, pushed out of sight and treated like an outcast. And he could do nothing about it. They wanted him gone, they wanted him to leave. They would go to any lengths it seemed, and even purposefully gave him the wrong dates for his exams so he missed them all. He failed his first big assessments. He was immediately on the back foot, and with glee they watched him struggle to recover.

'I haven't been able to do anything in Prague for six months. No meals, no movies, no coffee, no tourist sites. I have no money. So I sit in my room all day, read and draw. I can't even afford to phone home,' his eyes welled with tears. 'You are my first visitor. Thank you.'

'*Shucks* Gor, I don't want to leave you here.'

'It's fine, I am used to it now. Just having you visit has been a good reminder of what I can still look forward to.'

We spent just two days together. Doubt crept into my fragile optimism about his situation. I was hopeful he would survive, but there was a palpable projection of his depression. His unintended drain of my energy and grey, pleading grimace troubled me. I had seen those eyes before. They were fresh in my memory, but they had been bedded in a different head. They, too, had stared me into a chill just six weeks earlier.

Since 1995 I had been in and out of a long-term relationship. It had been fraught with disturbance and became a twisted point of collision. It failed, and was always going to fail. Much of the discord and pain was inflicted by and towards myself, and she was the inevitable casualty. I couldn't find safety and chased shadows of doubt in myself. Seeds of disease, embedded in the relationship, activated a toxic dynamic. In short, I doubted my worth and feared being rejected, so I pre-empted each rejection and broke up with her, many times. At the end of 1998 she finally cut me loose and rightly so. She overlapped our relationship with another, and for that I was devastated and relieved at the same time.

Then, inexplicably, in early 1999, she woke up one morning, felt for her heart, and turned a pistol into her chest. The fact she was left-handed saved her life by millimetres. Shock waves rippled around her community. I had visited her just before I left, and was left awash with guilt and remorse. Her clenched jaw had bit hard into the pain, and her eyes were cavernous and blighted. It remained a lingering, open wound that festered for a long time. It was also a reminder how the residue of my dad's abandonment had blighted almost all of my closest relationships.

So there I was on a bus leaving Prague and a thread

of dread had been linked between two people I had once deeply cared for, and thought I knew well. Through their eyes, I stared at my own vulnerability and noticed how fragile they had made me feel.

It didn't matter how many kilometres I had already covered and how much I thought I had prepared, I began to realise it was not all going to be easy. I was headed into a haze of unknowns. I was undeterred, but disturbed by a niggling question: *What makes me think everything is going to end well?*

Shaken back to reality, I wondered, for the first time, what I was hoping for. The stark truth of discord and disappointment with my dad flooded back in me. I had ignored our past for as much as I could, but it all felt very real from that point on. Not paying a cent, being completely dependent on my father, and being indebted to him before we had even started, had sinister connotations and consequences for me. From then on, I battled to subdue the discomfort.

The Reunion

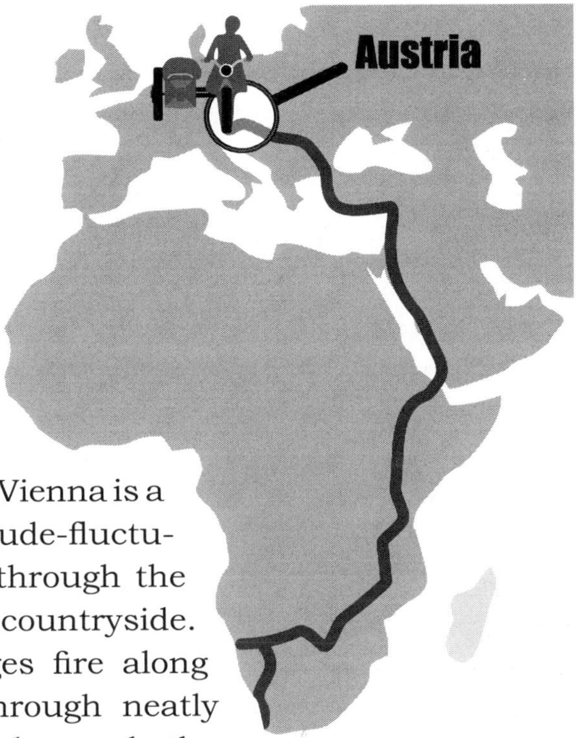

The train ride from Vienna is a meandering, altitude-fluctuating, roller coaster through the beautiful Austrian countryside. At times the carriages fire along an elevated track through neatly demarcated farmlands, and then squeeze and rattle between small hamlets. Everything in Austria is so deliberate and precise. As the train comes closer to where people live, the tracks drop below or high above ground level. On each side of the lines, there are recycled, lattice-work fences and glass frames that buffer the noise. Eventually, the Alps appear, bearded with spiny pines. The train weaves through the cracks and ravines. Direct sunlight disappears with only glimpses of yellow light high against the tall peaks. The cliffs rise sharply above the tracks as they hug the narrow ledges, and water seems to tumble out of every crack in the rocks.

My anticipation grew with each new station. I began to dwell on memories of my previous trip there in 1994. As commonly happens, I could only remember the good things; the festive meals, my distant family who were no longer strangers, the quality food, and especially the cold meats, schnapps and mustards. I enjoyed the prospect of never needing to repeat or spell my surname to anyone. They just got it. It all had a familiar feel to it, not quite home but very much a part of me. I was like a root that hadn't sprouted a trunk. The country was deep in my DNA but mostly hidden from me.

The town of Villach lies in an open quadrant of land between towering alpine peaks. It's an ancient town, with aspects of all the great empires of Europe and the near east. It has masks of a Roman past, a Turkish influence, a Nazi footprint, and an Allied occupation. It is the picturesque second town of the province of Carinthia. It is surrounded by mountains and lakes that have become thriving tourist attractions in both summer and winter. It is the happy state of Austria, where the citizens are proudly Carinthians first. They love their lands, their Alps, and their rivers, and assert their idiosyncrasies of culture through their own dialect and traditional dress. They almost exclusively drink beers made in their town. I was happy to be back.

Eventually, the train squealed against the platform at the Villach Hauptbahnhof. I gathered my belongings with my tingly nerves and stood patiently in the queue to disembark. I hadn't looked out the window; I hadn't seen him yet. I breathed in the crisp, snow-cleaned air that flushed the passage as we waited.

'Welcome to Villach! Half the size of the NY cemetery, and twice as dead,' there was Papa. His hands were buried in his pockets and he wore a meek smile behind his bushy beard. The beard had lost none of its imposing ruggedness but had turned a wizard's grey. 'So, how was the trip?'

I reached out to shake his hand, and pulled him closer for a hug. I instinctively knew he wouldn't take the lead on showing affection. It was an awkward hug. He didn't really know what to do, so he began to walk. We strolled in silence down the platform while I searched for a question or a phrase to kick-start it all again. I had nothing to say. After so much time and very little contact, he was a stranger to me again.

'Good, thanks. I have just been with Gor,' I said.

'Oh Gor, I remember him. What was his dad's name again, Ivan? Ivor...?'

'Igor.'

'Yes Igor, the Russian, that's right.'

I winced at that recollection.

'Actually, he has had a very difficult time in Prague because he is Russian,' I tried to keep the conversation going.

'Really? Shew, *ya*, I think I can understand that. You know those east Europeans are more racist than the Afrikaners in South Africa.'

'Mmm, maybe. That's exactly what he said too,' I ended it there, not wanting to rehash the story.

'So what's the plan for today?' I asked.

'Well, straight to *Tante* Inge now. She has made your favourite, chili con carne,' he said with a huff. He hated social engagements with his elder sister. He hated that she presumed what he and everyone else liked, thought and felt.

'My favourite?' I said, surprised, 'News to me.'

'Well, you know her; she has been cooking and baking all day. We will have to go, but we can make it quick, in and out.'

We strolled to the parked car. It was *Tante* Inge's car, of which my dad still had exclusive use. I took a moment to soak it all up. It was the beginning of our adventure together. That moment, as I closed the door and we drove away from that station, was the start of it all.

There was a distinct sequence of stories I always told people about my father. I recited them with boastful glee, and usually all in a row. I would fill with pride, and recount these tales with such fervour, almost without breathing, to ensure I had the attention of whoever would listen. It was clear-cut; my dad was my hero.

His life started with humble beginnings. The World Wars had inflicted relentless hardship and grief on the family. His parents had lost everything, twice. My dad felt trapped by post-war poverty, and restless with an intolerable wanderlust. So, in his 20s, he escaped what he described as a stifling and pedestrian life in Austria. In his search for meaning and excitement, the Alps had become an obstruction: impenetrable, unchangeable cookie cutters shaping his life. He wanted out of the small-town, small-minded, village soap opera. I imagined him flipping a map of the world on its head and seeing what came up in the place where Austria had been; kind of middle of the latitudes. It would have been Southern Africa. The circumstances of his departure were murky and tainted, but he never spoke much about that time. His story always began with his arrival in South Africa to satiate his enduring appetite for freedom.

He arrived in the late 1960s and quickly found a vibrant community of Germanic expatriates. They were mainly technical men who loved beer and were rough around all their edges; except for the waistlines. Southern Africa was in short supply of technical skills, and those European castaways traded theirs for a wage and took advantage of every privilege they could snatch. They were living on the back of the paranoid need of white South Africans to import more white people. They also exploited a prevailing vanity in the desire of that white minority to live a quasi-European lifestyle. They would stick any typically European name onto a business sign board and customers came to them in droves. Engineering firms took on German names, coffee and clothing makers were Italian, and so it went. It was that easy. Yet they had a silent contempt for the South African reality, mainly because it was Africa, and then because Apartheid was starting to exclude the country from the civilised world. They felt excluded and isolated.

There were legislated benefits to being white, no matter where they came from. That easily accepted sense of superiority, mixed with a heritage far from African soil, created a cocktail of wild recklessness that made them often unrecognisable to those who knew them. My dad was very much a part of that crew.

He had always sported a long and bushy beard. It usually stretched below his neck and spread out into two ponytails onto his chest. All my life I had only known him with a beard. There was a single picture of his naked face, taken when he was five years old. The beard suited the wild-man-of-the bush persona. It became the lifelong mark of his crazy, early days in Africa. He plied his trade as an electrical engineer, and relished the broad spokes of his travel routes across Botswana, Namibia, Zimbabwe, Mozambique and South Africa. He quickly developed a solid professional reputation too.

Once, on one of his many work trips, he was driving along the winding roads of the Eastern Cape in the pitch black of an early morning, when he fell asleep at the wheel. He woke in hospital with a shattered jaw that had been wired shut, and told the doctor the last thing he could remember was the inadequately short strobes of light leading the way from his headlights. He had been unbelievably lucky, they said. Most people wouldn't have made it. It was quite a miracle. It emerged he had aimed the old *kombi* through the barrier and launched it over the cliff. The *kombi* had rolled, bonnet over boot, in a single somersault and had landed on its wheels on a parking-bay sized ledge, 100 metres above a ravine.

Should his tyres have bulged a little more, while on that jutting rock, he and that hippie-mobile would have plunged down the cliff. But there he sat, knocked out cold in a shower of shattered glass. His face was cracked and disfigured from having repeatedly slammed against the steering wheel. Even once the jaw had healed, his chin and cheekbone were awkwardly lopsided. To hide the deformity he kept the beard, and at the same time pulled a rebellious middle finger to the establishment. His time in hospital was the only time in 40 years it had been shaved. He survived many similar incidents, and constantly dared life to curtail him. But it never could; he was that sort of an expatriate, who lived with an 'only-in-Africa' tag line to every escapade.

Through my younger years, there was so much for me to vicariously boast about. My dad was living the adventurer's dream. I deeply identified with that, and leaned on it. I think it was the bravery and old-world charisma I pinned my genetics to most. I seemed to have found an archetypal resonance in it all, a deep and pervasive connection. As a result, I sought his constant approval, and then, with my parents' divorce, I was deprived of all the time I used to have to please him. From the age of seven, our time together became intermittent and stifled. At each visit we would have to try and find where we had left off, and that took a lot of time. I became frustrated and more desperate. I could sense distance wedge between us, and I brewed a desperate need to mend it. I forced myself to make the most of the limited time we had together, but I was invariably disappointed, and then found myself become even more addicted to the need for constant acknowledgement. It felt emotionally blinding at times, overwhelming at others. Eventually I got used to the rhythm, but was never content with the result. Then, just as it all settled into a new normal, it all changed.

All I remember about that day is where I was when it happened, and the weather. We lived on St. Joseph's Road, in a quiet middle-class suburb. We shared an oddly constructed, A-frame home with my new stepfather. It was a home that felt strange and unfamiliar. The elements that day were restless and unsettled. Like music so often did, the weather mirrored my edgy, uncomfortable mood.

It was a week until my brother's ninth birthday, and my mother was frantically trying to establish the customary exchange of gift ideas with my dad. She had repeatedly tried to contact him and eventually called his employer in frustration. They, too, had no idea where he was, but they advised he had left with just a day's notice and had flown somewhere. No goodbye, no final visit to us, no warning. Just like that, he had packed up and literally disappeared. We were confused and unsettled – *what were his reasons?* We assumed he must have gone to a city close by, but eventually we contacted his sister in Austria, who confirmed he had come 'home'.

Because we were in a cycle of not seeing him for two weeks at a time, the rhythm was not immediately disrupted. For the first two weeks we were in denial. I certainly expected him to be back for his next weekend. But weeks passed. We heard nothing. No phone call, no message, no contact. Finally we heard word, through a simple telegram, the only one I would ever receive. Its brevity was stunning:

'In Austria, my father is dying. Be back in six weeks. Papa.'

The six weeks passed faster than expected, but he didn't return. After 12 weeks it became clear he had left us. I was 11 years old. He had just disappeared, a week before my brother's birthday, while living mere kilometres from our home, and had not said goodbye.

It was five years before we saw him again, and then for only four hours during his two-week visit to Cape Town. It was a surreal experience. We were floating in limbo, knowing he was in the same city as we were, and yet had so little time for us. I was deeply affected by that and it amplified my ringing narrative of loss. It felt almost cruel, as if he was purposefully trying to force me to hate him.

As always, I tried to make logical sense of it. I had always understood there to be two reasons for his sudden departure, without warning and without a goodbye. First, he had gone home to say farewell to his dying father. The second, he had been unable to tolerate the injustice and brutality of Apartheid. The 1980s in South Africa were raw and unpredictable. Revolution was on our doorstep. The white minority leaned on its military force and the nation struggled back. He left, I believed, to no longer be a part of that system, to no longer be an unattached Austrian who lived off the backs and privileges of a white Boer state. He made a stand. That is what I believed. It made me proud. That his father was terminally ill made sense to me too. I identified with those reasons but often wondered how many people actually heard what I was saying, or were in fact convinced by my intense loyalty and rationalisation of the devastating loss. My stories and memories were all I had. My reasoning helped me when I needed it to be okay.

In time I discovered I also had a deep and damaging belief he didn't love us enough to stay, and I wasn't worthy of his continued presence. For years I wanted to find a way to move on but I couldn't shrug the part of me that felt trapped in a whirlpool, being sucked deeper and deeper into sadness. I developed an aversion to intimacy and actively avoided feeling dependent on others. I pushed away people who got close to me and masked my own pain by inviting others to share all their hurt and anguish with me. I presented a persona of confidence and strength, clarity and purpose, and the whole world thought I was fine. Many people believed I was thriving. I still cried myself to sleep more than I cared to admit.

My dad's proposition, that invitation to travel, came 12 years after he had left. It sparked an emotional deluge of intemperate hope, need and desperation. I had no idea what I was getting myself into, but what I did know was for too long my naïve inability to heal myself had claimed chapters of my life. That invitation, to team up with the very perpetrator of my pain, seemed like my only route to salvation.

The Austrian Life

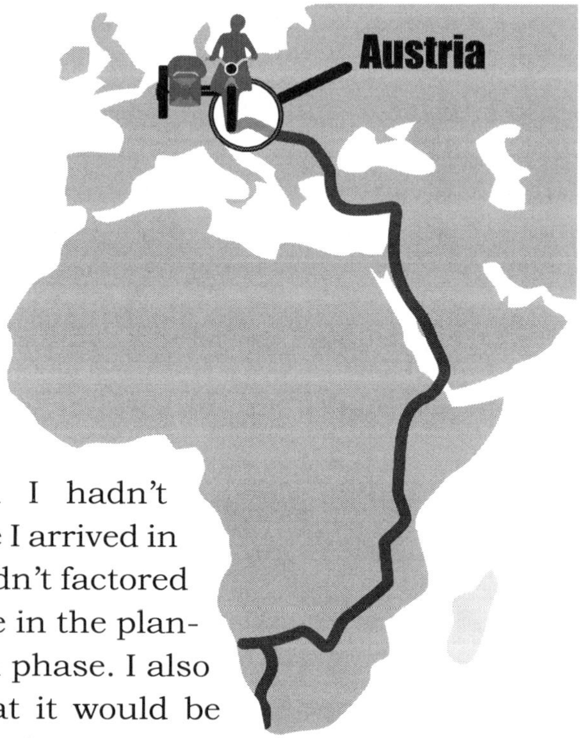

There was much I hadn't considered before I arrived in Villach. For one, I hadn't factored how long we might be in the planning and preparation phase. I also hadn't imagined what it would be like to live with my dad again. There were many aspects to that, but the most obvious was the renovation of the flat. It was the most bizarre conversion of a living quarters I had ever seen. He had built a shower in the middle of the bedroom. It was a glass capsule literally planted between the beds. One of which would be mine, but he had moved himself into the lounge. The entire wall was covered in my grandfather's hunting trophies. He had often threatened to take those staring skulls down, but they still cluttered and hung high up to the roof. It was a small flat, just about right for two of us. I couldn't imagine a family of five living there.

The other aspect I had not prepared for was how he would treat me. It became clear he saw me as the 11-year-old he had left behind, and not the adult I had become. It was a slow grinding irritation, and my sensitivity to his tone of voice and body language rose as the weeks went by. That pattern was not ad hoc or temporary, but seemed more deliberate and enduring with time.

Most days started in the same way. I would get out of bed and follow the aroma of coffee that slipped under my door. The percolator would gurgle in the corner of the kitchen, while Papa read the paper through a pair of glasses that rested on the tip of his nose. Most mornings, he would ignore me for a minute, as if annoyed by my intrusion, but then would eventually raise his head. Like clockwork, he would push his eyebrows up his forehead and smile. It was a micro movement on his face which I interpreted as disapproval. He didn't think much of my 9am wake up. But I was always so tired I couldn't help it, just like I couldn't keep up with the 'rounds' every night.

The rounds always began with a couple of '*kleine*' beers. They were smaller beers which gave us an excuse to drink more of them. It was always just two small draughts to start. There were a number of pubs, all within walking distance of my dad's flat. We would map our picks for the night as we left the front door and then head to at least two of them in an evening. By the time we were done, it was usually a six to eight-beer round trip. Too much for me to handle. Some days it was harder to wake up than others. On one particular morning, I stumbled into the kitchen closer to midday and the glare that greeted me was unashamedly mean-spirited.

On that particular occasion, we had spent the previous day in Northern Italy. Villach is just a short drive from the borders of both Italy and Slovenia, and we had travelled to a small wine farm outside Udine to collect caskets of Chianti. Each bottle had a small basket wrapped around its bottom half and a useful ring of glass at its neck suited for lifting. We had crammed the car's boot to its brim, with the back seat folded down for extra space. It was technically illegal to ferry that amount of liquor across the border, but we took our chances and made it through with a friendly wave of the hand. The joys of the European Union.

We stored the bottles on the floor of the kitchen, mainly because we had no space in the storeroom, and because many were destined for family distribution. We had over 20, five litre bottles neatly laid out in rows. That night we went drinking. I am not sure I remember coming home, but as per usual, at about 2am I needed a pee, a really big pee. As often happened, my dad and I would wake up at the same time and a midnight race to the *loo* would ensue.

'What the ...!' I heard Papa yelp, as he went into the kitchen to fetch a glass of water.

He was standing, as if stuck in mud, with the door ajar behind him.

'Oh no...' I croaked, as my feet stepped into something wet on the floor. We both stood in a very dark, soupy liquid that covered the entire kitchen floor.

'Did you knock a bottle and break it Marc?' His voice was heavy with disparaging annoyance, 'It's wine; there is a lot of the wine that has spilled out.'

'No, I just stepped in here ... after you, actually. Maybe you knocked one over at the door.'

'You must have knocked it when you went to bed then!'

He turned on the lights, and we discovered that, curiously, not a single bottle had been moved, knocked out of place or broken. I had wanted to spot the source of it first, but had nothing intelligent to say as I wiped the sleep from my eyes.

'Don't move; there may be glass in the puddle.' He leaned down and tipped the bottle closest to him on its side. It was empty, 'Strange, very strange.'

I sat on my haunches and looked into the glass caskets. More than half of them were emptied to the ankle of the bottle. Papa picked one up and the entire top of the bottle snapped off its base.

'Aha! There it is. Hairline cracks in the glass. It's the change in temperature that caused this. The bottles have expanded and shrunk again – and then cracked,' he moaned, annoyed at the loss. We cleaned and mopped until almost first light.

I nursed my coffee as midday struck and waited for it to kick-start my brain. I didn't care what my dad thought.

'Today I need you to go and mow the lawn at Drobbolach,' he instructed, finally breaking the silence. 'It must be done today. I have been waiting for too long to do it.'

'Sure,' I replied, quite buoyed by the thought. I enjoyed physical labour and had missed doing exercise.

'And you can go on my bicycle. I need the car. Okay?'

There was no mention of the wine debacle. He would have enjoyed blaming that on me. Either way, I really had no choice around my plans for the day. I was going to do some work. And I would be alone, which raised my energy.

Drobbolach is a hamlet that sits on the edge of a small inland lake called the Faaker See. Every time I say that name I cringe at the way it sounds aloud. Its turquoise waters are flanked in the south by a small beach, and in the north by a line of hotels. A small wooded island floats in the middle. The entire scene is set against the backdrop of a volcano-like mountain. It is a dramatic, photographer's delight, as you can tell by every postcard of the place. My father's family had owned property in the area for two generations, with the prize lot being a small plot on the hill. It was a parcel of land, equally divided between flat ground at the top and a steep drop off at the bottom. The point at which the flat land began tumbling down the hill was marked by a line of fruit and nut trees. In the corner was a small, wooden hut which was big enough to sleep up to three people. It had all the essentials, but no luxuries. From the small deck of that dark timber home was a view over the ever-descending roofs, the lake and the mountains. It was a beautiful place and it was quiet almost all year round. It was very important to my dad. That was his. His father had left it to him, and every tree had a memory.

The cycle ride wound out from Villach, through the peri-urban smallholdings, and up a little tree-covered hill. Cutting over the hill was an ancient cart track. It was the shortest way. The Romans and centuries of people since then had pulled their carts over that exact outcrop and so cut deep funnels into the stone. That became the pathway. I decided to push the bike along that part of my route. Riding felt disrespectful, and with each step, and the occasional slip, I navigated the bicycle along the moist, dappled path. It was very still. A good time for reflection.

I was yet another human being, passing over the same hill that had stood there for millennia. I had always felt small and in my place in the footsteps of history. I was reminded of the relatively short imprint a life has, and how so many before us had laid out maps and lessons, routes and pathways for us to lean on and follow. Walking up that path, watching the rubber and spokes snugly follow the trail in the rocks, I realised I had little idea what my journey was all about. I had no expectation of what groove I might leave behind. I was more focused on teasing my future closer to me. I had the habit of imagining who I would be when it was all over, rather than being present to what was in and around me. I believed I would discover more of myself, of my limits and my abilities. I tried to shrug that niggling discomfort about the role my father would play in all of it, but resigned myself to the idea he would need to change to make a significant impact on me. Or maybe not. Him changing was unlikely to happen, but I admit I hung onto the desire to be the one who prompted him to take accountability for what he had done. Pushing through the outer rows of the forest, I caught a glimpse of the imposing Alps, so high and dominant. So permanent. That time to myself was the first chance I had to reflect on my expectations, and that journey to Drobbolach allowed me to shed a childish blindness and begin seeing the trip for what it was, just a drive down to Cape Town. I felt lighter at the end of that trail. Drobbolach was also where I first met my motorbike.

The Bike

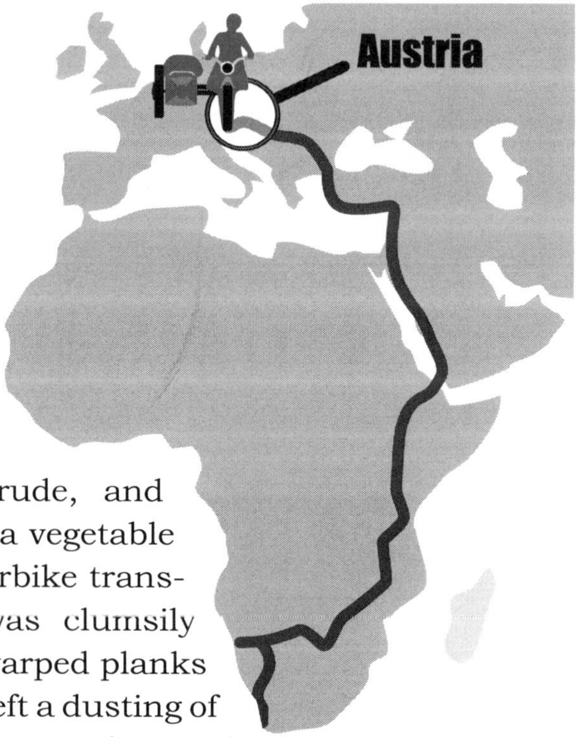

The crate was crude, and looked more like a vegetable carriage than a motorbike transporter. Each nail was clumsily hammered into the warped planks and the rough grain left a dusting of splinters wherever the crate bumped or rubbed against anything. There was straw poking out of every gap, like stubble on a hobo. It looked archaeological, as if it was ferrying ancient ruins. The sheer size of the thing suggested an Egyptian relic was hidden inside. There were Cyrillic letters branded on all sides, and randomly placed, bright red stickers warned us the cargo was fragile. That turned out to be a wild exaggeration.

It had arrived on a truck but when we saw it for the first time it was already in Richard's garage. He was my dad's cousin and neighbour in Drobbolach. My dad didn't have a garage and this was the next best option.

I don't know why, but I had imagined the bike would be wrapped in a specially designed, water-resistant tarpaulin. I assumed, whatever the packaging, it would be emblazoned with the bike's name and emblem – Dnepr

MT-16. What we saw, however, was everything but grand, yet that straw-emitting crate was charming and told a story all of its own.

'Where do we open it?' I searched for a door or a flap the Ukrainians might have closed after they had pushed it into its container. 'Is there even a door, do you think?'

'I think they just parked the bike on a wooden base, threw straw and blocks of wood at it, and then nailed it shut,' said my dad. 'Pass me that hammer, this should be fun.'

'Blocks of wood?' I asked, confused.

'*Ya*, look through there. There's all kinds of wooden braces and blocks, probably to make sure it didn't slide off and out through those wooden sidings. This bike weighs 650kg, and those planks wouldn't stand a chance if it tilted or twisted.'

'It looks exactly like your bike. Do they only have them in black?' asked Richard.

'Pink and zebra stripes were out of stock,' quipped Papa.

We had been riding around on my dad's bike for weeks already. There was an air of anticipation among us as we dismantled the box. I was very excited; that was my bike, a brand new version of a gravely dated design. A few nails popped easily from the corners but we had to vigorously assault the rest of the box to break it down. We pulled and smashed our way through the planks. Eventually all sides had been pulled off and we raked through the straw, pulling it off and into a small pile.

'Make sure we get all that straw off, and watch out for any loose nails on the floor. Last thing we need is either a fire or a puncture when we get this thing going,' Papa said as he used his foot to clear a short runway in front of the bike.

And then, there it was.

'There's your Harley, Marc! Just imagine, in 2002 we will take this to the US with Cyrillic letters spelling Harley Davidson on the side,' he chuckled. I had no idea what he was talking about.

'But let's get to Cape Town first, why don't we,' I said.

'Okay, let's get this thing started!' he trumpeted.

The Dnepr MT-16 was a vintage-style motorbike with a sidecar. They were not antiques, and were still in production. It looked as if it had been pulled from a World War Two movie set, but it had a bold *'1999'* inscribed on its manifold. There we no rounded edges, or clean lines of moulded sheet metal. Every panel was pop riveted and stretched by hand and hammer. The welding was coarse and irregular, and we could clearly see how they had used a grinder to flatten down the edges and hide their mistakes. There was no German engineering in those rip-offs. They were not original designs, but copies of the much vaunted BMWs that were used in the war. Apparently, as the Soviets advanced into East Germany, they seized the designs and copied them. Today, the Russians, Ukrainians and Chinese make motorbikes that look remarkably similar, each one a copy of the original 1940 design.

'You know what, maybe we won't get a chance to ride her today,' Papa said. 'Look at this stuff.'

He had inspected the entire bike and traced his signature into the dust with his finger. He followed the imaginary fuel through the pipes towards the engine heads, and double-checked each of the other parts within his view as he went. He was mechanically literate, I was not. With a few knocks and taps, he eventually stopped and stared up at us, his glasses poised to somersault off his nose.

'*Shit*, we're missing some of the electrics,' he said quite calmly, as if he had expected there to be a problem. 'Where is the distributor? Can you see it Richard?'

We both shook our heads.

The sidecar looked the neatest. It was closed up, with a taught leather patch which covered the seat. We pulled it back and found a pile of parts, with no instructions and no labels. Just a random dump of electrical components and some tools that seemed like they had been inadvertently covered and forgotten about by the assemblers in Kiev. We laughed at the thought and imagined how, distracted by a round of vodkas, that could so easily be close to the truth.

My father's cousin, who had the habit of looking past me to see me, chuckled and brawled out a few lines of a heavily-accented Austrian dialect I didn't understand. He offered us each a beer in commiseration, to ease the frustration. He was gnome-like, partly because of his stature and rounded body, but mostly because he seemed to be carrying the woods and elements with him. His farmer's hands rustled and chafed against all he touched. He blanketed his beer with large stubby fingers and in his protruding eyebrows he caught the light and wind.

My dad nodded approvingly. I had become accustomed to the fact if there was work to be done then there was a beer to be had while doing it. We all cracked open cold Villacher beers and paused.

'We are going to be here all day,' Papa's voice was heavy with resignation.

It was like completing a puzzle without an image of the final product. We collectively chattered and debated as to what each part was. Sometimes we simply had no idea. Most of the parts were tried in numerous combinations and on separate parts of the bike. We hit many dead ends. It was very frustrating, but with cold beer and a regular supply of cold meats and snacks, we kept ourselves calm and light hearted. I found it easy to be involved as a result, but my constant commentary and intrusions clearly exposed a distinct lack of mechanical ability. At that point, I really didn't give a damn and eventually we figured it all out.

With all our focus beamed at the bike, we hadn't noticed how the sky had clouded over. The humid, Austrian summer air hung low in the garage, and sunset was on its way.

'Okay, petrol in!' Papa called, with a slight loss of balance as he lifted a leg to climb on the bike.

'Keys!' I replied with a salute, holding them above my head.

'Are you ready?' he asked.

'Very ready, let's do it.'

It was just the three of us, but it felt like the room was filled with a crowd of expectant onlookers. The suspense was thick. It suddenly went very quiet; you could have heard a blade of straw roll out of the corner of the garage. We all stared at the keys and collectively sighed and smiled as the ignition light flickered a bright red.

'Helmet!' Papa barked, zipping up his leather jacket.

He mounted the bike, pulled the helmet tight around his chin and placed his boot on the kick-starter. He mock pushed it, and leaned down to open up the fuel line. He squeezed a few squirts of petrol into the engine, and then he finally did it. With only one violent kick, he brought that newly-minted motorbike growling to life. We looked at each other in astonishment; we hadn't expected it would start with such ease. As the smiles and clapping flashed around the garage, Papa yelled, 'Did we order a Harley!?'

It was a memorable moment and I banged my beer against Richard's, faintly picking up a mumble of congratulations from him. His words joined the din and the garage was filled with loud bellows of exploding fuel. Then suddenly, there was a frothy splutter, followed by a blue flash and wisps of smoke rising off the motley mix of parts in the bike's mid-section. The bike then died. My dad leapt athletically off the seat and we just stared at the smoke wrapping up and around the fuel tank. It made us cough and move back for air.

'I don't suppose we have a spare one of those?' I asked hopefully.

'No, *shit* man,' Papa turned the ignition switch off abruptly, 'the starter motor has burnt out. We might as well eat now. We need to get spares and that will take a few days.'

'Flip man!' I said, as I struggled to hide my frustration. It had been such an anticlimax.

Within a week, the parts arrived, along with a dog-eared, sketch-laden manual. It was more of a picture book than a detailed guide and our guesswork was still required. It took a full day to get all the parts in the right order and, as evening approached, we were ready to ride. My dad insisted on taking my bike. According to him, he had a better feel for those machines. I struggled to believe that, because each machine was so obviously an interpretation of a rough plan, rather than a carbon copy of a winning formula. But I chose to avoid the brewing quarrel.

We nudged the bends out of Drobbolach, down through the wooded hills and farmlands. The bikes punched an unfamiliar sound against the village air. Boom, rumble and groan. I felt like we were on a parade, but without the crowds. The entire place must have heard us as we came closer but never quite went away. I was liberated; free on the road at last. I felt a surge of excitement and anticipation. It was my first proper ride and with gravity dropping us down the slopes, I tingled as the speed built. It was riveting.

The road eventually flattened as we approached Villach,

and my heartbeat calmed to a flutter. We must have been quite a sight. In procession, one behind the other, two black gleaming relics bobbing about on partially-deflated shock absorbers. Mildly out of control and unpredictable. The air was fresh on my skin. The heat had fed rising thunder clouds that then blocked the setting sun and cooled the air that afternoon. My dad's bike had been nicely worn in and it was cruising under me. He was in front and I could see him nervously glancing at the back tyres, his hands hovering over the piston heads to assess the temperature of the engine. There was intermittent revving and braking as he swerved and turned on the straighter roads, much like they do in the warm-up lap in a grand prix. Everything was, at that point, in tip-top shape. I imagined him muttering with surprise into his helmet at the state of affairs. It felt so good looking at him, watching us ride together; it was like a test drive for the rest of the year.

It was ludicrous to expect it would all remain so calm and in control. But we revelled in it while it lasted. Then, without any warning, my bike started to lurch and stop, lurch and stop. I instinctively squeezed the brakes, which only exaggerated the jerks. I revved the engine too, but it kept cutting out. Each time it was about to die, it would find a spark of life and fire up again. I looked down and noticed thick white smoke rising between my legs. When a long flame shot at my crotch I lost control of the bike, and veered straight for the pavement. I ramped onto it, slammed on the brakes and narrowly missed the lamp post. I almost wrote myself off, but had no time to breathe with relief. The bike was on fire, the battery was engulfed in flames. It crackled beneath my seat and fire licked the petrol hose. It started to engulf the petrol tank itself. I panicked, and in self-preservation jumped away from the bike, half expecting it would imminently explode. My dad, however, continued going. Preoccupied with the clinging and clanging of the bike, he was blissfully unaware of the blaze behind him.

There was a split second where I had to decide to either run for my life, or douse those flames. I was paralyzed, and just stood there. I kept waving towards Papa's ever-shrinking silhouette. He was too far to hear me, but then I saw him slam on his brakes, and skid for far too long. He wrenched the bike around violently like a rodeo rider, clipped the pavement and slipped between the oncoming traffic. He screeched to a halt at my legs, hurdled off his bike like a 20-year-old and, with his bare hands, went for the guts of the bike. He ripped at the flaring, glowing copper wires that had melted against the frame and battery. The runny, plastic coatings burnt through his hands and sprayed off the ripped wires as they flew past me onto the road. Within seconds, the fire was out. And I was still just standing there.

'What did you do?' he shouted, clearly in pain, as the blood streamed down his arm.

'Nothing, it just started, just like that. I did nothing, really,' I stammered in shock.

We both breathed heavily in unison. That had been close, very close. Flames, fuel, five more seconds and that could have been it. Cinders and no more.

'Aha, the battery came loose,' he said, as he picked through the flaking ash of plastic. He sighed deeply, 'Look! That wing nut has popped off. I think the positive and negative cables running from the battery must have made contact and shorted. It's difficult to see, now that it's all *fucked* up!'

'I promise I didn't do anything,' I said meekly.

'It's fine, but let's hope this doesn't become a pattern, you know, you being on the bike each time it fails.'

The pungent smell of burnt plastic lingered in the air, like the pressure I felt layered on me. I was due another mechanical debacle, I just knew it.

We had to tow Papa's older bike back into Villach, and skulked home in the darkness. The first thing we did, after parking the bikes askance in the driveway, was to drink a sullen beer.

'Tomorrow, we will fix the bikes again and then go back to that middle man,' said my dad in annoyance. 'These bikes are *shit* man, we need to get everything right. He hasn't been honest with us. But it's a fair drive to get there; maybe we should just take the car.'

'But maybe that would be a good test, a little distance. Also, won't it be better to have the bikes with us?' I asked.

'Yes, yes, okay. We will take both bikes. If we can't make it that far then we are really in trouble.'

'Might be easier to do this trip on a bicycle,' I joked.

There was a growing list of peculiarities that needed to be checked and discussed, but it was still a 120km round trip to the Dnepr agent. That made me nervous. The next day we re-wired the battery and navigated our way through the Villach traffic and opened up into the highway. The bikes were cruising again. We headed into the lowlands along the rivers and wound our way northwards. We made it there without so much as a rattle or a fuss, and spent the rest of the day dissecting each possible frailty with our supplier. We stocked up on spares and parts that were most notorious for breaking. He was depressingly honest with us. With every question we asked, the middle man would reply, 'I think it should last, but you know, these bikes were not designed to go down Africa.'

It was a feeble disclaimer and painfully obvious to us after just a few weeks of riding them.

When we were done, we decided to return via my aunt

and uncle's house and we made a mid-afternoon start back the way we had come. I remember it was a quiet road, with green grazing plains on either side. The bang, when it came, was so loud it startled my dad to swerve in his lane. The echoes bounced into the crags and crevices of the cliffs circling our horizon. Then, with a second bang and as if shot through the head at point-blank range, my bike just stopped and listed forward. It felt like the closest a bike could get to collapsing in a heap on itself. It wheezed a last few puffs of smoke and steam and then went quiet.

The diagnosis this time was a blown cylinder head. The prognosis was that a full overhaul of the engine block was required. Fatefully, we had just collected two new piston heads but had no tools to do anything with them. The irony was nauseating. For the second time in two days one bike towed the other and both times I was the rider being pulled. My dad would have made yet another judgmental note of that.

We were so close to my aunt's farm we felt obliged to stop in, with maimed bikes and all. Besides, a clutch of schnapps and a *breteljausen* was certain to be outstanding, and anything predictable felt worthwhile experiencing at that point. We limped towards the small hamlet of Furnitz.

Onkel Hansi and *Tante* Rosi were pragmatic farmer types. They were almost self-sufficient. He had been an engineer on the railways for most of his formal career, but had continued the family tradition and farmed on the side. They lived in a spectacular farmhouse with a traditional mix of mortar and carved, heavy wood. It was nestled beneath a steep, wooded peak and sat between lush and muddy pastures. It was a small pocket of land, but just enough for the part-timer. He hunted, they farmed cattle, and he was the local, authorised butcher. He also made some of the most potent schnapps and cider too. For that he was also certified. These curled on the ice in winter, made every type of cured meat including curdled blood sausage, and were a feast on tap at any time of day or night. They were busy people, and did not suffer fools. I liked them a lot, but had not kept in touch with them over the years. She was my dad's middle sister, and had not made much effort with us either while we were growing up. Nevertheless, both of them had been warm and caring from the moment I had reconnected with them. Significantly, they had already dropped hints of concern about the trip. The first and only people to do so. I felt like they were in my camp, if there was such a thing. At the very least they were concerned about my well-being.

They had expected our visit but, on seeing us, their demeanour quickly frosted. *Onkel* Hansi greeted me, turned his shoulder and ignored my dad, who seemed unperturbed as he entered the house first and made a sharp turn into the bathroom. Looking grumpy, *Onkel* Hansi placed a glass of homemade cider on the table in front of me.

'Someone needs to speak to him,' he whispered. He became more visibly annoyed with each step he took. They were slow, shuffling steps of well-worn and weary legs.

'This is now becoming irresponsible,' he wagged a puffy finger at me. 'And you want to travel to Cape Town? *God!* You can't even get out of Villach! What are you guys thinking?'

He glared at my aunt who stared blankly back at him. It was a look perfected over decades. It was a wordless message of, 'I know, love, you are right. But again, you can't change it.'

I shrugged my shoulders and took another long sip of

cold cider.

'So who is going to tell him? What are you expecting to happen?' snapped my aunt, as she offered me a big slice of homemade cheese. 'You know what he is like.'

'Well, someone must, for Marc's sake. This is not right!' hissed Hansi. He looked at me and I sensed he wanted me to say something. I, too, had my doubts, but the chance to do that trip was still much too enticing. I was torn.

'I think we'll work this out. Better now than later for all this to happen,' I said diplomatically.

'We all know what he is like. When he sets his mind on an idea, there is no change in plan unless it comes directly from him. We know that about him,' said my aunt, trying to keep her voice down. It was too much for my uncle and he stood up and prepared to storm out.

'I really hope nothing happens to you Marc, I really do,' he said. Turning to Rosi, he repeated, 'I hope nothing happens to him. I really do hope we are doing the right thing.' And with that he left the room.

I attacked the *breteljousen* to divert my attention. It was my favourite meal, a broad selection of cold meats, cheeses, mustards and breads, served on a farm-style wooden board with a samurai sharp knife. There was a little bit of horseradish piled neatly next to the cured animal fat. It was more delicious than ever. We made small talk when my dad sat down, as if nothing was wrong. *Onkel* Hansi eventually stepped back inside, his eyebrows standing on high alert, the only visible sign of his repressed fury and frustration. He was still red in the face.

'So you still think this trip will work, do you?'

'*Ya*, no problem,' Papa smiled disarmingly. 'Better now than later for this to happen.'

I almost choked as I heard my own words replayed through him. *Onkel* Hansi backed off, but his disapproval was palpable. There was a long list of things about my dad he struggled to make sense of. I was only at the start of discovering those things myself.

The Crash to Reality

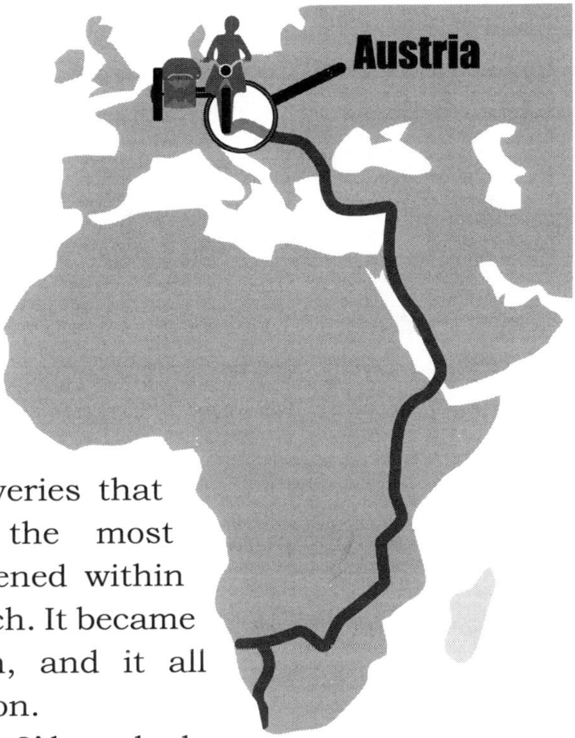

One of the discoveries that unsettled me the most about my dad happened within my first week in Villach. It became a daily conversation, and it all started with a question.

'Do you want a shot?' he asked as I shuffled into the kitchen. He was tightening the lid firmly on the bottle, with a fresh, thumbfull of golden whiskey already sloshed in his glass.

'Um, no thanks.' It was the third morning in a row I'd declined his offer, but he still pushed me to succumb.

'You sure you don't want any?' he persisted. 'It's just to clear your mouth, to fight off infection. It's like all those mouthwash things you get,' he said, as he tried to justify what made a stiff shot acceptable on an empty stomach.

'It's not to get you drunk you know, it's just to start your day,' he explained.

I wasn't convinced. Not at all. I was alarmed that every day he would twist the tall, green Jameson's bottle top and admire its golden label as he swirled a sip around his mouth. So it went on, and every morning he would wash down his night breath with a shot of alcohol, mostly whisky, sometimes schnapps. It was normal to him. It had clearly become an acceptable habit.

Habits, in my observation, have a way of narrowing our curiosity and discovery. We find ourselves skipping from one sequence of auto-pilot actions to another. Before we know it, our entire day is massaged and guided to be similar to what it was yesterday, last month, maybe even last year. That happens quite easily too, mainly because habits lull us into feeling safe, and yes, that dreaded word – comfortable. Of course the hidden danger is we often don't face our reality as a result, and never make changes, don't alter the course of our experiences, and invariably get stuck.

Habits are mostly personal too, and yet we often assume everyone is like us. In reality, habits are often small, intimate actions, behaviours, twitches and even sounds. In combination they can often define a person. It can be what makes him or her unique, or peculiar, or weird. They are quite selfish in that way. They express themselves in the way we eat, where we eat, what we eat. In a nutshell, they represent our surrender to a panel-beaten life, but they are also *damn* convenient. It makes our sense of what we can control so much easier to believe. And that makes us feel very safe, even if the habits are bad for us. They become, in contrast to much else, reliable.

Habits are so close to us we often don't even know we have them. It's as if we have developed a habit of ignoring our habits. They have then gone into stealth mode as they blend into who we think we are, and from that point on we don't know the difference. In all cases, and I say that with confidence, our habits are best exposed by the people around us. Usually, we believe we have hidden the unhealthy habits, the unreasonable habits, and the offensive ones too. And darn it, those ones always seem to sneak out and trip us up. Exposed, for all to see.

I discovered within those first weeks my dad had a daily diary filled with habits. Much like a poor writer leans on paragraphs of clichés, so my dad stumbled from one repetitive behaviour, comment and joke to another. Initially it was charming, but it soon became quite painful.

It was the drinking habit though I noticed with most alarm. It wasn't I had a problem with drinking. In fact, my sense of the Austrian culture was a swig of liquor and a few mugs full of golden beer were more about rounding out a meal or occasion than about getting drunk. It was commonplace and I had begun to quite enjoy the comfort with which I could sip away at a superb cold beverage just as the clock ticked past midday. And I wouldn't be alone either. I would salivate at the sight of a busty waitress, cradling a *breteljausen* with treats avalanching off its edge. It was the top and tail of a strong schnapps that gave the meal its credibility and gravitas. As everyone kept telling me, a *stampale* of homemade, fiery fruit schnapps was medicinal after all. I was serving my health, it seemed. Hard to argue with that one.

Growing up in South Africa, I'd been subjected to a Calvinist and puritanical obsession with control and obedience. It was bullied into us, and it cast a shadow of resistance in my younger self. Unlike my uniform-suffocated peers, I didn't fight this battle blind drunk, with vomit drooling out of my nose. I struggled to just let go like that. I also had a history of alcohol abuse in my DNA, but it was more than that; alcohol had killed people in my family. The serpentine syrup had a lot to answer for. I was young and had never met those deceased family members, but what I did have was the stifled lament of my mother. When I look back, I can't imagine what it must have been like for her to watch her eldest child enjoy an activity, over and over again, when it was exactly that 'sociable' habit that had killed her father. In truth, it made him kill himself. The merciless irony of choice and circumstance. I was oblivious to it all at the time, but my mom held back all her pent-up guilt and anger to allow me to normalise my relationship with liquor. But, like a matron, she kept a keen eye out for signs of an emerging habit. She never said that, but she couldn't help expressing it somehow.

There I was in Austria, primed to adopt that habit. If the breakfast shot was to start my dad's day, then it was the love of 'doing the rounds' that crowned the night. There were no plans, no need for a meal, and no calls to friends to hook up for a beer or nightcap. The 'rounds' were an excuse to drink and that was it. It was a problematic habit and it eventually crashed into broad view, quite literally, on a cool spring afternoon.

It was a Saturday. Papa had cycled into town late in the morning. I took a breather, and declined the invitation to join him. I savoured some time for myself. It was a quiet and peaceful morning, and then I heard it. The hollow clang and sound of metal against metal. It came from our apartment block entrance. It was a brief, chaotic mix of sounds that abruptly went to silence; until I heard a clumsy clatter of keys prodding against the wood of the door. Our door. It must be Papa, I thought. The door slammed shut in a way that would have normally drawn his wrath. The glass in the door chattered to the brink of a shatter. All the movements around the door were then slow, brash and heavy. Only then did I question who it might be. I heard heavy breathing, and then a fast, indelicate and disruptive series of sounds followed. I couldn't make out where those noises might be coming from. Then it went silent again for long enough to make me curious to investigate. *Had the person left? Surely it was Papa, but something was definitely wrong.* I tiptoed into the kitchen and moved the door ajar. I stopped when I heard a commotion in the bathroom and stepped towards the front door to investigate.

The first thing I saw was blood. A patchy, broken line of drops and larger puddles from the front door to the bathroom. I could see where the person must have stood for longer moments. The blood pooled in those spots. My dad's sunglasses lay bent and cracked on the floor leaning against his bloodied leather purse. The front door had been slammed so hard its locking mechanism hadn't had enough time to bite, and the door swung open with a draught of air.

'Papa, is everything okay?'

There was no response. I could hear the tap running and muffled wincing and sighing from behind the door. My dad's face unexpectedly ballooned through the doorway. He bashed his way out of there. His face was brutally swollen with a deep gash above his right eyebrow. I saw the bath draped with a blood-soaked towel. Alcohol fumes wafted against my face, and it seemed like the entire room was an equal mixture of blood and alcohol, both of which appeared to be dribbling out his nose and over his separated lip.

'I fell off my bike,' he slurred, using the handle of the door as a crutch, and stumbled past me into the lounge. He collapsed on the couch.

'Should we go to the hospital, or a doctor?' I asked with rising concern.

'No no, just shut up. I am fine!' he barked, waving his hand to dismiss me from his quarters.

I saw blood had leaked onto the couch and I grabbed a towel to catch the flow. I gingerly lifted his head and stared straight into the wound above his eye. Small crumbs of tar were lodged in the flesh around a dark well of blood above his brow. He had grazes running from his chin across his cheek and pulling back towards his ear. He didn't seem to know I was standing there. I pushed the towel further beneath his head. Blood was brushed from his knuckles onto my shirt. There were more wounds too. Some were seeping through his jeans, others on his elbows and more on his hands. By the time I had completed my short scan, he was snoring deeply and had passed out.

He had clearly banged his head on the ground, and was losing lots of blood. He must have fallen hard, possibly as he skimmed a bend, and then slapped the pavement with his face. It was 2pm and I went into his room every 15 minutes to ensure he was still breathing. His thunderous snoring made it easy to monitor, but it was in the silent spells, when he turned over or just stopped breathing, that I perked up. On each inspection, I saw his left eye had begun to swell and change colour, and the cut had become smudged with a mix of dry scabs, road debris and flesh. He remained fast asleep throughout the night.

The following morning, I found him sitting and cradling a coffee in his uninjured hand. His face was pale and puffy and, despite the early morning light, he wore dark, tear-drop sunglasses. His head wound had been cleaned and plastered but his grazes had become more prominent as they scabbed over and reddened. He didn't mention anything and for the first moments we both avoided talking about it. But then we heard a stony tapping on the kitchen window.

'Oh no, not her again,' Papa sighed, 'Every day, every single day, *Tante* Inge has to come round and she is doing this more and more now you are here.'

I wasn't sure if that was a good or bad thing. Maybe good for me, but clearly bad for him. He found her incessant chatting and interest highly annoying. To me, her daily visits showed she cared.

'Oh my *God*,' she said with alarm in her eyes. 'What happened to you?'

Like a peacock, my dad pushed his chest out and turned his grazed face in her direction, giving her the full gory view. It seemed to please him for a moment.

'Were you in a fight?' she asked. 'Who did this to you?'

The question made him recoil in embarrassment. I chuckled to myself. A fight would have been the perfect alibi, even if it was unlikely to happen more than once a year in this sleepy town.

'No, Inge, I wasn't in a fight. When last was I in a fight? I don't fight. I actually fell off my bike coming back from town,' he tried to sound matter of fact. 'Now you can see why a helmet is so important.'

'And do you need stitches? Did you go for stitches?'

'No Inge, I am fine, I just needed these plasters. It looks a lot worse than it is.'

'But what about infection?'

'Inge, I am fine; please stop this, I am fine. Okay? Did you want to speak to Marc?'

She shook her head and handed him a bag of fresh bread.

'Just some lunch for you two,' she said. She shook her head, and wandered down the road.

Sometimes the best form of distraction is the truth. He conveniently omitted the state of his inebriation as being the cause of the accident and no one ever asked. I was the only one who knew, and it gnawed at me.

The bikes had already proved to be more of a liability than I could have imagined, and I began to wonder what baggage, what stuff, my dad was carrying around with him that would make him just as much of an unpredictable burden. His abuse of alcohol was a clear habit.

The Battle of the Cage

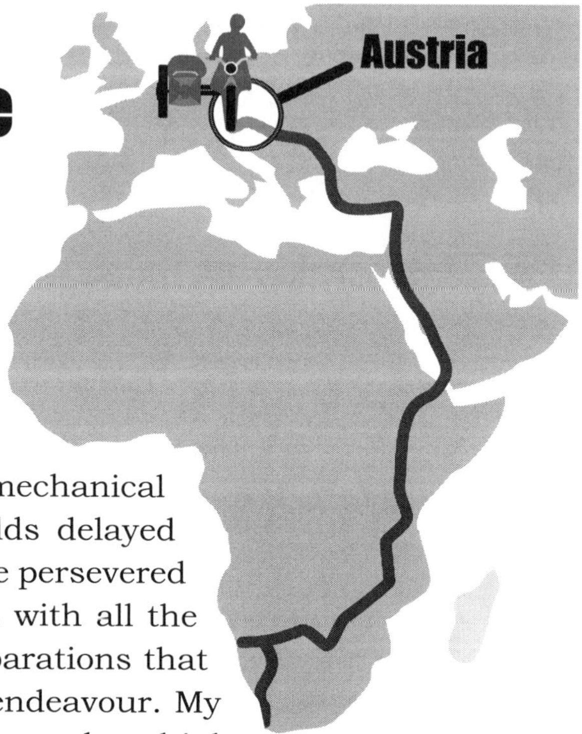

The regular mechanical faults and rebuilds delayed our departure, but we persevered and busied our days with all the other plans and preparations that go into such a long endeavour. My dad painstakingly mapped multiple routes through each country, and calculated everything from total kilometres to gaps between petrol stations. That second figure was more an estimation than fact; he assumed most dots on a map that looked bigger than a hamlet would have fuel. That was all essential to think through beforehand, and it had a direct bearing on our eventual route. The bikes only had a range of about 350km per tank of fuel.

Next, we methodically recorded all legal and trans-border document requirements. From visas to motorbike licences, ownership records and insurances. From international drivers' licences to export documentation and medical certificates for every possible grizzly disease. We also applied for a handful of visas and underestimated how long those bureaucratic lags would be. In some cases, sending off our passports would mean weeks without them, only to repeat the steps again at another embassy. We would have to apply for most of the African visas on the way. Ethiopia turned out to be the perfect place for that.

With extra time on our hands, we turned our attention to the design and functionality of the bikes. The engines were untouchable as we had chosen to do the entire trip on the originals. If there would be anyone to blame for choosing those rickety contraptions and keeping them unmodified and unmodernised, then it would be only us. But there were storage solutions and carriage options we wanted to explore. On such overland trips, there were certain items that needed to be easily accessible. Spares for example would need to be readily available at all times. The bike modifications should ensure that was possible.

For such a long trip, and despite a careful geographical plot of all fuel stations, we worked out we needed to be able to comfortably survive with 450km worth of fuel. To make that possible, we had to carry two 20-litre jerry cans and an extra can of motor oil. The bikes were already fluid incontinent, as the pools of oil that stained the roads wherever we parked had proved. Extra fuel and oil provisions were essential.

The bikes came standard with a spare wheel bolted elegantly on the back of the sidecar. That was the only relatively flat space we had to work with. We created a new seat for the spare wheel which then proudly hung off the front flank of the side car. We built a metal saddle for the oil can opposite the spare wheel. The jerry cans were then mounted on a wooden base on the flat spot and covered with canvass protectors, made to specifications to ensure they didn't get too much dust or exposure to the sun.

Throughout all of that work, from the conceptual

planning to the actual building, I was, at most, a junior assistant, a hanger-on, a real lurker. I would scramble to get the correct tools in the right order after every short command. Most of my ideas were ignored. I just watched and waited. I became frustrated, but I was used to that feeling. When it came to mechanical, technical things, I was seen as pretty useless. That was at least how I felt. It was how my dad made me feel most of the time.

The net result of my fringe participation was all those preparatory activities, such as buying supplies, tracing maps, modifying bikes and spending money, made it even easier for me to simply hand the lead role to my dad. In the beginning I didn't think I had a choice, but within a few weeks I was frustrated by my lack of involvement. It was above all, tediously boring. I itched to write my signature into the trip and became restless in my isolation. I wanted to have a say about our route, which towns we would see and which we would bypass. I wanted to rebalance the equation and put my wishes on the table. Of course, that meant I would need to be more vocal and risk annoying and challenging my father.

As I wasn't sure how I would do that, I started with my bike. I believed it would have the least effect on him, it was a softer target. Papa had shown no interest in my ideas and expected me to copy what he was doing. He was after all, the engineer with decades of experience jump-starting 4x4s in the desert, building machines and contraptions, MacGyver style. He was the self-proclaimed expert and I was the sissy who had grown up with his mother and never quite learnt how to do more than wield a hammer at a nail. His general response to my more technical ideas was patronising. In truth, I didn't really know too much, but I would have appreciated some help, rather than disdain and ridicule.

That dynamic soon escalated into a competition, smeared with needle and grit. We didn't admit to it, but we slowly started to enter into a low-grade battle to outdo and outsmart each other. That had become my intention at least. My initial tactic was to delay all of my efforts and inputs. I would wait for him to start a new modification or implement an idea to the point when I believed there was no return; or when it made little sense to start over. I would then move in and, with his design in mid-build, try and trump his idea. I went Japanese on him, and tried to improve on what he had done by noting the problems that emerged and then celebrating how I solved them. I don't think he knew explicitly what I was doing, but he must have sensed my growing lack of cooperation.

The most notable example of our competition played out around the cage. We had become increasingly aware of the value of the goods we would put into our sidecar. After each purchase, we began to worry about how we might lose it, or that it might be stolen. Security features were our next challenge. The bikes simply had no way of being locked or secured, and with the sidecars becoming our storage compartments, the thin fake leather covers provided little resistance.

We gathered our thoughts on a sunny summer's day in the basement below the flat.

'We need to build a lockable sidecar,' said Papa, 'and we have a few options.'

He didn't share all the options, just focused on the final idea he would pursue.

'I'll weld us each a cage that will fit securely over the top of the sidecar and will be easy to lock.' He showed with his hand exactly how it would slide into the sidecar and where the locks would rest.

The problem for me was I had no idea how to weld. As

a result, I would be unable to improve the design. It was a disastrous start.

'What other options did you think of?' I asked, fishing for additional ideas.

'*Ag*, don't worry. I had a few other ideas but the cage is the best for now.'

I was losing my grip on the possible solution. Welding was way too advanced for me. If defence wouldn't work, I decided to go on attack. I needed to find possible weaknesses of the welding design and force a rethink. But I had to keep him on his track of thought to ensure he would still build his original weld option. It was intensely petty but I couldn't help myself.

'The problem with a cage is people can still get their hands through the gaps,' I pointed out, almost hoping he hadn't heard me, 'and it won't be waterproof either, will it?'

That was my sucker punch, but I was concerned I might have given too much away. My dad threw a sharp, annoyed look at me.

'No, the gaps will be small and the cover will go over the cage, of course,' he snapped.

Shit, why hadn't I thought of that? I hadn't prepared what I was going to say next, but it frothed out of my lips in contempt, 'I have another way of doing this security thing, so don't worry about welding me a cage.'

In truth, I had no idea what I would do, but I was resolute in my desire to do something for myself. For the next three days we each worked tirelessly at our inventions. Papa's cage began taking shape, and it boasted many desirable features. It was a strong, well-built, smart modification. I, on the other hand, only knew how to work with wood, and spent much of my time sawing and sanding my idea into shape. We didn't talk much.

When we were both done, it was clear my wooden trapdoor, which was the best way to describe it, would resist very little penetration from both weather and criminal. It was heavy and sat awkwardly over the seat of the sidecar. It just didn't fit properly. In comparison, Papa's cage ticked all the boxes. He said nothing. It was gleaming with black metallic spray paint, each bar and bend in the metal was equidistant and precise. It sunk into its seating like a finger into jelly.

I had noticed his odd smirk, but he didn't tear into me, he opted to just let me be. It was a fleeting, fast dissolving tonic for my sagging confidence. But it didn't last. The daily grind of feeling watched and out of place ate at me. Yes, the details of the trip, and the regular rounds, shifted my attention away from our relationship tension, but they didn't last long enough to make me feel altogether better. It was inevitable I would crack under the persistently heavy sense of judgement, and it was no surprise a specific trigger would make it burst out. I kept my creation without making any further modifications.

With the bikes fully kitted, and the last of our visas returned, the countdown to our departure day began in July 1999, many months later than planned. I had been in Villach for four months already, and as the starting line came closer, my wheels came off. It started and ended with Papa, 18 days before our scheduled departure.

I remember everything being finc until I stepped back into the flat and began welling with uncontrolled emotion. It was an awkwardly deflated response to a short trip to the train station.

'It's for business,' he had said. 'I have to go; the money will help, you know.'

'So what am I supposed to do? What do you want me to do while I wait here?' I had asked.

'Just relax and take it easy, we are all set, it's no big deal.'

That was it. It was a twist of forgettable proportions, but nevertheless, it was a further delay to our departure. All the previous delays had been shared experiences, but this one was different. We had grown used to waiting together for parts to arrive, we toiled side by side fixing and modifying, planning and preparing. We even sipped a beer in resignation after every false start. I had secretly celebrated most of those delays with a mix of relief and frustration. But that final delay was different. It happened so quickly. He had heard the news and within a few days we were at the station, en route to the airport and then he was gone; to Kenya for a week. Sure, it all made sense. We were in no rush; the bikes had no evident expiry dates, although each weld and crooked part was symptomatic of a coming demise. The Millennium would come, wherever we were, after all. So what was the issue? There really was no need to rush, but gee, I felt livid, and I wasn't entirely sure why.

I dropped myself on the kitchen chair in the empty flat. The fury fuelled a cocktail of belligerent moods. 'Flipping lucky *bugger,*' I mumbled under my breath, thinking about my brother's declining of the invitation. Kenya was to have been the switch, the predestined halfway point on the original plan where he and I would swap. The way I felt at that moment, I faced rabble-rousing resentment in my thoughts. Then I let rip.

I can't remember if I swore my way around the flat, or wrote it down first, either way I vented. And I was alarmed at the viciousness of my rant. It was a confusing rush of emotional leakage.

'*Fuck* him. *Fuck* him!' I shouted until I was breathless. 'I don't want to do this. *Shit* man, I can't do this. No ways, 12 months, 10 months, three months just with him. I can't take it!'

And then I started writing. I addressed it to my mom, in a journal entry of all my concerns and regrets. I scribbled it all down, unedited and uncut. I revisited it all, and with each deeper engraving of the pen into the page, I spoke my mind, truthfully, to absolutely no one.

'Dear Mom

I came all the way across the world on a plane filled with strangers. My plan was to go back all the way round the world on a bike with my dad. Today, my dad is still a stranger to me. I am sick and tired of feeling this. I am not going to do this trip. That's it. I am pulling out. Stuff him. He can do this without me...'

I paused as I decided right then I was done. I was not doing that trip with him, and as I made that decision I felt a release of tension and intolerable expectation. Like jumping off a cliff, I felt in flight and free. Months of turmoil, with no one to talk to, filled the certainty of my decision. It wasn't a hasty idea. It had been brewing for months; I just had not been able to offload the burden of my hopelessly mismatched expectations. I thought he would be different, but he was worse. But I had done what I had always done: grinned and endured it. Too scared to make a stand, too frightened to lose the small chance of being accepted, I had simply rolled with it all. But on that day I exposed the net effect of keeping it all to myself. On the first day I was not with my dad, the flimsy veneer of normality was shattered and my deepest projections and desires flooded out like a drum full of serpents.

I ended my letter.

'So I suppose I will see you very soon. I need to find some money for a flight home, please call when you can. I am serious. Love Marc.'

I dropped it into an envelope, addressed it directly to my

mom and sealed it. She was the only person who would understand. And then I shredded it with calm, slow scissor strokes. It was as if I had emerged from a psychotic episode. I went to the phone and dialled home. I had left all the venom in that letter and felt completely normal. When my mom answered the call, she immediately asked how I was doing and I authentically replied, 'I am feeling much better now. I am ready to get on that bike.'

The Departure

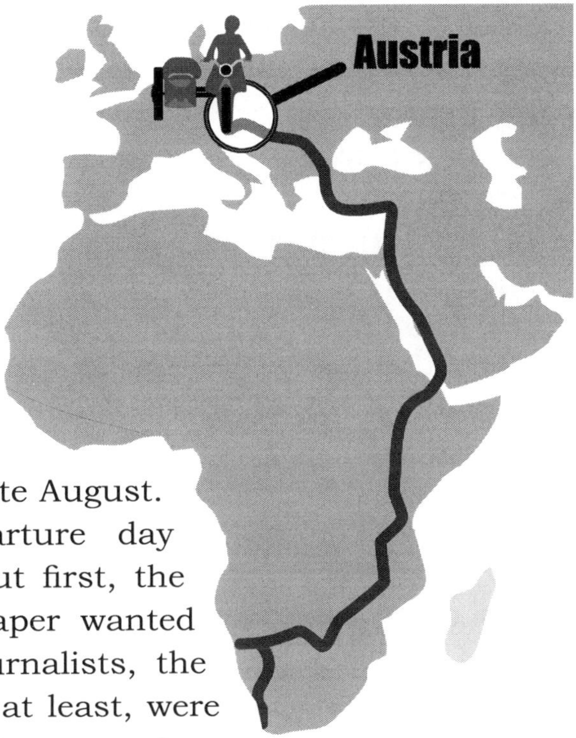

It was eventually late August. The elusive departure day finally stood still, but first, the local Villach newspaper wanted to speak to us. Journalists, the small-town versions at least, were a peculiar type. I had never met one in the flesh before, but they seemed overly enthusiastic and awed. I always imagined them being more cynical and worn, but the pair that met us were in a constant state of disbelief at our plans. They gasped when they saw the bikes, and rolled their eyes in a mock coma when they heard of our proposed route. They rocked their stares between the bikes and us, like spectators at the net of a tennis match. They took photos and wrote full and lengthy notes. They wanted all the juicy details, like the name of the most dangerous place we might visit and the number of times the bikes had already broken down. They even probed for a laundry list of our deepest fears and anxieties. That we believed we would charge into Cape Town on 31 December was the part they found comical. But we believed it. It had always been the end date, and with a few longer days in the saddle and a couple of short cuts across the map, it was still likely.

After shooing the media away, we visited my aunts and uncles to say goodbye. I hoped I would see them again. Papa hated goodbyes. He didn't believe in them. They were a nuisance, a social obligation that had no meaning to him. We rushed each visit, and eventually arrived at the pub for an early dinner. By 1am we were still dancing on the tables and totally out of control. It was more celebration than farewell. I didn't understand the mood, it felt part fatalistic, almost like the final night before a sentenced man goes to prison. On the other hand, it was possibly also about accomplishment, about feeling like the achievement of actually being able to leave was worth a celebration in itself. Whatever the trigger, it was an unplanned, uninhibited and wild night, and the next morning we nursed the consequences and were forced to delay the start by yet another day. We hid from the world. That morning the local paper ran our story, with just one picture and a smattering of text. To all who read it, we had already left.

When we finally did get going, our route took us north-east. Surprisingly, my dad insisted we say our farewells to my half-sisters on the way. Yes, I have half-sisters, two of them, both more than 10 years older than me. They had lived in South Africa at one stage – one was born there – but they were as Austrian as skiing. I didn't know them well. I had only met them on a handful of occasions. Of course, I also had nieces and nephews. As can be expected, my sisters had their own painful relationships with Papa. There was an awkward similarity between their story and ours. But I always felt there was envy, maybe even hostility, that they did well to hide when they were with us. For the 11 years my dad had lived with us, he had been away from them. Then the tables turned. I don't even remember if I had known I had sisters until I was a teenager. It was complex to explain, my mother said. Something about a messy divorce that was the ex-wife's doing. I never really listened or cared, but I did see them as family; they were siblings, and I discovered we had a lot more in common than I had ever appreciated. One experience was consistent though. Every time we met, it felt like my brother and I were seen to have been favoured by my dad; that we were the golden boys, and they had been forgotten. It was more complex than I allowed myself to face.

Maria, the eldest, lived on a farm high up a slope in the foothills of the Alps. Her husband divided his work with the seasons. In winter he ferried tourists up to the local ski slope in a horse-drawn sled, and in summer he was a wrangler, herding the local farmer's livestock to greener pastures beyond the inhabited slopes. He took them deep into the Alps. They lived a simple rural life, tilling and farming the land using traditional tools in the age-old pastoral ways. They used real horsepower for all their hard labour and were, to all intents and purposes, self-sufficient.

We wound through the forest in the late morning on our first day of travel. It was peaceful and picturesque, the thick pine forests blanketing each hill and slope. Their farm was all slopes, with not a square inch of naturally level ground. Their fields were all leaning with the camber of the hills.

'This house is older than Cape Town,' said Maria, as she sat on an old wooden bench with a mug of coffee cradled in her soiled hands. 'Well, you know, older than when Europeans first got there.'

We hadn't said much beyond our greetings. I had

quickly been kidnapped by my niece for a tour of their livestock, and arrived in the house just in time for some stove-fired coffee.

'Wow, that would make it over 400 years old,' I said.

'Yes, close. Actually, more like 500,' she said with a broad Rogatschnig smile. 'What was his name again? The man who arrived in Cape Town?'

'Jan van Riebeeck?'

'Yes, that was it. Are you surprised I know that?' she asked, holding the cup to her lips.

I was. Only a South African would know Jan van Riebeeck was the first white settler at the Cape of Good Hope.

'I could even speak Afrikaans when I lived there you know. I was growing up like a South African, like you I suppose.'

That was the most I had ever spoken to her. I sat leaning against a metre-thick wall. The ceiling was made of hand-sawn pine planks, as was the front door which had probably been high enough a few hundred years ago, but was awkwardly low in modern times. For a short while I mused at the historical juxtaposition. I lived in a city that was younger than this modest house. Where I lived everything had changed, but that house had been there, all the same. Those peculiar observations stretched me between my South African and Austrian identity. Every time I waded into my family history, it was a mix of paradox and irony. There was so much that was opposite and so much that was the same. It was always the human stories that were timeless and spanned beyond borders, language and nationality. To me, the only link between South Africa and Austria was in my extended family.

I found connection and similarity in our experiences within and between the two hemispheres. The story was firmly anchored in the footprints of our father and his journey between them. I sat there that day, surrounded by the only family I knew that had both countries in their blood. It wasn't meant to be significant, there had been no nostalgic plan to it all, but I believe it was more predestined than any of us realised at the time. The journey ahead had more meaning to us all...

We drove late into the night on that first day and slept in a small and comfortable guest house. We were both physically shattered and we awoke stiff and strained, having tweaked and pinched muscles that weren't used to that much attention. It was the physical discomfort that finally made it all feel real. Our trip had begun, and each day would pretty much end the same way; in a new place we had never been to before. The anticipation was palpable.

On day two, we picked the autobahns as our most direct route towards the Hungarian border, and it was hair-raising. Three lanes of traffic hurtled around us. The trucks were the most startling, and I was mentally drained within the first hour from the concentration it took to stay in my lane. I had also underestimated the mental switch I had to keep making between driving on the left-hand side of the road, which I was used to, and driving on the right. In Villach, I had become used to the well-driven routes, but the autobahn was all new and I was doing mental gymnastics to keep within the correct place.

That is probably why I almost didn't notice it happen. At first I heard a rattling sound from the back of my bike. It was only as it grew louder that I registered it might be something I should worry about. The moment I looked back to see what it was, I saw my number plate tear off and cartwheel down the road behind me. It clipped the bumper of a truck and shot back into the air. It spun and then slid beneath the cars. I had to focus on the road in front of me and didn't see where it landed. There was nowhere to stop. The road began to bend and I lost sight of that stretch of it altogether. After about two kilometres we pulled over at a roadside stop. The traffic was thick and swarming past us.

'Oh *shit*,' said Papa, stepping off his bike, 'was that your number plate?'

'Yip.'

'You have to go back and get it,' he said. He was still wearing his helmet and his voice was urgent. 'We have problems if you have lost it. We will have to go back to Germany to get a new one, because we will not be allowed to leave Austria without it.'

'Okay, I'll just walk back down the side of the road and fetch it. I think I know where it ended up.'

I jogged back around that bend and expected to see the number plate pushed to the side of the road. But I couldn't find it. There was no sight of it. I wondered whether it had maybe taken flight and landed in the opposite lanes behind the thick plants of the centre island, or maybe landed in the foliage itself. It was difficult for me to see anything in the outer lane furthest from me. It then dawned on me the multi-lane barrage of hurtling vehicles would make retrieving it near impossible anyway. I was stuck. I had no plan and no idea what to do next, and paced up and down the side of the road like a dog waiting for its owner to throw it a ball. On the verge of desperation, I spotted a small yellow telephone booth neatly positioned on the edge of a small glade of trees. It looked like a roadside assistance booth. It seemed to be my last chance, bar getting back on the bikes and driving up and down in both directions.

As I trotted over to the phone, I realised I would be

speaking to someone who most likely spoke only German. Although my German had improved, it was still a bit stringy. I could get by, but struggled to be conversational, let alone technical.

'Hallo, can you help please?' I shouted into the receiver, pressing the phone hard against my ear. I had rehearsed that first line and it rolled out in perfect German.

'Yes, what can we do for you?' said the man politely, but with a heavy colloquial accent, the kind that changed the German language to an unrecognisable dialect.

'I have left behind my plates that have numbers on them,' I said, starting to get lost in my translation.

'You have what?' said the man. 'This service is for traffic emergencies sir; please do not call us with false problems.'

I paused and tried to work out how to rephrase what I was trying to say. I could hear the annoyance in his voice, that year-round agitation so typical of officialdom.

'What are you talking about? Are you camping? Why are you camping on the side of the road?' he asked.

'I with my motorbike and my plates flew away from me,' I said, trying to find the correct German words, but I knew something was wrong.

'Listen, this is a line for emergencies.' He barked more admonishment, but I only understood bits and pieces. He was becoming more and more annoyed. And then came the warning, 'If you are playing games then I will have to call the police, do you hear me?'

'Sorry, sorry sir,' I apologised. 'You see, my motorbike has a plates and they fell off the road. They are German platters and my German is disgusting. I speak only English.'

Again, I knew it was all wrong. He was silent for a moment and then started to chuckle, building up into loud, belting laughter. I couldn't help it and joined in. We echoed each other's mirth.

'Okay, just wait a minute,' he said in broken English.

In the background I heard him banter with a colleague. He had muffled the phone with his hand, but I could hear activity. I searched my German vocabulary for the correct translation for 'number plate', and tried to practice what I needed to say. *Is it even called a number plate*, I wondered? *Maybe they call it a licence plate?*

'Hallo, are you still there sir? Did you lose a German licence plate, or German platters?' he chuckled again. There it was, the label that had eluded me: licence plates.

'Yes, licence plates. I have lost the licence plates.'

'Oh, so you didn't lose German platters, with, say, bratwurst and speck on them?' he joked. 'You are in luck then. I have a trucker on the other line who says he has just picked up a German, Munich-based licence shield. Is that yours?'

'Yes, yes, so sorry, my German is terrifying. Thank you, that is mine.'

'Great, and yes it is terrifying, it is so terrible,' he said, emphasising another phrase I had butchered. 'The trucker says he can see you. He will stop at the phone where you are now and give it to you.'

I was so relieved I spewed the best of my English manners at him. I didn't care anymore. He just chuckled and with a quick goodbye, hung up. As I put the phone down, a small delivery van pulled in and the driver held the plates out the window for me. Again, my English thanks poured out. *What luck, what a start, what a damn relief!* Thank the Lord it had happened while we were still in Austria.

Before we pushed off again, I cable tied, with triple strength, my number plate back on. We were now acutely aware the gruff rumble of those engines would rattle many components off over time. Luckily for some, I would no longer be expected to speak German either.

The Eastern Gateway

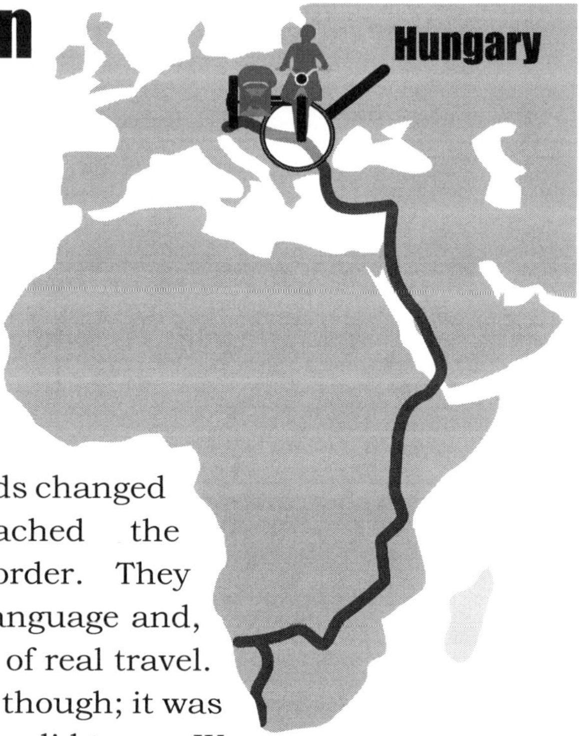

The roadside boards changed as we approached the Austria-Hungary border. They were in a different language and, for me, the first sign of real travel. My edginess shot up though; it was what border crossings did to me. We had a file full of papers to present, with stamps and signatures and official letterheads. They were all translated into multiple languages, except Hungarian. There were so many pages and details within each document, the potential for an inaccurate or incomplete form was high. That, coupled with grumpy border officials who often behaved like zealous uber guards and protectors of their civilisations, made the outcomes murky. It meant a slipped pencil mark, smudge, spelling error, or something as arbitrary as the sight of our teeth could present them with plausible reasons to bar us entry. I had once been fined for wearing sunglasses while I drove in Mozambique. The man told me they obscured my vision. We needed all that documentation to be without a single error. But my paranoia was misplaced; we sailed through, without hassle or debate.

Just beyond the border we found a campsite in an old orchard and assembled our stretchers between the trees. Our mosquito nets hung off fruit-laden branches. We had a long and peaceful rest on that first night beyond the home country. Hungary turned out to be a pleasant place. A country with neither edges nor strife, nor deep scars. At least we didn't see any of that. It had no real claim to fame, other than its part with Austria in a century-long empire that dominated Europe in the second millennium. I later discovered it was the birthplace of the inventors of the Rubik cube, the ballpoint pen and plasma TV; and that the language is closest to Finnish.

We toured the country with ease. I learned two critical survival tips on a night we camped at Lake Balaton, the largest inland lake in Europe. Firstly, when Papa and I shared a tent, I had to be sure to go to sleep at the same time as him, or earlier. If I didn't, which was the case on the lake, his bellowing snores would keep me awake. Secondly, he followed the alternative, hippie tradition of eating garlic at bedtime. To survive the herbal stench that choked the tent after he had gorged himself, it was essential to be unconscious. My bedtimes would therefore be at my dad's chosen hour, no matter how early or late.

The weather was unpredictable, but offered us a prime opportunity to test our bikes. They slogged in sweltering heat, battled the buffeting of gale-force winds, and sloshed through torrential downpours and flash floods. We suffered sunburn and marginal heatstroke, battled with stiff shoulders and arms while we hunched over our handlebars to wrestle those elements. Our boots filled with water and the bikes spluttered along but never gave up. That made us proud and sent a deep-tissue sensation of relief through me. We ended each day with diesel dust smeared across our faces and the smell of oil dyed onto my nostril hairs. We would debrief all the close shaves and near misses that had tested us along the sharp bends and with passing trucks and tractors.

On our last night in Hungary, we discovered a neat and manicured campsite. Our wooden hut on stilts was surrounded by giant pine trees and overlooked the empty, eerily quiet travellers' village. There was a single caravan with dim light parting its curtains. The sky was dark and moody, like a distinctive horror movie setting. Fringed by a blackened forest, isolated and empty, it was more than a little creepy out there. The caravaners must have felt the same discomfort, and within an hour they popped over to invite us to join them for dinner. Better the creepy axe murderer you know, than the vagrant gypsy bikers you don't, I supposed. It was a kind gesture, but suspicions of poison and an ambush were in my mix of wicked thoughts. They were harmless; a grey-haired German couple, probably in their 70s, touring Europe.

We gave them the pitch and boasted about the effortless start to what had begun as an ill-fated trip.

'So far, despite the number-plate saga, we have had no hitches or troubles,' Papa said. He was in high spirits, obviously relieved things were going so well.

'You are very lucky aren't you?' said the white-haired, hippie granny. She looked vital, with bright-coloured eyes and lips.

'Yes, we are, actually. We had so many issues before we left. These bikes are actually pieces of ... well, they are not great, not very reliable, let me say that.'

He paused for a moment, as if he was mindful of the bikes being within earshot and maybe hearing his insult. A plausible, superstitious consideration.

'These bikes have a German designer you know. Long time ago, but these days they are built by the Ukrainians.

If you look at them, you can see there have been many short cuts in making them.'

'I wasn't talking about the bikes,' she said, pushing a deep row of bangles up and down her forearm. 'I mean, you are lucky in other ways, aren't you?' She turned warm eyes on me, 'You are so very lucky to be a father and son, doing this trip together, as a team.' She sipped her beer. 'It is such a privilege to be with each other, and to have the time and the energy to explore the world in this way.'

'And only you will know what this journey was. You will share that for the rest of your lives,' added her husband, speaking for the first time. 'My wife and I will share this special trip, but we are old and our lives are near their end. You have your entire lives to be bound by this great adventure.'

'That is a unique and a very special gift isn't it?' asked the woman.

Papa looked at me and started in a way that sank straight into my heart, without him knowing it.

'Yes, this is probably the journey of a lifetime,' he said slowly.

Maybe even the journey for a lifetime, I thought to myself.

They were right of course, but within the task-focused run-up to our departure, I had lost sight of the bigger journey. My dad and I were travellers now, first and foremost. Yes, we were estranged family too, but that had pre-occupied me for most of the prior months. I again entertained the possibility of closeness between us. It was as if meeting those and many other strangers made it more evident we were not strangers ourselves.

We would cross continents and hemispheres together, and have it all to ourselves. We could feast on the challenge and the incredible opportunity that lay ahead. I hadn't noticed it before that conversation, but it seemed we were no longer competing as much. We were collaborating and showing signs of becoming a fledgling team. We were all we had. I was grateful.

The Romanian Knives

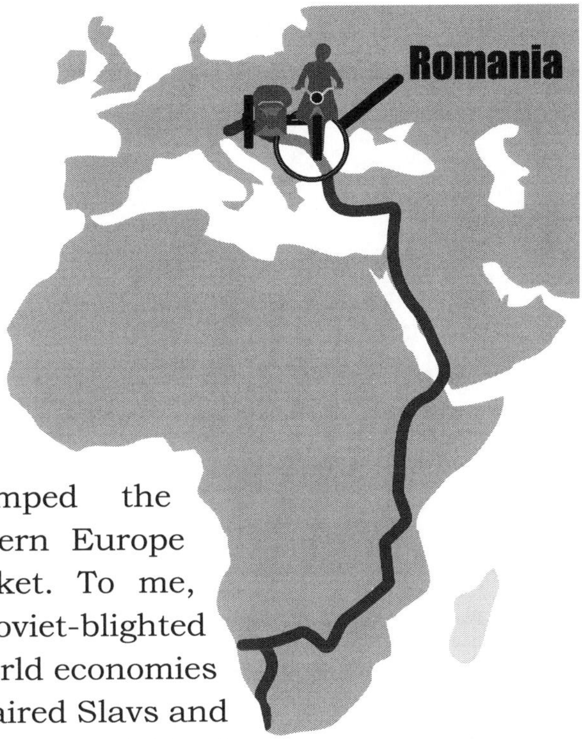

I had always lumped the countries of Eastern Europe into the same basket. To me, the region was a Soviet-blighted swathe of second-world economies inhabited by dark-haired Slavs and gypsies. That was an astonishingly prejudiced view, no doubt influenced by Cold War-era Hollywood movies. The languages were complex too, but to my ear they all sounded pretty much like Russian. Again, a broad swipe of generalisation. I often wondered why it had not been called West Russia, or Western Asia instead of Eastern Europe.

Hungary stood in stark contrast to its geographical siblings in the European east, but I doubted Romania would have such a distinct identity. In my mind, Romania was only about the Roma people who caravanned around Europe, living off the goodwill of strangers, or skirting the edges of the law to make ends meet. I had experienced three run-ins with gypsies in my time, and had developed an enduring suspicion. The most harrowing was being chased for kilometres through the streets of a small

Italian village after I had faked a coin drop into a busker's collection hat. We escaped through a labyrinth of railway platforms and skulked in the shadows for hours to avoid their prowling search.

Romania, as its name suggests, has as much Roman lineage as it does Roma habitation. The ancient empire gave the country not only its name; it dotted much of Europe with its distinctive architectural signature and in Romania, as in Italy, its language persisted too. Modern Romanian is the closest of all languages to pure Latin. It is believed the gypsies were originally from the Asian subcontinent and possibly of Indian descent. Their rich and colourful culture is a blend of traders and travellers. The remnants of all that history could be seen everywhere.

On arrival in Romania, unlike other places, we noticed the main highways were consistently lined with magnificent, well-tended trees. It was a vibrant, sensory experience to drive down those avenues, flanked by narrow orchards, their blossoms and sweet aromas hanging in the air. There were large, old nut trees – gifts from the gypsies, it turned out. Over decades, and most likely centuries, the dominant Roma travel paths were planted with trees that served to feed and sustain the community. They were Roma farms on public land, and everyone knew it. The understanding was no one person or caravan of travellers was to strip any one tree of all its gifts. Everyone could have a snack, but should then move on. And it seemed to work. That part of the world had been shaped by centuries of occupation, war and strife. It had been torn and trodden upon, and yet the ancient traditions persisted, much as they had done centuries ago. The more we travelled, the more interested I became. I had many times hoped we could skip Eastern Europe, but driving beneath those blossom-scented sentries, I was pleased to be there.

Just as each country offered unique experiences, our bikes had quirks too. There were many oddities, and even some absurdities. Each was a mix of parts stripped and borrowed from other bikes, or so it seemed on those Ukrainian rip-offs. On the one hand, there was the charm of wheels with spokes, and sprung shocks, and then the pain of a postman's bicycle seat, and that elusive, thumb-sized hooter. Each mechanical and electrical plan was simple and understandable, even to a non-petrol head like me. In fact, it was all so rudimentary we could patch and mould, fix and fiddle with anything we wished. My dad liked to tinker; it was an almost daily, troubling pattern. He would tighten a nut here, pull back a wire there, and even switch a few things around, seemingly out of boredom. Then with a mildly pleasing predictability, that area of the bike would begin to moan and malfunction.

The headlight of the Dnepr MT-16 was proudly mounted to the steering wheel. It epitomised all of the bike's frailties. Its casing tapered towards the back, and was nestled neatly in front of the handle bars. It had a vintage look to it, was pitch black and had bottle-thick glass that dramatically snuffed the light into a faint yellow glow. Either way, the old world appeal was lost on us, particularly when we needed light. It became dangerous and risky when dusk closed in, and the sun spat thick soupy rays from the horizon. What made that even dicier was driving east when those coming in the opposite direction were staring into the setting sun. That could be fatal, in particular in Romania, where they had a habit of overtaking at impossible odds, and usually couldn't see our lights at all.

On our first day in Romania, we found ourselves in the ideal head-on collision scenario. The time of day, combined with the deteriorating roads, a steady stream of heavy trucks, and the fact we were lost and thus quite distracted, made it reckless to continue. We pulled over at the nearest bar to find some directions and get help. Bars were more common than petrol stations in that part of the world. Without a word, Papa walked straight to the wide-eyed barman, who must have wondered if he was still wearing his helmet indoors as a disguise for a robbery, or if he had simply forgotten he was wearing it. I had the sense he might be clenching his fists into a karate stance below the bar, just in case.

'Hi, two birra please,' Papa tipped his head and offloaded the helmet.

The barman snapped his wrists and the bottle tops flicked off.

'Oh man, I know I say it almost daily now, but this beer may just taste like the best beer ever,' I gurgled as I opened my gullet for a beery watering. 'The first sip is still the best.'

We stood there quietly. The stares from around the room confirmed we were the focal point of the attention in the small locale. We nodded our heads and smiled at the stubbly cheeks and toothless grins and grimaces that rubbernecked at us. I assumed by the gritty and grubby look of them they were all truckers and farmers. Once we had greeted them, the chatter and hum rose again, and we were left alone.

'Excuse me,' Papa beckoned to the man behind the bar. 'Excuse me, can you help us please? Do you know if there is a campsite anywhere close to here?'

The man just smiled, pulled his hands out of his pockets and flapped them about in that universal answer of 'I have no idea what you are saying, but I will smile even more so you don't feel bad about not being able to speak my language'.

My dad repeated himself, but just a little bit louder.

Again, the man grinned and chuckled. He looked intently over our shoulders and searched for someone among the motley crew behind us. He was probably trying to find a translator. It was a quick browse of the faces, and clearly none were a match, he turned around and disappeared into the kitchen. We stared at the swinging door. He did not return.

Papa shrugged, 'Okay, that was interesting. Well, cheers then to our first day in Romania, and I hope we don't remain here.' He squeezed his eyes in amusement and kept on swigging his beer. That old 'Remain Here', Romania joke again. I laughed, as I always did.

I sipped at my beer and looked around the bar. We had no idea where we were; I couldn't even work out the name of the pub. It was one of those moments when we really had no plan. We had no address, or name of a hotel. We had no deadline, nowhere to be, and no one waiting for us. It was a unique feeling of true and raw freedom, with the liberty to be and choose without any obligations or expectations. At times it was a scary, anything goes, boundaryless sense of opportunity and potential. It was an addictive, fleeting sensation that entices all travellers to seek ever further and more remote places to disappear, and live unfettered from their past or future. In our case, no one knew we were there. It was as if we had fallen into a black spot on a map of Europe. We were forgettable strangers and real travellers at the same time. Either way, we were clearly just passing through. We were neither here nor there, and that made us eerily dispensable. We were in the moment, with no imagination of a next destination to intrude into the present. It was the opposite of wanderlust; it was about just being. I felt good, and fully alive.

We were both in deep thought when a timid voice spoke in my ear.

'Hello Mister, how are you today? Do you need help? Where are you going? What can I do for you?'

He was young and slender, maybe in his early 20s. His neat shirt was opened three buttons from the collar to reveal a bulky gold chain. He smiled and giggled nervously as he prepared himself for a chat.

'Hi,' I said cautiously, 'how are you?'

'Good, good, good,' he replied, nodding his head and looking around the room.

He seemed on edge, constantly looking down at his hands. In each hand was a cell phone. At first I thought he was trying to peddle them to us, and shook my head to show my lack of interest. They were large, bulky and scuffed old technologies. One of the screens was shattered from the corner outwards. It seemed as if he was half in conversation with us, and half waiting for his phones to ring.

'*Excuzzi*,' he said, before answering one of the phones that had begun to flash in his left hand. He spoke for no more than three seconds, in abrupt grunts and single-word sentences, and then hung up. He bashed at the buttons to kill the call and then switched his attention to the second phone and waited. He was oblivious to us watching him. One second, two, three, four ... on the fifth second the phone began to ring. Again, he spoke for just about three seconds, and then hung up. Five seconds later he answered the other phone again. That went on for a number of rounds. With each micro chat he got louder and more animated. His tone of voice became more panicked and agitated, as if he was trying to force his per-second word count beyond the athletic abilities of his lips. But there was something else that was nagging at him. We just sat there and watched him.

'I am so sorry,' he said as he caught his breath. 'So do

you need help? How can I help you?'

Again he scanned the room, and looked intently at the other patrons. His gold chain swung across his chest. It was like a trophy he wanted us all to see. It made me more nervous. That part of Europe had a pretty tarnished reputation and I felt like we might be in the cross hairs of a stereotypical con man. My suspicions had begun to grow with each ring of his phone. *Who was he speaking to? What was going on?* I was convinced he must have been talking to someone about us.

'Where can we find a hotel?' I asked firmly. 'We just need to know the name of a hotel or campsite.'

'No, no hotel, and no campsite in this town,' he said adamantly. Again he looked at his hands and picked up one of his phones. That time he stared straight at me as he juggled the lines. It was unnerving. He spoke very little, just answered the phones, nodded his head, shrugged his shoulders and watched us. My suspicions turned to dread.

'What do you think he is doing?' Papa hissed.

'I'm not sure, but I don't trust this guy for a ...' I cut myself short as he hung up his phone.

'No hotel, no place for sleep here. You must come with me now,' he said, and signalled to the door. We didn't move, so he tugged at my shirt. It was dark outside. Riding at night was a lottery anyway, especially for my dad with his dodgy eyesight.

'No, don't worry, we are okay. Thanks!' Papa turned back to the bar to try and separate from the conversation.

'No hotel or place to stay? Mmm, this guy is playing games with us,' I said. 'Look at these people and all those trucks; there must be a place to stay here.'

Just as quickly as he had arrived, the young man disappeared, but we instinctively knew he would return. We knocked back the last quarter of our beers in preparation for a hasty retreat out of there.

'You must just follow me,' he called as he burst back through the doors. 'I know where you can stay. It is safe place for you and the motorcycles. Please, please, come with me. Not to worry.'

He could see the doubt in our eyes. We were in a defensive position, but it felt like we had very little choice at that point. We had no idea where to go and it was pitch black outside. What we had was a guide, albeit a dodgy scammer in the making. We had no map and we weren't even sure which town we were in. We had no alternative plan and had given too much of that information to him already. What could we say as an excuse not to go along with him? At what stage would we be rude, maybe even insulting? We were lost and at a loss.

'Okay, we will follow you,' I said, resigned to circumstance. My dad looked fidgety.

As we fired up our bikes, the young man appeared in a light blue Toyota Corolla, gleaming with wax-polished pride under the flickering street lamps. He gave us the thumbs up.

'Just keep your distance,' Papa warned, 'and if it begins to look like we are moving away from the town, away from buildings and people, then stop and let's turn back.'

'Good idea. Let's take it easy and slow,' I replied.

We drove for about five kilometres on the main road. The blue Corolla often streaked ahead of us and then backed off to keep the gap between us free of cars and trucks. He constantly looked back and continued to juggle his phones from hand to ear. Eventually, we made our first turn into what looked like a suburb. The roads off the main route were drowning in watery potholes.

We would have struggled to make a quick getaway, I thought. There were no street lights. A dim glow shone from the small square windows of some of the houses. The brightest light of all came from the Toyota. In my rear-view mirror I saw my dad stop dead behind me. I slowed down to a halt too. That would have been the ideal opportunity to use a two-way radio system between us. There was a 40-metre gap between us and the car, but it began to hastily reverse and close the gap. Our faint headlights created a dancing flash of light off his reflectors. I held my breath as he pulled up next to me. It felt like we were in a stand-off between faith and foolishness.

'Everything okay?' he asked, as he leaned out of his window.

I smiled and nodded as he again flashed the thumbs up at me.

'You don't need to worry my friend, we are very close now, very close.'

He drove off, for no more than a 100 metres, and then turned into what looked like a driveway to the left. I heard my dad's bike rev and rumble closer behind me. 'I'm tired,' he called. 'Let's see what this guy has got for us.'

It was a cottage, much like all the other small buildings we had passed on the road. As we turned into the entrance, our headlights lit up a long driveway, covered in vines that snugly blanketed the blue Corolla. To the left, there were three steps leading to a tiny landing and a green front door. On either side of the door were single windows. There were no curtains. The lights in the room closest to us were on. The young man beckoned us up the driveway and closed a ramshackle gate behind us.

'Hello, and welcome to my house. You are welcome to stay now tonight; we want you to be our visitors,' he said with pride. 'There is no good hotel here, it is a dirty and dangerous hotel and much safer to come and stay with me.'

An elderly couple peered through the window, nervously scouting the commotion in their yard.

'This is my father and mother,' he announced. 'We welcome you for eating and sleeping.'

I felt my guard drop. Seeing that elderly couple, dressed in day clothes but wiping the sleep from their eyes made me feel safe. We exchanged pleasantries and made an awkward attempt at small talk. Neither of his parents spoke English, but they smiled and nodded their heads. The front room was the kitchen, and three small, floral plates sat neatly placed around the table in preparation for a meal. They were expecting us. I felt welcome.

As we set up our stretchers on the wooden floor of a spare room at the back of the house, I pondered the meaning in it all. 'How amazing. I didn't think for a second this would happen to us tonight.'

'*Ya*, incredible,' replied my dad. 'How old do you think his parents are? Or are they maybe his grandparents? They could be in their 80s, and they are still up, almost at midnight.'

'I feel safe. Do you?'

'Yes, that is important isn't it? Up to about five minutes ago I was very nervous and worried.'

'Me too, but I think we will be fine.'

We both sighed in silence as our anxieties gave way to gratitude. We were strangers to them, and they must have been anxious too, and yet they hadn't shown it at all. We had misread the young man whose generous heart had brought us together under one roof.

We ate a meal together and tried as much as possible to get to know each other. We drank potent, local schnapps and laughed heartily as we stumbled over words, translations and sign language. It made the jovial banter slower and longer than usual. We finally went to sleep early in the morning.

Despite the late night, we both woke early. The morning sun streamed through the uncurtained windows and reflected brightly off something lying next to my stretcher. I rubbed my bleary eyes and eventually made out the shape of a knife placed on the floor. It was neatly laid on top of a light brown, leather sheath. I reached for it. My dad had already picked his up. As I drew it closer I noticed it had a bronze handle, carved into the shape of a lion's head. The detail was intricate, but rough and unpolished at the same time. The lion's head looked towards me as I held the knife in my palm. It was heavier than any knife I had ever held. The leather sheath was adorned with exquisite geometric patterns and detail. I stroked my finger along the blade; it was icicle sharp.

'Did you see someone put these here?'

'No, they were there when I woke up.'

'They look the same. Are they?' We held the knives next to each other. They were similar but not identical.

'It's beautiful and unusual,' I said, flipping the knife over and over in my hand. The weight of the lion's head made my muscles flex.

We packed up quietly and ventured out when we heard voices in the adjoining room. A big breakfast spread awaited us, with thick black coffee gurgling in the corner and fresh fruit piled into two baskets in the centre of the table. Cheerfully, we picked up the thread of a few tales from the night before. It was clear the family had pieced together the details from the late-night conversation, and wanted to know more about us and our adventure. What was of most interest to them was we were a father-and-son team. They listened with curiosity and had many questions. Despite the language barriers we felt able to converse. We asked them about themselves, and about

Romania. The young man's name was Chris and he was a student. We also discovered that in Romania there was a loophole in the cell-phone industry that made it possible for people to make free, three- to five-second calls.

Time passed quickly, and we could feel the heat of the new day's sun already starting to rise. Leaving too late was risky for us. We finished our meal and they handed us a basket of fresh bread and fruit and a bottle of white liquor, a home brew made from cherries. I had to ask about the knives.

'Chris, we found these knives next to our beds,' I said.

'Yes, you are welcome to keep them,' he said. 'It is a gift. My father was making these knives all night. He was making them from the beginning. They are new knives, made just for you.'

'He made this knife himself? And he made both knives last night?' I was amazed.

'He tells me to tell you it is our ... how do you say?' He paused. 'It is our culture to give a knife to people who travel.'

The old man stared and smiled at us.

'They are absolutely beautiful. Please thank him for us,' I said, clasping my hands together and nodding my head in that universal language of gratitude.

'Yes, he was working all of the night,' said Chris proudly. 'He was also praying for you when he was making them.'

I held back some tears, just. The old man said a few words which Chris translated, 'In the knife is God, and he will keep you safe.'

The Soviet Hotel

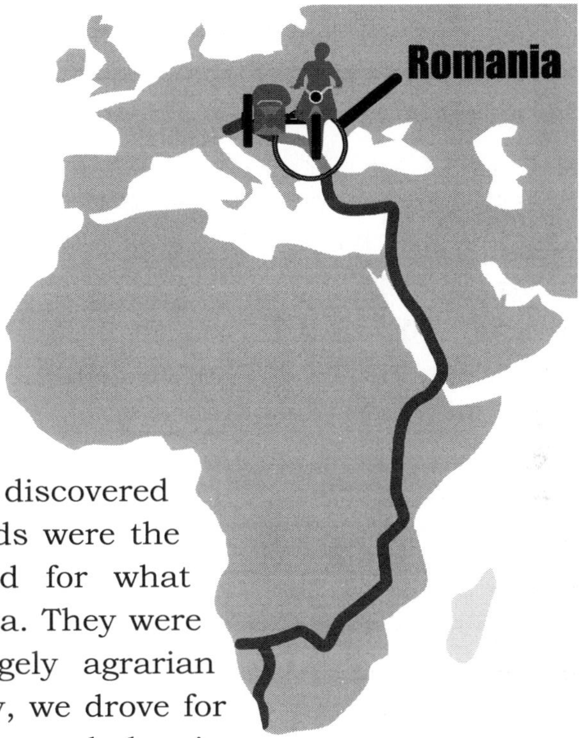

We soon discovered Romanian roads were the ideal testing ground for what was to come in Africa. They were terrible. In the largely agrarian south of the country, we drove for an entire day banging and clanging over thousands upon thousands of holes in the road. With each kilometre, small parts of the motorbikes shook loose. Items of luggage rattled free and our bodies took a hefty beating. Having to hold those half-ton machines steady and make last-minute turns and stops strained our backs, necks, shoulders, hands and arms. After a long day toiling in the heat, the idea of sleeping under a roof rather than the stars was appealing.

We neared the Romania-Bulgaria border at dusk. It was too late to cross, and we began looking for a place to stay. We hadn't seen a camping sign or clearly-marked overnight accommodation for much of the day. That was no surprise really, because we had decided to go off the main routes and had drifted into the bland and uninteresting hinterlands.

I suspect I might not have noticed the place if the sun hadn't been setting. It was a large, grand building of which only the western edge was visible from the road. It glowed a warm yellow as the last rays slipped beneath the thick pine trees and reflected like a pot of gold in the distance. It looked square, about three storeys high, and was lined with windows. Each had a small, wrought-iron balcony, with flower pots spilling plants or weeds down the walls. It was set back on some kind of estate and was guarded by a suitably ornate gate. It might have been a farm once. Either way, it looked nice from afar, but the partially crumbling perimeter wall made me wonder if it might turn out to be far from nice. Its state of decay made us more confident it would fit our price range.

The guard at the gate looked very surprised to see us. He was less interested in the bikes, and more curious about us, actual people, knocking on his gate. We slowly wound up the gravel path in first gear, straining to keep our wheels on the narrow track. We pulled up against a ramp which curved alongside wide steps that led towards two large wooden doors. The handles had been painted gold but were scuffed to the bare wood by countless grasping hands. A chubby man in a faded uniform, who was part bellboy and army general, welcomed us. He looked like a player in an historical re-enactment. He was unkempt and spoke almost no English, but was able to tell us the price of a room. As we entered the foyer, we noticed most of the lights were off in the sprawling mansion. Above us, a splendid chandelier illuminated the burgundy-coloured carpets underfoot. The walls were a mix of reds and off-white, some painted, others wallpapered. Large paintings of local scenery and history hung crookedly along the walls. The building smelled of an acidic mix of cigarette smoke, spilled vodka and greasy meals. But it was the emptiness that raised my suspicions the most. I slipped my newly acquired knife into my jacket pocket just before we began lugging our most essential belongings up the stairs. The lifts had not been working for a long time, the red-faced fatso told us.

Unsurprisingly, the rooms were no different to the rest of the hotel. I felt I'd seen a place like it before, probably in a James Bond film. It was rudimentary and functional, with hints of Soviet-era nostalgia. I imagined an overweight KGB major reclining on the bed, his belly bursting through his vest. Around him would be nubile lady friends, each wearing a single item that represented his prized position: one, his jacket; another, his hat; the next, a tie. The grubby room was deeply impregnated with the smell of tobacco that seemed to ooze from every corner.

'So we are sharing a bed again,' I said with mild irritation, spotting only a double bed in the room.

'We need to make sure our bikes are safe,' Papa said, ignoring me. 'I am not sure what we can do, but we can't leave them outside there. Did you see any security? Just that guy at the gate?'

'*Ya*, I didn't see anyone. It's a bit creepy, isn't it? There is no one else here either it seems. Pretty desperate.'

We heard a faint knock at the door. The bellboy, and for all we knew the only other person in the building, urged us to come with him. He muttered to himself as we followed him back down the spiral staircase and into the lobby. He then pushed open the front doors and walked purposefully to our bikes. He put his hands on the handlebars and moved as though to push them up the ramp. His under-sized shirt unfurled out of his pants as he did that. He repeated the action and pointed to the large double doors.

'Ha, problem solved, I think,' Papa said. 'Is he saying we

can park them inside?'

'Yes, I think he is actually telling us to park them in the foyer.'

Slightly bemused, but cheerfully compliant, we pushed the bikes up the ramp. Another young man appeared to help us. It took four grown men to do the job. They opened both of the wooden doors and we could just squeeze the bikes through. We parked them on the carpets, in the middle of the lobby, and right up to the front desk. We tried to move them out the way as much as possible, but were ordered to keep them exactly where they were, in the way. Although it was far safer than leaving them outdoors, we still stripped as many loose items as we could from the bikes and hauled them up to our room.

The man who took our booking at the front desk was also our barman and waiter. Maybe he was the chef too. We ordered a simple toasted sandwich off a curiously all-English menu.

'So far so good, hey?' Papa knocked back half his beer in a long, single gulp, 'We are on plan, on time and the bikes ...'

'Please don't jinx it,' I interrupted.

'*Ya ya*, but I think the bikes are feeling more at home these days, closer to the motherland, you know?'

'Things should just get better and better the further east we go, right?' I said hopefully.

'Let's not push it. For now, we have had some good luck for sure. Last night was just amazing good luck. I never imagined it could happen the way it did.'

'Maybe if we focus less on the bikes then we can enjoy more of the places and the people,' I suggested.

'Maybe. Hopefully. But we have only covered about one and a half thousand kilometres, on good roads and in cool weather. Well, mainly good roads.'

'When should we write to people back home and give them an update?' I asked.

'When we can, but we really don't have to,' he answered. 'I am enjoying feeling like we have disappeared; like it's just us.'

He was right. We were gone and lost to all those who knew us. I felt heartened by the comment. He was happy to be just us, the two of us, and that was it. I couldn't remember him ever saying that before in my life.

The MacGyver Moment

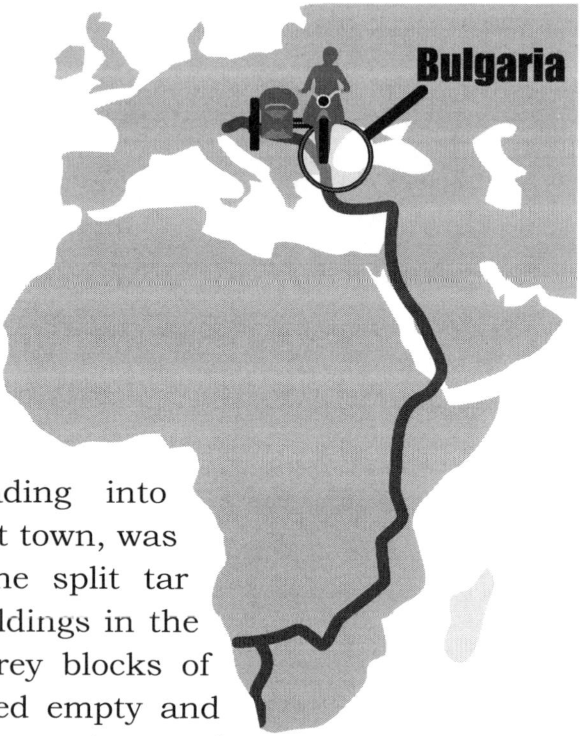

The scenery leading into Razgrad, the next town, was as regrettable as the split tar beneath us. The buildings in the valley below were grey blocks of concrete. Each looked empty and industrial. The litter on the weedy road verge had begun to break down in the summer rains. Muddy grooves dropped deep off the tar and were filled with stagnant, oily water. Dirt trails were scribbled across the surface where cars had dipped their tyres in the mud. Most of the paintwork on the buildings, the signs and the road markings, had peeled like the pages of a dog-eared book. It was a town I was looking forward to driving right through. The dreary urban sprawl was endless. There was no natural backdrop such as a hill, or a mountain, or even an horizon to soften the cement blocks that day. The entire view was shrouded in grey clouds. Like children going to a dentist, we cautiously made our approach. My focus was on any road or signal that invited us to skirt the city's edge and drive on. But desire and destiny were estranged bedfellows in our little world and it happened again, just as we knew it eventually would.

At first I felt that familiar, yet mild and almost forgettable jolt. The power temporarily faded and then surged again. It was probably a clot in the fuel line. My instinct was to pull a little harder on the throttle, to give it juice and feed it with petrol. The fading effect however became more prominent until eventually the harder I tried to accelerate, the less the bike responded. As the bike's momentum was lost altogether, there was nothing, no response at all. It died like a cat with nine lives, with the promise of a resurrection and an even more certain promise of repeated death.

'Aaaargh, not again! These *fucking* pieces of ... aaargh man!' I shouted in despair. I signalled to my dad with a slice of a finger across my throat. He knew exactly what I was referring to.

'Oh *shit* man, not again,' Papa lamented, shaking his head.

Yes again, for the third time. It sounded and felt like the piston had blown. I could hear it in the way the engine hissed and puffed, like a hyperventilating jogger. The air that was meant to compress into a small space at the top of the cylinder had escaped through a hole in the piston head. The spark would light the fine spray of petrol that filled that gap, but the explosive force of fire dissipated through the hole. When it all worked properly, the explosion would push the piston down the chamber, which then turned the engine; but with the air and fuel leaking through the hole, the explosion happened both in the small gap and in the chamber. That left no direction to the power, and the engine basically vomited in its own mouth.

'I can't do this again,' I said, exasperated. 'I think you jinxed these bikes last night, seriously! We should never ever say anything hopeful around these old ladies!'

Papa just shook his head. 'They are taking turns,' he said, reflecting on our calamitous day. 'Let's try and get to that parking lot down there, I'll tow you in.'

'Do we even have another spare piston left after this morning?' I asked.

'Let's just get down there and then we will make a plan.'

It was a case of deja vu. That morning, as we crossed the border post, my dad's bike had whistled and hissed and died. We had spent most of the day stripping that engine, and had replaced the piston. Actually, I had spent most of the day playing mechanic.

I usually did the grunt work; it was the established norm. I would do whatever he instructed me to do. I would lift the bike, put muscle into loosening and tightening, and reach a cup under a leak to save the oil. I was the one who lay in the dirt, took sprays of oil to my face, and rubbed loose tar into the back of my head. I would stand at awkward angles while I held tools and parts, or contorted to get to a pesky nut or electrical connection. I struggled with all that mechanical stuff. I had grown up with a single mom, and an intellectual and emotionally awkward stepdad. His slight figure and spectacled head of curly, fluffy hair were the antithesis of real masculinity. He never taught me anything about cars, bikes, tools and being tough. From the start of our trip, I'd been the *de facto* apprentice. I was made painfully aware I was many scars and greasy fingers short of being the real thing.

We wheeled the bikes into the parking lot and piled our belongings into neat batches that would be easy to pack again. It was always a tedious exercise. Such a waste of time. We also had to factor in the time it would take to repack which, after a long delay, was often the most tiresome. Security was always an important consideration. It meant we would have to split our attention to keep an eye on our exposed belongings, while at the same time trying to fix the bikes. We unlocked the metal saddlebags, pulled out the ammunition boxes, found the right tools and started to work, like robots. The spares were left untouched in the back of the side car. We always made a diagnosis first, and then initiated the last steps of a total unpacking process.

We knelt down next to the bike and waited for the engine to cool. The wet, grey air helped to speed that up. We noticed small melted strands of rubber squeeze out the edges of the cylinder heads. That was a sign of overheating, and usually signalled a wider range of heat-related problems. We became increasingly impatient until, despite the piping hot metal plates and covers, we began to loosen the first nut. As the nut fell out, the entire rubber gasket drooped out of its seating too. It was melted and disintegrated.

'We may be in luck,' said Papa, 'it looks like we only need to replace the rubber gasket. Did you see that it was melting earlier today?'

'Gee, I didn't notice it earlier, but I also didn't really look. It could have been slowly melting all day. I probably would have smelled something though, wouldn't I?'

I was being as hopeful and optimistic as I could be, but I couldn't brush away the, by then, habitual dread that accompanied any breakdown.

'Well, let's check,' Papa pushed the kick starter with his boot. Up and down, up and down while I watched the tappets flap within the cylinder heads.

'Can you see or hear any air escaping anywhere out the exhaust? Or anywhere else?'

'Nope, all seems fine, actually.'

'Well, we are in luck then,' he said with a victorious smile. 'The piston is still fine; it's just the rubbers that have gone.'

'Flip, that is such good news,' I replied, looking up at the sky as the clouds drew over the mid-afternoon sun. 'Is that rain coming? Should we move somewhere under cover?'

'We're almost done,' Papa said confidently, 'this will be our quickest fix yet.'

He put his hand on the seat of the bike and pulled himself up off his haunches. He began to straighten his back and his knees rocked forward. He misjudged the gap to the bike, and knocked the front of the cylinder head with his kneecap. The cylinder moved, ever so slightly, from the impact. We noticed that micro-movement, and for whatever reason, it looked unnatural. We both leaned down and watched intently as my dad knocked the heads again with his palms. This time on purpose. Nothing happened; it didn't move at all. He clenched his fist and gave it a sharp upper cut. That time it moved and we both recoiled from the bike in frustration and disgust.

'Oh *shit*, oh *shit*, oh *shit*! We have problems!' He dropped back to his haunches and looked up at the sky for a sign, 'Maybe it's just a loose nut or something; maybe it's nothing too serious, but that would explain why air was pushing out of the cylinder, I think.'

His voice became muffled as he peered in to have a closer look. I watched him, as I so often did, not knowing what part of the bike he was looking at. I usually couldn't name the parts, and I certainly had no idea what their Ukrainian-engineered purpose was. I waited for the next instruction. He pulled and pushed on the cylinder head and eventually was able to make it rattle more freely.

'Okay, I have it, I have it!' he shouted, raising his hand high in the air. 'This is it. It's a loose nut; it's just a loose nut.' He sat up and inspected it.

'It's a size 12 nut. Can you look in the top ammunitions box for a size 12 nut? It looks like the thread is stripped, so it isn't able to tighten. Basically, the cylinder head cannot be tightly sealed, and that is why air is escaping.'

He smiled at me and sat back on the tar. I prodded my fingers into the box and pulled out anything that felt round and small enough to be a nut.

'Oh *shit...*' he said again through a clenched jaw, 'it's a size 12, but it's got a fine thread.'

I, too, sighed, and pretended to know exactly what the implications of that fine thread were for our day. I waited for the explanation. My search of the top box was unsuccessful but I started the search again. The second time I focused on fumbling for fine-thread nuts. That meant I had to look very carefully at the inner side of each nut. It was tricky to see anything in the twilight.

'I've found a size 12, but not with a fine thread. I can't find anything with a fine thread,' I moaned.

'We have to find a size 12 nut with a fine thread,' he barked. 'We have to find it on the bike then if we don't have a spare. Let's look at the electrics, like the lights maybe. Just look for any place where you think there might be one. Otherwise we have to order one *fucking* nut and get it delivered by DHL!'

'That would be funny ... kind of,' I mumbled.

DHL were our direct link to the stream of spares we kept needing. All trip long we were either waiting for a delivery, preparing an order, or anticipating both.

Frozen in thought, we glared at the tools in our hands. *Firstly, where the hell were we going to find the nut? Secondly, where on the bike would a nut not be needed?*

Above us, the sinking dark clouds threatened imminent rain and nightfall.

'Okay, let's first try one more time in our spares. Look in

all the toolboxes again. Let's start there,' Papa pointed to a pyramid of ammunitions boxes. 'And we'd better make it quick. We have maybe 20 minutes before it's lights out.'

We tipped out each box and sent all our tools and spares sprawling across the tar. We were close to frantic. I didn't have the eye my dad had for judging those sorts of things, and needed to pick up each nut and measure it into a spanner. Some were ridiculously over or under-sized, but I tried relentlessly. We found nothing.

'We have to move through the entire bike, starting with the light fittings, and don't worry about the size, just find a nut with a fine thread.'

'Actually, I have one already, Papa, a size 14 with a fine thread,' I said, giving a thumbs up. 'It was tucked in behind the headlight. It's one of two nuts that fasten it to the steering rack. I think just one of those will hold the light just fine.'

'Brilliant! Wow that was quick.'

Once I held that nut in my hand it dawned on me what we were about to attempt. With the file in his left hand, and a set of pliers in the other, my dad turned to me. He took the nut, tightly nestled it into the pliers, and handed me the file.

'Now you start filing. Always rotating it so you keep the edges as straight and sharp as possible. Don't let the edges get rounded at all,' he instructed. 'You must concentrate for this one, okay?'

That was our solution. I had to literally grate layers of steel off, millimetre by millimetre, with a fine-grained file. After almost two hours each edge was equidistant, clean and sharp. The nut had been transformed to a size 12, with a fine thread. It was pitch black by the time we were done, but the rain had stayed tucked in the clouds. We felt our way around the engine and groped at the tools in exhaustion. The nut fitted and it worked. The bike roared boldly to life. We savoured our success.

'Ha! Now that was real MacGyver stuff, hey?' Papa was triumphant. 'When we put that head on the last time, we must have rushed it and probably forced that nut on too hard. That is what stripped its thread. Lesson learned!'

'How about a schnapps before we pack it all up?' I suggested, trying to ignore what I interpreted as a jibe.

We sat in the deserted parking lot, filthy with grime, dust and grease. The bikes looked dishevelled and untidy. The schnapps to our lips toasted another day of endurance. I felt proud of myself, like a real man. In places I couldn't see what was blood and what was grease. I had a Marlboro grin on the inside.

'That looks like a hotel over there,' said my dad, pointing to a bright sign beaming off the tallest building in town. 'It looks smart, and I don't care how much it costs. We are sleeping there tonight.'

The Untold Story

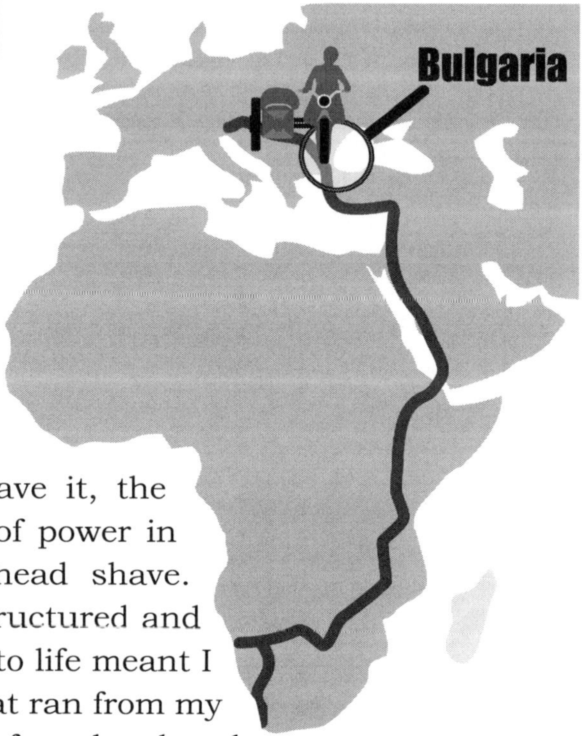

As luck would have it, the shaver ran out of power in the middle of my head shave. Luckily, my dad's structured and organised approach to life meant I had a perfect line that ran from my nose over the back of my head and to the centre of my neck. Half my skull was clean shaven, while the other remained a stubbly hemisphere. I looked like a newly-inducted member of a gypsy circus. Combined with my dad's ever-drooping, snowy beard, we made the oddest of couples. As if our bikes hadn't drawn enough attention to us already. We were in Nesebar, Bulgaria, a destination we had looked forward to for weeks. Within a day of arriving I contracted the flu, my first on the trip, and we decided to take the opportunity to rest for as long as it took for me to recover.

We found a private, two-bedroom apartment, just one road back from the beach on the Black Sea. We were a short walk from a huddle of restaurants, had satellite TV and no pressing damages or issues on our bikes. It was like a mid-trip holiday, and then I took ill. We did as much admin as we could in that time, which included shaving our heads, catching up on emails and diary entries, sleeping late, eating out and having a daily dip in the sea.

This pause in our journey initiated a period of reflection; an unmentioned and almost unnoticed part of our rest. We had space to be alone if we so chose, we had long periods of silence and very little to distract us, in contrast with the previous weeks of activity and pace. We both seemed to go inwards for a while, culminating on one unforgettable evening. Like so many evenings before, we had strolled up the clean, beach-hugging road between rows of double-storey apartments and homes. Twilight brushed a pink blush onto all the buildings. We kicked small pebbles along the gutters and passed what had become our local grocer. The owner was packing away the fresh produce from the crates that were stacked under a large, yellow umbrella. As we marched up the steep steps to a small double-storey restaurant, we looked over terracotta roofs. All we could see was white sand that trailed off like a tail into the distance. Far away, where the beach seemed to vanish, we saw a cluster of buildings. The lights of the main town were brightly contrasted against the flat, dark waters of the sea. A handful of cars had parked in the lot, and we could hear music invite us in for a meal. It was mid-autumn, and there were only faint echoes of a bustling summer season left.

We elected to sit indoors that night, next to a window that looked over the veranda and across the sea. It was a familiar view, similar to the one we had from our apartment. The town's glow defined a line of life on the edges of the Black Sea. There were small dots of light scattered across the blackness of the bay, fishing boats most likely, and maybe even the odd yacht. The air was still, but it had a cool nip to it.

I slipped my feet beneath the table, dropped my sandals and ordered a beer. It was a night for a beer but the sangria was free, and so we had both. Within about 30 minutes, most of the cars in the lot had driven off, and the restaurant emptied. We were the last ones there, and the sun had only just set. That aloneness, near the end of a pause in our action-focused journey, was like a reflection gestation, and it birthed an evening of honesty.

'You know, I have no regrets,' Papa said, out of the blue. He tugged at his beard and folded his arms. 'I really don't have any regrets. I look back at my life and every part of it was a choice for the best.'

As I didn't have a reasonable response to that statement, I kept quiet and stared down the neck of my beer.

'The first time I was left behind, I had no idea it was going to happen,' he continued, cradling the beer on his waist.

'What do you mean, "left behind"? When were you left behind?' I started picking nervously at the edges of the beer label, 'Was this in Austria? I don't remember that.'

'No, no, I'm not talking about now, not on this trip. I'm talking about a long time ago, before you were even born.'

I stopped fiddling with my beer and sat forward. My dad had a charming habit of repeating the same, albeit large, library of life's stories. That one, however, I had never heard before.

'It happened in South Africa, but before you and Daniel. Even before your mom,' he said, and paused in preparation for his opening line. 'It was because of my first wife.'

Our food arrived and I began to eat. He held off, choosing to rather deliver the story. It was that important.

'When I first arrived in South Africa, I came with my first wife and my eldest daughter Maria. Hilda was born there. My jobs were always on site. That is how engineering jobs were. So we moved around a lot. In the beginning she, my first wife, was okay with it, but she began to struggle as time went on. It went on like that for a long time,' he took a long sip of his beer, his meal remaining untouched.

'I was having to work six days a week then, which is how it was on site. They were projects and the faster they finished, the more money the bosses made. So I worked very hard. We were lucky though; because we had children, we were given a proper house. Everyone else got one of those made-up houses. What do you call them again?'

'Prefabs? Prefabricated homes,' I said.

'Yes, prefab houses, I was thinking pre-fabulous!' he laughed louder and longer than usual. I was tense in my seat. He paused with the beer at his lips, and then continued.

'One day I went to work, as usual. On many of the days I could go to the house for lunch. That was really great. I mean, the children were still small, not yet at kindergarten, and I would go home for a family lunch sometimes.'

I noticed a change in me that was best described as confused envy. Hearing him talk about this entirely different family was weird. It was probably the first time we had spoken about the other children in his life. It just bubbled up. He didn't look at me, just stared out the window. He had a habit of wiping clean his moustache after every sip of beer. He had done that a lot already that evening.

'I will never forget that day,' he pulled ever harder at his beard and stroked his moustache. 'I got home that lunchtime and our neighbour was there. She was often there, because she would help with the children. But she was there alone that day and she was crying.'

He paused for a long, long time. He seemed to find it difficult to look at me, raw emotion leaked out through the wet of his eyes. I could see it, even though he tried hard to hide it.

'She told me, the neighbour told me, my wife had packed up and just like that she was gone,' he said, letting the words hang in the still air. '*Ya*, they were gone, just like that, gone.'

'Where to?' I asked, as I cleared my throat after a long silence.

'She had gone to Austria, just went straight to the airport and gone. She was gone with no goodbye and no note.'

'But why?' I asked.

'I had no idea, I didn't know why. I also didn't know why she had left Hilda behind.'

'What?' I was shocked. 'Who was the elder child?'

'Maria was the eldest. Our neighbour had tried to stop her doing it, but Hilda was left sleeping in her room. No goodbye, no nothing.'

The pain flickered in his eyes after all those years. Emotion tried to make its way out, but was denied access to his face. The tension was palpable. It was a brand new story, but if felt familiar at the same time.

'She just left the baby with me. Can you imagine?' His voice rose with a controlled burst of anger, 'It was so cruel. It changed my life, and Hilda's too; it was a terrible thing to do.'

I had heard my half-sisters had lived in South Africa and that divorce had forced them to move back to Europe. That story was however an altogether different set of circumstances. The harshness of the abandonment punched off every one of my dad's sentences. I could see he was still trying to make sense of it all, that he hadn't quite figured it out. I was trying to make sense of it too, a story that echoed the one that had happened to us.

'But why? What was the reason she left like that?' It felt as if I was discovering an evolutionary link in my dad's psyche. That conversation and the intensity of the emotion was an artefact of his past I began to believe might help me to understand so much of the broken man he was. I was overwhelmed with pity and then empathy. The scorn came later, much later.

'I began living like a single parent with a small child. I had the help of our neighbours, and Hilda and I lived together. I did it all, just the two of us. I was Mom and Dad. Sometimes I had to go away for a few days and even a week. Sometimes I would take her with me. We made it work, we all made it work, and I think she was even happy,' he delivered each word with tenderness. 'But then, after a long time, I came home from work ... and Hilda was gone. My wife had come and taken her ...'

We sat in silence. I struggled to digest what I had just heard. He then picked up his knife and fork and began to eat. He seemed to have changed gear, putting that all behind him, as he had done all his life. I was stunned and just sat there.

'But you know, even with that stuff that happened I regret absolutely nothing I have done,' there was a hint of cold-hearted venom in his words.

I am not sure what he meant, or what he was trying to say. I can only assume he was speaking generally and broadly, but what I heard was close, specific and very painful. I felt numb. *What did he mean? Was he saying that, despite being abandoned himself, he still had no regrets about just leaving us behind when we were little boys?*

All the emotion that had been neatly packed deep inside began to boil again. He showed no remorse. All that simmering emotion that had rolled out of his lips just moments earlier evaporated into a rain of selfishness that doused my flame of empathy for him.

The Rift Widens

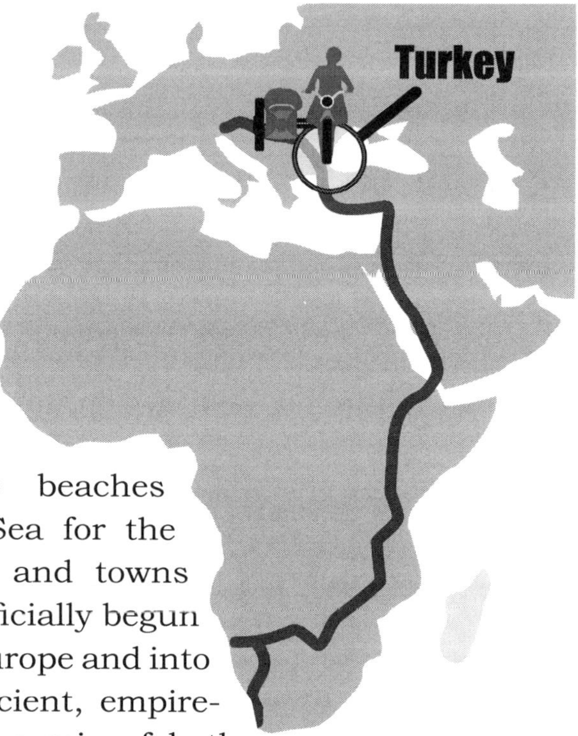

We traded the beaches of the Black Sea for the ruin-strewn villages and towns of Turkey. We had officially begun the crossing out of Europe and into the Middle East. Ancient, empire-making Turkey was a mix of both continents. It has a unique language and culture that is not considered Arabic yet the mosque spires, reaching like long fingers to touch God, clearly make it a Muslim country.

Our trip into the country was uneventful. We crossed the border and slept in a petrol station forecourt on our first night. After that wakeful, neon-lit slumber we meandered along the coast, reluctantly bypassing Istanbul as it was too far from our planned route. Turkey was so diverse and enchanting it was easy to move on from that disappointment. We found it a tranquil place to visit and spent our days sightseeing in a leisurely way, feeling welcomed wherever we ended up.

There was an empty campsite which stretched between the Mediterranean and a low grass bank. It was long and clean, and for the first time on our trip, I watched the sun set into the ocean. Sunsets evoked many fond memories for me. I had watched countless days end with the sun splash into the sea, either as I readjusted my floppy red hat to block the lowering rays, or as I surfed my last waves in the fading light. That campsite sunset made the evening feel more familiar than it turned out to be.

'Beer?' asked Papa, tongue-in-cheek.

'I wish. That would make this feel right, wouldn't it?' I said, lamenting the fact we had none.

'*Ya*, maybe a schnapps will have to do.'

Alcohol had been our third travel companion. It seemed as if each point on the map was celebrated either in a mug, shot glass, over ice, or just straight out the bottle.

'So what's for supper? What do you feel like tonight?' I asked.

It was my turn to cook that night. We had a system. It wasn't quite as structured as it could have been, but in most cases I just knew it was my turn.

'Surprise me,' he said as he started to unpack the stretchers and sleeping gear.

We sat on our undersized camping chairs, sipped at a warm schnapps and watched the sea ripple into small waves. The water swirled around the pebbles in the shallows. It turned a darker green as twilight descended. I had been so distracted with setting up camp, I hadn't gone for a swim and by the time the light had faded the thought became less appealing. There was a crisp chill in the evening breeze. The pot began to boil, and as I reached over to measure the maize meal, Papa blurted, 'Yes, *kaffir pap*! That is exactly what I feel like!'

His words jolted me. I had chosen not to challenge him for months around that word, but enough was enough.

'You know, Papa, that word is no longer PC in South

Africa,' I said, not looking at him.

'What word? What is PC? What is that?'

'*Kaffir* is a word that is just not used any more. Times have changed and it is very offensive now.'

I wanted to sound assertive, but I sensed I had not made an impression.

'And PC means politically correct. So it's not considered appropriate to call black people names like that. That is what it means,' I said firmly.

There was a long pause.

'You know Marc, the Germans ... even today, still use the same national anthem they did under Hitler,' he said, looking down into his lap. 'You can't just rub out history and change everything people know to be normal or what they are used to.'

We were headed for another argument. Granted, this was a debate that had been brewing for a while. It had festered for months and what made it even more intolerable was I had believed the false assumption that my dad had in fact been overtly anti-Apartheid. The reality was greyer.

'Okay, firstly, let's try not to get confused here,' I said, raising my voice as I switched into debate gear. 'If you want to compare South Africa to Nazi Germany then let's ask ourselves if the Germans still force Jews to wear gold stars. Huh? No, they don't! Calling people *kaffirs* is a label that is just as painful! It's just not on anymore!'

'I don't care Marc! When I was in South Africa, we called all black people *kaffirs* and "boys", to their faces. This is how I grew up. It was not political, and it was just the way it was. And besides, not a single black person had a problem with that – they never said anything.'

I struggled to hide my discomfort around his flawed logic.

'But times have changed, Papa. What you learned in

those days, in the 70s and 80s, at the height of Apartheid, is no longer acceptable. It's illegal to use that word. You have to change!'

'But why should I? Everyone I know down there still calls them *kaffirs* and no one is going to jail. They have no issues. There is even a *kaffir* president now Apartheid is over, so what is the problem?'

Stalemate. We both thought we had arrived at a checkmate scenario. I'd claimed the law and my dad had played the 'all has worked out fine for black people' card. We sat in silence. The blood pumped against my temples.

'And besides, *kaffir* is an Arabic word that means unbeliever, so what is wrong with that anyway?' he added.

That comment, plus the tone and nature of the debate, was reminiscent of so many I had battled over time. It had been most common in the transition periods, even with Mandela at the helm. There seemed to be a lingering assumption that if you were white, there was license to speak about black people and South Africa in a disparaging way. I had chosen to not be a part of that, but most white strangers didn't care. I recalled the most glaring example of how intertwined racism was with people's identity that was enacted one night on the fringes of the Kalahari. I had been a student, touring southern Africa with a friend. We couldn't find a campsite and decided to pitch tents on a dusty roadside, but a farmer with typical Afrikaner hospitality offered us a room in his farmhouse.

As we entered the house, there was a switchboard, with direct lines to each farmer in the region. All their names corresponded to a button on the board.

'Any *kaffir* wants to cause trouble with me, he has to deal with all of us,' he said with glee, as he swept his hand across the multi-coloured spaghetti of wires. 'In minutes those boys would be here and those *kaffirs* would have no chance.'

We nodded our heads politely and contemplated what we had just walked into.

'It's war out there you know; they are still the enemy, even if Mandela is president. History across Africa has proved they are barbarians. They love to kill, don't they?'

As the evening wore on, our liberalism leaked out. We couldn't help it. And so he kicked us out of his house and forced us to sleep under the stars. He felt unsafe with us in his home, he said. We were sympathisers with the enemy, after all. Although unacceptable, I could understand why many Afrikaners might have thought like that, but it made no sense with my dad. He was a foreigner who could come and go as he wished. He had no right to have a beef with anyone in South Africa and yet he had absorbed the prevailing rhetoric. He had been as much a part of the system as any other white person. And he certainly had not left us behind because of Apartheid. He was more complicit than opposed. That rattled me. Deeply. The entire story of his hasty retreat was a myth. That took a lot of getting used to and raised questions I preferred to not answer. *So why did he leave?*

'Papa, whatever the original meaning, it is no longer okay. When you use this word it makes me feel very uncomfortable and uneasy,' I said, trying to make it less political and more personal.

'Well, that is your problem. You expect me to change, then you should also change. Maybe you must show more respect to the older people who built South Africa, to the white man who made it more first world than the black man ever could have. We did all that!'

'But South Africa was built on the backs of black people and they now have their freedom. With no war or bloodshed. They have asked us to stop using that word ... it's pretty simple, Papa!'

'It's actually not that simple Marc. Africa is a mess, and South Africa will go that way too. You are either with them or against them. Maybe Mandela is different, but after him, there will be trouble.'

I stared into the boiling water, my hand fought the mielie meal which was clinging to the heat at the base of the pan. The more the heat, the more I needed to turn the spoon; the less it wanted to move, the more it got burnt. Each swivel of the blade made the wooden spoon bend and with every turn air popped through in large sticky bubbles. I tried to let it all go, and kept quiet. *A lesson from the mielie meal?* So I turned down the heat on the debate and just stopped. *Maybe on another day*, I thought.

Those clashes, and there were a few, left me panting for air. My entire body tensed into a hyper vigilant stance. Fight or flight. It all felt like an overreaction. That night, as I dozed off to sleep, I carried a foul mood to my pillow. There was a chasm between us and it irked me. We were supposed to close the gap, not widen it further.

At first, distance is only something we can measure. But then we learn distance, as they say, also heals. It can bring relief and after some time, supports our ability to face reality again. It can help us cope, and make us feel as if we are managing. Distance is charged both with joy and hurt. It can intimately affect us. Sometimes we can't get close enough or far away enough. That is what can make it polarised and polarising. It can literally drive us mad.

Distance is also a measure of time. It represents the revolutions of time that sync the predictable and metronomic cycles of the moon and sun, day and night. Each passing cycle separates what is 'now' from what was 'then'. Sometimes, the more time passes, the more our memories fade, until we either forget them completely or bury them temporarily. A curious memory design flaw prevents us from knowing how distance has shaped recollections of events, people and experiences. We live between certainty that a memory has been eliminated, and nervous anticipation that, at any moment, a memory will flood so vividly back to us, we realise the time changed nothing. For some, that is comforting, for others it is terrifying.

Distance can also be about understanding. There are times when stepping back, or pulling away, allows us to see more clearly. Distance gives us a new perspective, like standing on a mountain. We may see what influences us. We may spot hidden habits, reactions and thoughts that form and confirm our beliefs.

As a teen I chased a burning need. I believed one day, not too far from then, I would close the spaces between my father and me. I was convinced when the geometric distance was gone and the gaps in time were shortened, I would be cleansed and in a real relationship with my father. I assumed I would control those things someday, that I could choose and decide what I wished. I just wanted to let go of the hurt, forget the disappointments and reshape the tatters of our kinship.

Sitting on that beach, I collapsed with emptiness, as if I had been drained of a bloated sense of myself. There we were, as close as we could have been. The distance between us was mere centimetres and yet, I felt the furthest apart from him. As if distance was destined in our blood. I heard a lonely echo of yearning that bounced between us.

I wondered whether that was a male phenomenon, that men opted for the most expedient approach. That showing up was all it took, was all that was needed and expected. Right? Wrong. Actually, in the end, distance was more about the length of the scars. And their depth. To be there was secondary. What we both grappled with was the uncomfortable possibility that there were scars we needed to heal for each other. That role was certainly something most men didn't understand. The evolutionary male code dictated we inflict wounds, not repair them. It was pre-destined, and almost habitual. To heal was the responsibility of women, and so often attempts by men to mend were stunted and incomplete. Their attempts to neutralise the instincts of the hunter usually failed. It just never made sense to them.

As his son, I expected him to be both hunter and healer, and it may have been that my father had no capacity to be both. But that didn't stop the yearning within me. I simply wanted to be heard, I longed for him to be interested, for him to dwell on how I was feeling about my place in the world. I wished for the banter of bravado and the tears of empathy. I couldn't help myself; I needed that all and I was unforgiving in my expectation. And the more I looked for healing, the more I felt haunted by the hunter, pierced by the spears and arrows that had maimed me so long before.

I stroked my wounds with the only healing I knew, avoidance. I was on the run from myself and others, hyper vigilant to any markers of intimacy. I could feel the target on my heart, and I did all I could to shield it.

In the end, for all those years, distance had been both a curse and a cure; the reality I now faced was the healing had to come from me. And just like my dad, just like many men, I didn't know where to start. That I had no idea how to begin, or what to do, made me feel more empathy for him.

I watched him sitting there, his glasses tipping off his nose as his podgy fingers traced a line along a map of Turkey. Without looking, he slid his other hand to grip the ear of his cup. With slow, measured movement, he pulled it to his mouth and then brushed the vapours off the trimmed beard on his upper lip. I watched him as he stroked the grey curls down his chin. Gravity pulled his flat hand against his chest. He let it rest on his heart, while his eyes bored into the detail before him.

He was very calm, very still. There was a tenderness in him. And I liked him again, but only for a moment. It wasn't long, but it was enough. No matter how racist, how arrogant or careless, he was my father, despite all the distance. For the first time, I both hoped he could change and expected him to stay exactly who he was. The hardest parts of the trip so far played out within me.

The Discovery

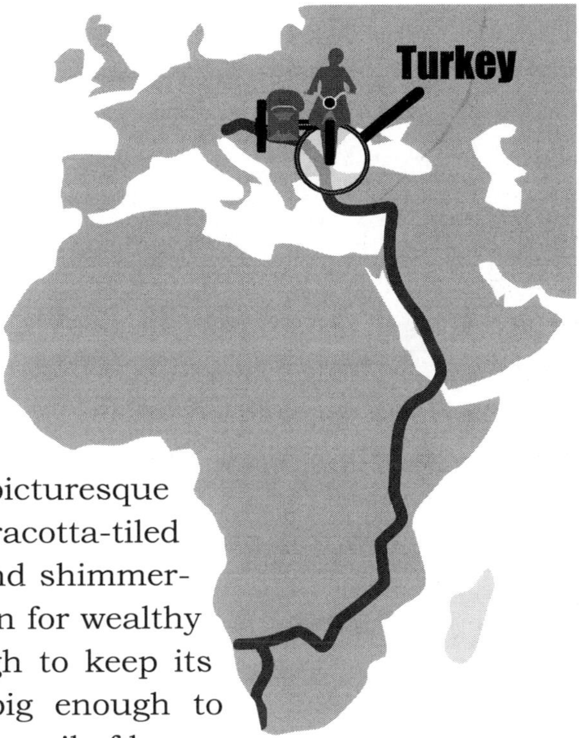

Marmaris is a picturesque collage of terracotta-tiled roofs, white villas and shimmering blue sea. A haven for wealthy sailors, small enough to keep its rural charm, but big enough to wrap each visitor in a veil of luxury. We planned to spend at least a week there, the longest single stay of our trip. That was partly because we had the opportunity to live on a yacht with a butler, but mainly because it was all free. However, our stay there didn't start well. We arrived a day too early to gain access to the yacht and spent a single night camped just out of town, in a bustling and revelling place, with a party that continued all night long. By the time we dragged ourselves into the yacht club, we were desperate for some rest. It made us appreciate our luck even more, and a little bit of good fortune went a long way with us at that time. We lived in luxury with not a care in the world. It was a sanctuary. We were in walking distance of the quayside restaurants and feasted on delicate Mediterranean foods, pasted with humus and light, fragrant vegetables. We drank wine and beer, and I spent much of each day in the crystal clear waters.

All in all, it was a calm yet lonely stay. The heated debate of a few nights earlier had not left my thoughts. I was still processing what it meant and remained confused. I began to feel a patronising tone start to filter into the conversations again. My dad seemed to purposefully take an antagonistic position to everything. It was childish, but Marmaris had space and allowed me the freedom to define the rhythm of my own days. With the bikes parked and up for a clean and re-pack, we could do what our hearts desired. Papa pored over maps, lost in a stoic and silent agenda. I wanted to be alone to explore, and I did just that.

It was also the first time since leaving Villach we had a chance to completely unpack the bikes. We discovered many items we had forgotten about. Some useful, and others not so much. When we had started the trip we'd tried to think of every eventuality and had packed as much as we could, cramming it in. Then, as the trip began, the layers of packing began to reorder themselves, based on the frequency with which we needed certain items. Predictably, all our tools had to be as handy as the cooking and sleeping gear. Many other items then settled permanently in the base of the sidecar, and were easily forgotten. We also needed a full stocktake of our spares and accessories. We had tried to guess which parts might fail first or break the most, but were nervous about the high attrition rate already eating through our back-up parts. The sobering realisation was we needed to restock urgently.

As we had to make another call to the middle man, we ventured beyond the moorings to find a bank, exchange some cheques, locate a phone and do some grocery shopping. As in many smaller villages, everything was in walking distance. We had a simple map of the road – one of those bright tourist maps that aren't very useful or even accurate. We lost ourselves in the childlike aerial view, but were not bothered in the slightest. It was a place soft and appealing to our eyes. We moved slowly, enjoying the chance to melt into our context rather than trundle through it, without the pressure of time to grasp at its tones and scents. The town was green with trees and the roads were lined with rows of double-storied houses. Flower pots at their windows spilled blossoms over their facades. The warm breeze pushed the leaves of an autumnal shedding around our ankles. There were few people around that day. It was still. The traffic was scarce and a handful of cars were parked between the chalky-coloured walls down the lanes that crossed the main street.

We eventually cut across a dusty intersection towards a bank machine in a wall. I stepped onto the pavement and up a low, sandstone ledge to the bank's door. Out of the corner of my eye I noticed a pile of cardboard boxes stacked about waist height to my left. A familiar shape caught my eye. It was a thing so unexpected that I stopped, mid-step, and stared in disbelief. My dad followed the line of my gaze.

'What is that?' he asked, suddenly as curious as I was. 'Is that what I think it is?'

'Well, yes, but it looks like it's damaged, and definitely abandoned.'

We stared at each other in amazement. I walked back down the steps and leaned forward to pull the first box away.

'It's red,' I said with surprise, 'but it looks different from ours. It's not like ours; that's for sure.'

'A Ural, I think,' Papa said as he lifted the next cardboard sheet away. 'I can see the badge there. Yes, it's the Ural, the Russian version of our bikes. You can see the quality is better than ours.'

We looked around to see if anyone had noticed us picking away at this most unusual discovery. It was an intact bike that leaned unguarded against the wall of the bank. The pile of boards had gathered seasons of leaves and had become a home for many small insects and spiders. The wheels had exhaled all their air and were stretching away from the rims.

'I think there is something else under there,' I said.

'Yes, you are right, look there!' Excited as a child on Christmas morning, he pointed to what looked like another wheel, a fourth wheel.

'Two of them, and obviously they have been here for quite a while. They seem to be in good condition, though,' I said.

We didn't know what to do next. The unexpected find had raised some questions. *Whose bikes were they? Why were they there? And what could we do with them?* The latter question was the most urgent to answer.

'Do you think these parts would fit a Dnepr?' I asked.

'Well, it would be a good idea to try, at least. I mean look at this, we may need so many things, especially those shock absorbers, maybe even the tyres. I would take some bulbs and who knows, maybe the pistons, rings and valves too. The only way to know would be to strip the bikes and try, I suppose.'

What a stroke of luck, I thought. *Who would have imagined that, right there, hidden from all, would be our personal-parts harvest?*

'Hallo,' said a man resting on the doorknob of the bank's door. 'Can I help you? Do you know these bikes?'

'Yes, I mean no,' replied my dad, startled to see the man. 'We have two of these bikes ourselves, actually.'

'Okay, so do you want these bikes?' asked the man

directly.

We looked at each other, surprised at how abruptly the question had arrived.

'Excuse me, what do you mean?' I asked, genuinely confused.

'Two people left these bikes here. Right in front of my bank and without permission. I am not happy with this. Look look!' he said, snarling at the litter. It was an eyesore.

'What happened? Why were they left here? Do you know?'

'There were two people from another country, but I am not sure where. They had no money left for taxes, or something like that, and they just left them here. First they were parked on the road, but that was too dangerous. So now they just lie here. Do you want to buy them from me? Do you want to take them away for me?'

The bikes had everything we needed: new tyres, spare shocks, extra bulbs and cables. I quickly noted what could be scavenged and grew excited at the idea of basically an entire bike available in spares. I hadn't processed the practicality of it all, such as the challenge of piling dismembered bikes onto and into ours, but if we could avoid having to buy spares from Europe, that would be a bonus.

'We will come back tomorrow to speak to you,' said my dad, cutting the conversation short. 'We need to think about it.'

That night we chatted to our butler, the only Turk we knew well enough to trust. We couldn't hide our excitement and surprise. The potential spares coffer would save us not only money, but time too. We had already created a list of items that would be feasible to extract and carry with us. A battery, if it still worked, would be very useful. A few handlebar covers, some accelerator cables. We could take all of the more generic and smaller items. The more animated we became, the more the butler shook his head. He then made it clear if we broke apart those bikes and stowed away the spares, without legal ownership of them, or indeed without the original legal papers of the bike's registration, we might be at risk of a smuggling charge. We both doubted the Turkish border control would be sophisticated enough to spot this; to match parts and serial numbers and compare them to registration papers, but his concern was the original owners might have already sold the bikes or asked people to look after them. Either way, the sense big brother was watching us was real and we decided to play it safe. The opportunity was lost, but it did provide a worthwhile distraction.

The drive out of Marmaris was a mix of satisfaction and sadness. It had been the most serene and balanced week of our trip. The bikes had been pampered by a spring clean and my dad had avoided his compulsion to fiddle with the mechanics. We were cleanly packed, as light and reconfigured as possible. We had mastered a new packing sequence, rearranging the most and least-needed spares and supplies. We felt and looked quite smart. Like starch in a new white shirt, we had an air of freshness about us. It was hard to leave, as we had fallen in love with Marmaris. It showed off the very best of Turkey – balmy, eastern and cheap.

We left the coast and travelled through a forest redolent with the faint potpourri of sea and pine. About 10 kilometres from the twinkling marina, reality bounced down the road in a flick flack of sparks. My dad's exhaust sheared off without warning and hopped towards me. We spent the next hour watching Marmaris wake up below us, while we wrestled with the metal to reattach it. It was indisputable: no matter how much we polished and pimped the look of a first-class ride, we were always riding coach on those bikes.

We cruised the Turkish coastline for days, taking in each of the many small villages and larger towns, like Antalya and Anatolia. We kicked dust through the ancient ruins along the way, and slowed down to savour the views from the long and winding banana-covered mountain passes. We saw beaches and swam, drank sweet tea and devoured Turkish delight. We slowed down, ate fine food and shortened our daily mileage. And yet again, after a short stay in an idyllic, hippie, tree-top commune, my dad's bike vomited its gearbox all over the main arterial road. We spent yet another long day picking through gear shavings, misshapen nuts and warm oil as we separated the bike from its sidecar and overhauled the gearbox in the blaze of a brutal southern sun. We had stopped fighting that reality.

The next stop was Syria and the desert, which would bring heat, dust and long, lonely stretches of road. If finding our groove had been the challenge thus far, then steering those cold-weather bikes through the desert would be our next. With a petulant need to overheat, the bikes were not designed for warmer climes.

The Jordanian

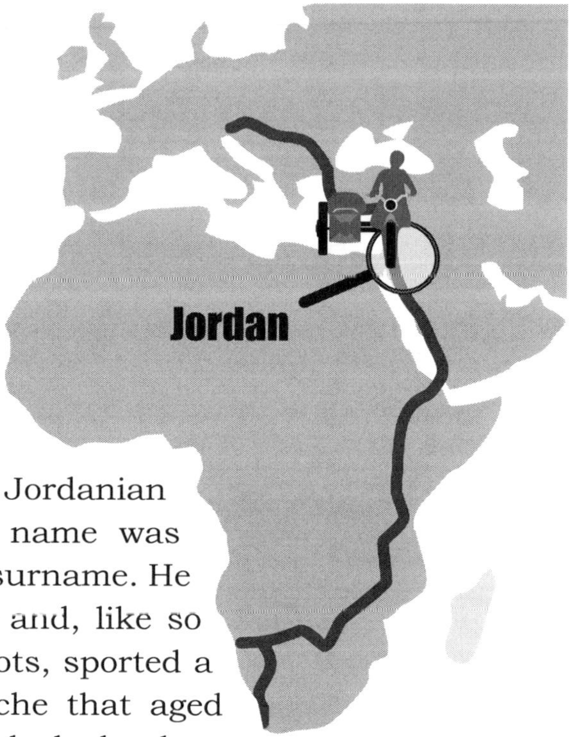

He was the first Jordanian I had met. His name was Feroz. I never got his surname. He was a cheerful fellow and, like so many of his compatriots, sported a plush, black moustache that aged his young and boyish looks by a decade. He wore a white shirt and blue jeans, with white sneakers and white socks, every day I saw him. We met him on our first night in Amman at the internet café and assumed he was the resident nerd, the *techie* in charge.

Amman was to be our home for an extended period. Our mission was made most simple by the Saudi Arabians and their inexplicable lack of empathy for Ukrainian engineering. In short, our visa allowed us just three days to cross Saudi Arabia – a distance of about 2000 kilometres of desert, at a daily average of almost 700 kilometres. That would be impossible on our bikes. Well, not totally impossible; we could drive for up to 18 hours per day, but the unpredictability of our bikes and the searing heat presented the biggest risk. And there would be trouble if we missed that three-day visa validity. As the Saudis were an intolerant officialdom, we had to think of an alternative plan. We would have to ship the bikes somewhere. Africa was the obvious destination. If Saudi Arabia was out, then our Middle-Eastern crossing had come to an end. We considered Egypt and Ethiopia as hop scotch south.

Feroz became an indispensable aide. Initially he helped us orientate ourselves in the city and then became something of a guide and translator. He didn't do it for money. We think he did it for company. At first we felt uneasy about it, feeling like we were taking advantage, but he always volunteered and made it his own choice to join us on many of our daily missions.

We toiled and traipsed across the capital, from shipping to travel agents, from embassies to freight handlers. We gathered multiple versions of what was possible. After numerous interpretations of interpretations of legalese and travel rights, from Arabic to English and then to layman's terms, there was a clear set of impossibilities. There were time challenges first. We had to find a solution that would allow us to travel as close as possible to our bikes, but every country in the region required an extensive visa application and processing period. The timing of these submissions with calculations of exact travel dates proved immensely challenging. Money was an issue too. All options were expensive, but there was a file full of plans that would have blown our budget, so sifting through the variables and then balancing them against a budget of finite time and money became the bulk of the work. Feroz helped us most with the final challenge – the ever-present trust deficit we had in all our interactions with local Jordanians. At times we didn't know what or who to believe. We heard options that contradicted each other, flights that from one person were available in a particular sequence, and from another person were not available at all. Feroz was part inquisitor to reveal the facts, part 'the-local-guy-who-couldn't-have-the-wool-pulled-over-his-eyes', and part the gut-feel guide. We trusted him implicitly. If he felt discomfort, he walked away and we followed. That went on for weeks.

In the final analysis, we whittled down our options to two possibilities. Plan number one: We could ship the bikes directly to Cairo, but pretty much nowhere else in North-East Africa. However, with enduring troubles in Sudan and a war brewing in the breakaway state of Eritrea, passing from Cairo to Addis Ababa was possible but not advisable. Not only was war a deterrent, but the Sahara was a potential swathe of sandy death we didn't have the confidence to pass through. The only other option was to get the bikes to Addis Ababa as directly as possible. That was through Sanaa, the capital city of Yemen. That would be flight number one. Then, we would have to cargo the bikes across the Red Sea and on to Addis. Throughout this planning I was learning of towns and countries I had never heard of before, like Djibouti. I loved that name. But in plan two, there was a catch. We couldn't fly directly to Addis from Sanaa because it was hellishly expensive. So we decided we would hop over the Red Sea to Djibouti and then catch a lift to Addis. From our optimistic assumptions we worked out it would take two weeks to get all those plans finalised, and maybe another two weeks to execute them. With a certain and clear objective, we became even more industrious, ticking off a long list of actions, hour by hour.

Between the long waits for paperwork and authorisations, we also had a chance to explore that ancient city of Amman. The busyness had a predictably biased pattern. It kept our focus on the future and the depth of conversations to the surface. It fed its need to be doing, to be going, to be planning. We wandered through the streets of Amman, and every so often, we slowed down just a little. It gave us a chance to notice the epic history of that hilly city. It was a time to breathe in, to unhinge my trailer from the force of adventure and look at myself and my father for who we were. The more I thought about it all, the more it choked me from being able to say anything. I just heard him say it over and over again: 'I regret nothing, I regret nothing, and I absolutely regret nothing.'

I didn't want to believe it, but the punctuation of certainty in that phrase made it difficult to dispute.

He regrets nothing, I thought to myself. *Then what have I been trying to fix? What do I think I could mend? He doesn't even think anything is broken.*

He has chosen it to be this way and he is content, satisfied and justified. So what am I fighting for again?

I stood between towering walls and columns of Roman origin. Time and history made me feel small and I grappled with the choices I had to make. I was lost. This was an outcome I had never believed possible. I had imagined a reunion, a deep, apologetic recommitment of parent to son. My entire compass on myself had been demagnetised and, without my daily refuge on the bike, I had to face him and that reality all day and every day.

But the thought of Africa, just down the map, energised me. It felt like a leap into the known and home. And with every day, we got closer and closer.

The Medical Certificate

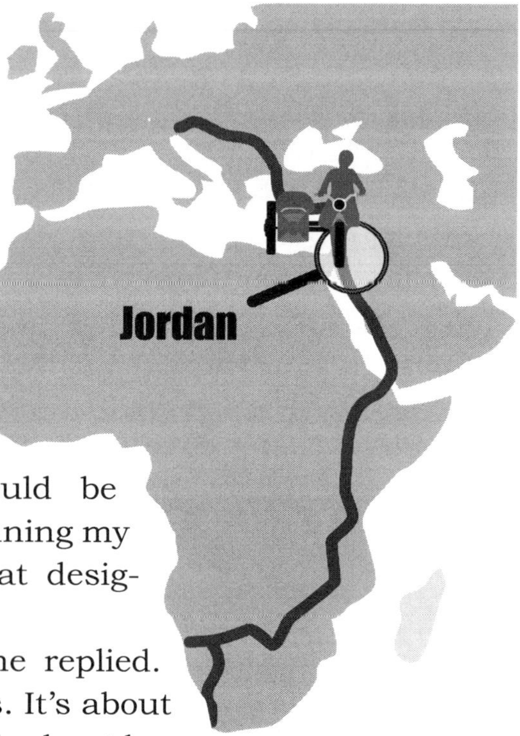

'I didn't think we would be doing this,' I said, running my hand along the tape that designated the queuc.

'It's a pity, isn't it?' he replied. 'But that is what travel is. It's about getting there, not so much about how you get there.'

'But we won't have done it all on the road. It feels like cheating, doesn't it?'

'*Ag* well, our plan is to get on a motorbike to Table Bay. We were always going to have to go by plane or boat over the Red Sea anyway, so not really such a problem. We just have to get to the Cape.'

We stood in silence as I brushed my shirt with purpose and tried to flatten a persistent crease out of the cotton. The more I pushed at it, the more I noticed all the stains. I picked at a few frayed threads and stuck my baby finger though a small tear. We had dressed up for this flight, the best we had dressed in many weeks, but we still looked like ragged road hogs.

'Passport?' asked a friendly-faced man behind the

Yemeni Airways check-in counter. His white head scarf dropped over our passports as he filed through them. He flicked each page with professional pride. He held the check-in stamp with the delicacy of a Swiss watchmaker, and bore it into the boarding passes with the force of a carpenter. He flicked a page or two further and then upended the passports and shook the pages repeatedly. His smile quickly turned to a frown. My first thought was money. We hadn't slipped any between the pages.

'Medical? Where is your certificate?' he asked, suspicion draining his eyes of that initial charm.

'For what?' we both asked in unison.

'To get on the plane, of course!' he said with irritation. 'You must have a medical with your visa. No medical, no fly. No Yemen. Simple.'

We were stunned, we were stumped. We watched him rip off the baggage stickers and roll our bags off the belt. He scribbled a scratch against the boarding passes and then swiftly tore them apart.

'Maybe see you again sometime, but no flight for you today,' he said with a smile.

We were turned away. There was a no-*bullshit*, no-arguing vibe about that whole airport. And so we just left. No arguments, no valiant stand against traveller injustice, no rant at how many tourist dollars were spent, no threats. We just left. That was a first for both of us. We had paid for tickets, we were all set, all packed, and the bikes had already been shipped. When it dawned on us we were about to become thousands of kilometres removed from our bikes, the idea of being cheated out of a flight became the least of our concerns.

The delays had become predictable. We should have known. We headed back to the city to regroup and find Feroz. We needed to get forms from the Yemeni embassy, and only God knows why we hadn't got them when we'd been there twice before to deliver and collect our passports. Apparently it was all in the fine print. Eventually we identified the obscure 45-minute visitation slot that was set aside once a week to collect medical certificates. It was all pretty harmless in the end; needles, gloves, small vials of thick red life dribbling out our veins. Tagged, signed, double-checked and re-signed. We were each handed a long, Arabic, perforated slip in return for our blood. It read, *'Tuesday at 14:00'*. That was collection day.

When we arrived at the hospital on that Tuesday, we were asked to wait outside the doctor's room. The nurse handed me a sheet of paper and a tenderly nibbled HB pencil. We scribbled our names in the column marked with an X and she walked off, her nurse flops clapping a rhythmic beat on the vinyl floors. With each step down the empty corridor the echo doubled back towards us. Even when she had turned out of sight, it was her gait we followed with our ears. We listened and we waited.

At some point, I became aware we had entered a large and busy hospital. The entrance had been a push and a squeeze, and we had navigated our way with the help of symbols and pictures. We were preoccupied until we arrived at the collections desk. Or so we thought. It hadn't seemed at all strange at the time, but we were pointed along a long corridor, across a small landing, and then again down an ever-emptying part of the building.

We ended up sitting in silence in a quiet corner. There was no one there but us. Ten minutes, 20 minutes then 30 minutes passed. The sun streamed through the window onto my shoes and I noticed how much dust I had displaced. The floor was sandy and unswept, so atypical of a hospital. In fact it all looked quite deserted.

'Is this the right place?' Papa asked. 'Did you see

anybody in there?' He pointed at the door between us with his thumb.

'It's the only door, so this must be it. She told us to wait here,' I said, anxiety rising in me.

Time continued to pass. Our wait moved to 40 then 50 minutes. Still there was no one. Just the two of us.

'Mr Marc,' mumbled a deep voice from behind the closed door. 'Mr Marc...' The person's voice trailed off to silence.

It was the 60-minute mark exactly. We heard a door slam behind the door we had waited against. I stood up and hesitated, uncertain of what I was supposed to do.

'Did someone call me? Or us? I couldn't hear properly.'

After a short pause, the voice came again, 'Not Mr Hans. Just you Mr Marc.'

In the glum, paint-peeled corridors of a state hospital, my anxiety thumped in a loud rhythm in my chest. I could see in my dad's face a projection of utter emotional confusion, part smile, part terror. The edges of his lips curled upward, but his eyes stretched to the limits of his sockets.

I edged in and greeted a man seated behind a long desk. He didn't stand up. He just watched me intently. He and I both stopped breathing, like in those few seconds before the whistle blows at the start of a match. I instinctively smiled but his bristly lip, covered in thick dark hairs, stayed resolutely down. He broke the silence with a knock of his fingers on the wooden desk that was empty but for two pieces of paper. He kept knocking his hairy knuckle on the page closest to him.

Knock, knock, knock. Then he stared at me again. Knock, knock, knock.

'You Mr Marc?' he asked in a prosecutorial tone.

'Yes, Marc. I am Marc Rogatschnig, yes,' I said, almost breathless.

'Okay, good. You take this and stand there.'

He held up one of the pages, and skim read it to check it was my name at the top. He then waved it slowly until I took it from him. There was no other seat in the room, but he pointed to the wall behind me. I assumed he wanted me to leave again.

'No, you stand there, in the room, next to the door,' he commanded. 'Mr Hans, you come in now. Slowly, very slowly please.'

He pulled open a draw and deftly slipped on a face mask, then stretched a pair of latex gloves over his stubbly hands. By the time my dad entered, the man was dressed in protective gear and he had pushed his seat to the wall behind him. He was as far as he could possibly get from us, but the focus of his attention was my dad. He had lost his calm demeanour and looked more like a cornered animal than a respectable professional.

'Stop!' he shouted. 'Stop right there. Don't move, don't move any closer to me.'

Papa stopped moving. He stood stiffly to attention just within the entrance to the room.

'Mr Hans, I have some news for you,' he stood up. 'You are sick, you are very sick!' he almost shouted, then hastily adjusted his mask to ensure it was over his mouth.

'What? What are you talking about?' I exclaimed.

'Just let him finish, Marc,' said Papa calmly. 'What do you mean, Doctor?'

'Mr Hans, you are a very, very sick man. You are also now a danger to all people. The truth is you will also die in a few months. There is nothing for you; there is nothing we can do because there is no cure for this disease,' he threw the other piece of paper at us.

As I leaned over to pick it up I heard him whisper, 'Mr Hans, your blood is with a deadly disease. You have HIV. You have Aids! And that means you have a very short time to live. You will die, very soon!'

He then stood up, muttered something under his breath and left the room through a back door. I am not sure how long we stood there, but we didn't leave immediately.

'It can't be true,' Papa said, forcing a smile. 'Let me look at that. Where does it say this?'

I handed him the sheets, and there it was in black and white. He clutched it all the way to the hotel. We didn't speak. I had no idea what to say, or how to comfort him or even deal with that news.

The Deportation

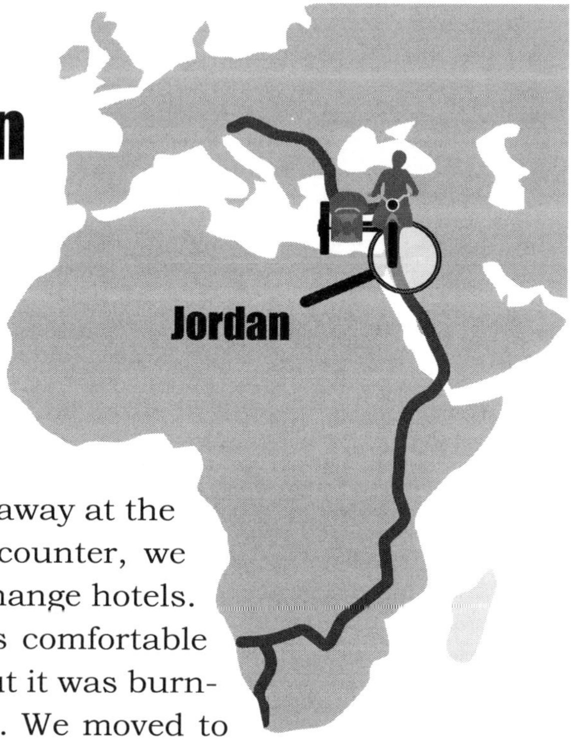

After being turned away at the airport check-in counter, we had also decided to change hotels. The previous one was comfortable and quite a luxury, but it was burning through our cash. We moved to a twin-bed room and shared a much smaller space, which wasn't ideal for me. My dad snored like a truck grating its gears. The room had a fan, expertly pointed at the beds from the corner, but there was no air conditioning. There was a small, grainy TV and an unusually large balcony. That was the feature we were most happy to pay for. We spent many days avoiding the heat out there. Every morning we would run our errands, and then in the evenings we splashed our faces and headed down one block for dinner, which had become a ritual feast of falafels and coke. It was a quaint takeaway that locals clearly favoured. The décor, signage and menu were forgettable, but the smells of fried chickpea and garlic-imbued humus lured us in the first time and didn't lose their grip on our taste buds throughout our stay. It was excellent value every night and that made it harder to be more adventurous with our meals.

The day my dad was diagnosed with Aids was no different. We headed to the local for a meal but he tried harder than usual to steer the conversation away from the day's events.

'So, we have the medical certificate, and tomorrow we fly out. I must say I will be happy to leave this place,' he reached for another pile of serviettes to wipe his greasy, falafel crumbed fingers.

'I've had a good time here, actually, even though it's the one place I didn't think I'd linger in.'

'*Ya*, it's almost like a halfway point, but not, if you know what I mean.'

'I think so. Next stop, Africa.'

'Next stop is like a homecoming for me. We will have fun there, in Ethiopia, I mean,' he said with a smile.

'But we still have a way to go before we get there,' I noted pragmatically.

'*Ag*, it will be fine. Within a few days we will be there, and then this will all be behind us. It will seem like it never happened.'

As he said those words, my body stood vigilant, like it had been pinched back to reality. I had almost ignored the diagnosis for the duration of the meal, but it clapped at my awareness very loudly. Aids was more final than fine. I looked at Papa, trying to pull up scraps of stories and experiences he had shared that might be a clue to whether this was in fact a possibility or not. Dread filled my veins, as the disease filled his. My realisation in that moment was it was very likely he did have Aids. A single man in Africa has needs after all. My mind raced in all directions. Given what I was thinking about, I realised that for now that news was probably our secret. I could tell no one, and he wouldn't want to talk about it again.

Wandering in a pensive mood back to our hotel, there was no way of predicting what would happen next.

'Police, open the door!'

That gruff command started a night of bewildered survival. Within minutes of our departure, that doctor must have triggered an alarm. The news fed through the security services. Regular policemen were ill-equipped, and the special unit, SWOT-like, came knocking at our door. That there were nations on earth that condemned Aids sufferers to prison camps beyond the city limits ignited a mild sense of injustice in comparison to our arrest. Never before, or since, had I faced the muzzle of a gun, and been as violently disempowered as we were that night.

Fear brings instant clarity. It negated all pity or concern for my father's health and lifted a warrior energy in me. All our resistance was futile and, in the end, watching my dad slump his heavy frame against the white walls of tiles in the cell, broke something in me. I wanted to hurt someone, to make someone pay for separating us, I truly felt loss. I felt wounded by the last sight of him, and my inability to help, or rescue, or console. I felt pure love, and panic. So much of my annoyance and frustration with his inability to connect with me melted into my hyper vigilance.

In those final moments, where we were separated, it was the word *deportation* which I held onto. It was a curve ball, and had never been an eventuality we had planned for. My mind raced. *He had the money, he had the bank accounts, and he had the contact details.* I was consumed by only one question: *where would he be deported to?* I also had no idea of when he would be deported. My flight was booked for the next day. I didn't know what to do. *Should I cancel it? Should I postpone it? Should I go back to the police station and at least see my dad off? What is the right thing to do?* I had no idea. I tried to work out what he'd been trying to tell me as the cell door was closing. It sounded like he wanted me to come somewhere. The only place that came to mind was the police station.

I was alone. And I was feeling it. I felt paralysed in no man's land. Confused, shaken and short on a plan, I lay awake trying to figure out my next move, trying to make sense of the best next step. Over a period of 20 hours, everything we had planned and depended on had been tossed into the shredder of circumstance. And we had been separated. There had been a few times on this trip where I had wanted some space, but the rasping nature of that night made me feel at my most vulnerable. I actually needed my dad. We were a team. He was the leader. Without him, I was forced to make all the decisions, and what lay ahead was the trickiest part of our trip. The impending transit through Yemen, with a bike re-routing and a hitch-hike to Addis was a prospect within which each kilometre was new territory, and very uncertain. It was the general lack of information that was most unsettling in all of that. There were so many doubts, so much I didn't know. I ruminated over the same questions: *Where will they send him? When will they send him? Is that the end of the trip?*

The bikes were already off to Yemen, with only one of us to manage their transit and then possibly keep them rolling south. I had been relatively hands off on the planning of that shipment. *Do I know enough? Do I have enough to work with? Do I have enough money?* With each passing hour the ticking got louder and the intensity of the decisions I needed to make became more debilitating.

I had no idea who to call, except Feroz, but I didn't have his number. I couldn't sleep so I was up early and on my way to find him. With a goal and someone to contact, I felt I had enough of a plan to stay calm. I hadn't thought how he could help, or what I wanted from him, but I needed someone to know what had happened. The internet café was not open. It was way too early. Amman was just waking up. Time was tight for me; I needed to be at the airport at 10am which meant I had to leave the hotel at 9am at the latest. I had an estimated 40-minute window to find Feroz. If I didn't, then I would have to leave. I sat on the café steps and waited, lost in my thoughts.

'Hello Marc,' said Feroz, in his quiet voice. I turned with relief, and felt tears well up in me.

'Feroz, oh thank you. Morning Feroz,' I pulled off hiding my anxiety for a few seconds and then dropped the facade.

'Is everything okay? Do you have some problems?' he asked with concern. 'Are you not leaving today?'

'We have a problem Feroz, and I need your help, please.'

He took my hand and led me into his shop.

'Come inside, let me get you some tea. What is happening? What is wrong?'

I refused the tea and wouldn't sit down. I was fidgety and impatient. He stood very close to me in the centre of the dark shop.

'My dad was arrested last night.'

His eyes flew wide.

'My flight is at noon and they are going to deport him but I don't know where, they wouldn't tell me, they treated us very badly,' I rushed my sentences into each other. His face shifted from calm to intense, his moustache was squeezed tight against his pursed lips. 'I have no way of finding out what is going on. Please, can you help me, Feroz?'

I wasn't just asking for help, I was pleading for it. He listened intently, confused and curious. I wanted to, but just couldn't tell him why my father had been arrested. Perhaps I was ashamed, or embarrassed, or feared that he might not help if he found out. It felt wrong to question his loyalty after all he had done for us, but this was about survival. He didn't really need to know why; he just needed to help me find my dad. That was my primary goal.

'Please go to the central police station and find out what they are planning to do. I don't have time – I have to pack and get going.'

I scribbled down my dad's details, 'Here is his name and my email address, but I will call you when I arrive in Yemen. What is your number? Do I have your number? And your email address?'

That was it. No pleasantries after that. I hugged him and held him. I felt my tension shake through his bony back. I needed that. He anchored me and I breathed deeply in the embrace. He stood stiff and awkward, in a way that showed how unusual that kind of affection was for him. I did it without thinking. I stepped back and stared into his eyes. The tears began to well up in me again.

'Thank you Feroz, I really hope we will meet again one day,' I said, attempting to soothe my shock and discomfort. 'I will be okay.'

He dropped his head as I left. There was such a slim chance we would cross paths again. I believe we both felt that. I knew he was going to help me and as a result I didn't feel alone any more.

The Troubled Transit

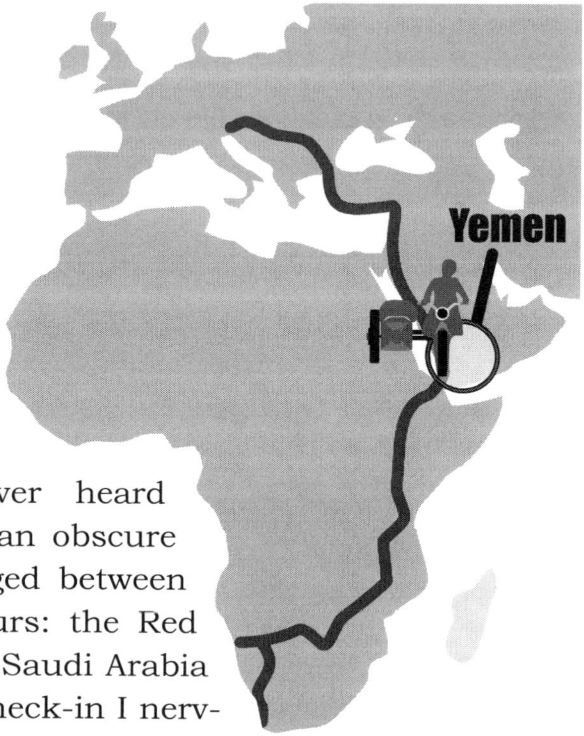

I had actually never heard of Yemen. It was an obscure desert country wedged between its famous neighbours: the Red Sea to the west and Saudi Arabia to the east. At the check-in I nervously pondered what that counter had triggered the last time I had stood there. I was operating on a shot of adrenalin and found a purposeful energy I rarely felt. I was in that 'get-shit-done' mode. I had compartmentalised my dad's likely experience of the prior 24 hours into the back of my mind and focused on what I needed to do. Buck the *fuck* up, get to Yemen, find the bikes and kick some *arse* if necessary, to get them back on another plane.

My anticipation and drive slowly melted into nervous concern as we began our approach into Sanaa. As we landed on the short and bumpy runway, it was difficult to distinguish the sand licks from the tar. The desert was in charge there, and as far as I was able to see there was sand and stone everywhere.

The arrivals terminal looked more like a bus stop than

an international port. We disembarked, strolled across the open tar and wandered through a broken door to our luggage. Passport control was a single row of school desks, situated just before the conveyors. There were people everywhere and most of them did not look like officials. They slouched about wherever they could find shade and cool air, and crowded around the small number of fans that worked. The taxi operators tried to catch my eye before I had even moved through passport control. There was no order in any of it. It was hot but bearable. I have always loved dry heat, and this felt like Namibian heat to me; dusty, dry and second nature.

It was a Friday, so quieter than usual. That is what my taxi driver later told me. It seemed I had been lucky to arrive that day. I couldn't imagine how much more chaotic it could get if the number of passengers and hangers-on were to double. I stood and guarded my baggage from what felt like the entire airport trying to get my attention. That is when I noticed them for the first time. It was a significant detail I had missed as I first tried to find my bearings in the building. It was also peculiar to males only. Basically, each man was armed and carried what looked like a knife or sword at his waist. The weapons were strapped to their belts, in ornate and sickle-shaped sheaths. There were machine guns too, and rifles worn like rucksacks. No matter who they were, or seemed to be, either an official or a member of the police, or army personnel or a taxi driver, it seemed a knife and a gun, were standard accessories for anyone. *Welcome to the real third world,* I thought to myself.

My friendly taxi driver told me about the tribes that still ruled most of the country. Their traditions had become the foundations of the modern laws, and it had created centuries of conflict. As he shared that history and we got closer to the centre of town, the more I prepared myself for a brutal visit.

The drive revealed kilometres of squalor, decay and dirt. The only frame of reference I had for comparison was *Mad Max* movies. The place was wild. There were people living behind walls and barricades of rusted car bonnets and roofs. Many settlements had used piles of tyres as fences for protection. There were barriers made of exhaust pipes and red, rusted tin sheets which created a patchwork of industrial grit. It looked bleak. It made me feel grim. The roads were simply foot and tyre-flattened paths that wound between where people worked and lived. They were in such poor condition I had a lot of time to capture each image vividly as we inched along. There were no signs in English, nothing familiar to me at all. It was as foreign as it could get and my defences all switched to high alert. What had seemed like a potentially straightforward administrative task of rebooking and forwarding our bikes began to look murky, complex and very challenging. By the time I arrived at my three-star hotel, I had already begun playing mental chess with actions and scenarios that could play out over the course of my week-long stay.

'You here for seven nights?' asked the young hotel receptionist.

'Yes, I hope not more.'

'We wish you a pleasant stay,' he said warmly. 'This is a beautiful and historic city. There is much for you to enjoy.'

'Really?' I said, unable to contain my surprise.

'Yes sir, we have a world heritage site here. When you go to your room you can look outside your window and you will see the old city below. You cannot miss it. It is like it was thousands of years ago. I think it will make you feel better.'

I must have missed it, I must have driven right past it, I thought. I hadn't seen anything that was remotely beautiful or pleasant. And what did he mean by 'make me feel better'? That was a curious observation. He said it in such a way that made me think he actually cared. It warmed me to him. Truth was I was not in great shape at all.

'But today everything is closed,' he explained with a broad and helpful smile, 'because it is Friday. Prayers day for us. Tomorrow it will be better.'

I dropped my bags and opened the windows of my room. Below I could see a procession of at least 50 people carrying a covered coffin above their heads. The funeral procession moved down the empty road towards an archway. I watched them, mesmerised and still. The road entered the old city of Sanaa, with buildings estimated to be over a millennium old. It was so close, and it felt like my first lucky break. It did make me smile, just as the young man had said. *It was like living in the Bible*, I thought. As the crowds moved, I saw a dead dog, half decayed and with swarming flies. Part of its skull was showing through its flaking hide. Reality again.

I tried to phone Feroz but couldn't get through. I then decided to make a collect call home. I held the phone close to my ear and looked out over the smoky glimmer of Sanaa's city lights.

'Hi Mom, it's me,' I said, overwhelmed with relief she had answered.

'Oh, Marcovich!' she gasped my nickname. I could hear the excitement and joy in her voice.

I wasn't able to call that often and I knew each day was agonising for her as she tried to imagine how we were and where we were. She worried about us a lot. She worried a lot about me. She was as cautious as my brother was when it came to the trip.

'How are you? Where are you? They said you were

calling from Sanaa, where is that?'

'It's in Yemen.'

'Yemen? What are you doing in Yemen? Where is Yemen?'

'We had to come here to ship the bikes, remember. I am here to physically check the bikes in again to get them to Ethiopia. It's a pretty crazy place this. South of Saudi Arabia – have a look on a map – mainly all desert.'

'And then what? What is the plan? How long will you be there?'

'Then, if all goes well, I will follow them to Djibouti, and then to Addis.'

I could hear I had lost her for a moment. Most of those places meant nothing to her. Really.

'Basically I have to ship the bikes across the Red Sea and I will then follow them to Ethiopia.'

I paused for a little longer than usual and she picked it up in a flash, the way mothers usually do.

'What's wrong Marc? What's happened? Are you okay? Where is Papa? You keep saying you will have to do all these things ... are you alone? What's going on?'

I breathed deeply and sat down. I lifted my feet onto the window sill. The sky was already full with stars, bright and blinking. It was the first clean view of my day. Then I dropped the bombshell.

'Mom, they deported Papa yesterday from Jordan,' I tried to drain the words of alarm and drama.

'What? Sorry Marc, what did you just say?'

'They deported Papa from Jordan,' I repeated more slowly, 'and I don't actually know where they have sent him. I have no idea where Papa is.'

'What? What are you talking about?' I imagined her sitting stunned, grasping for the sense in what I was saying.

'I had to come here to get the bikes, because we sent the

bikes a few weeks ago, but last night they arrested him, and I just don't know where he is. They wouldn't tell me,' I explained.

'Are you joking? Please don't play these games with me. What's really going on?'

'I'm not joking Mom, it's all true. It's all crazy, actually.'

'But why? How did he get deported? What happened?' There was the beginning of panic in her voice.

She knew she couldn't help. For many years she had endured calls from across the globe from me. In almost all cases they were easy and jovial. Over time she discovered that, however dire my situation, I had a habit of always keeping those calls light and devoid of alarm. She had learned I would act calm to ensure I didn't raise any maternal angst. But after every trip I would spill the beans on the white lies I had told. Some of the stories of what had actually happened were too good to keep secret. She had been on guard ever since, and had begun to imagine the worst behind each call. On that evening, she was confused by the tone behind what I was sharing. It must have sounded serious, almost overly serious, and maybe even exaggerated to her. I was as blunt and honest as I could be. I couldn't pull the wool over my own eyes, let alone find the energy to do it to her. That is partly why she couldn't believe it; it all sounded too true. There was a long silence and in that gap, my throat felt the pressure to burst out crying.

'*Jesus* Marc, so what are you going to do?' she exclaimed. The fact she'd sworn brought me back to the present very quickly. Her question focused my thoughts: *what are you going to do?*

'Well, I need to get to Yemeni Airways, find the bikes and re-ship them,' I said calmly. 'I have 2000 dollars to make it all happen. It's going to be fine, Mom, I think I am going to be okay.'

'Okay, how long will that take?' she asked.

'I don't know really, but I have booked myself in here for seven nights.'

'Do you have someone who is going to help you there?'

'No, I have to do it all myself, that is the only tricky thing on this side.'

'Is 2000 enough money?' She fired off rounds of pertinent questions, 'Are you sure you will get by with that?'

'I think so. It's all I have, so it will have to be enough,' I said, appreciating the chance to think out loud. Her action-focused questions helped me move into my plan for the following day.

'And Hans, what about him? What can I do?'

'Maybe you can call *Tante* Inge?' I suggested. 'Maybe Papa phoned her?'

'And what about money? Can I check how to get money to you? Do you still have your blue credit card?'

'Yes, that might be the easiest. It's a MasterCard, but I think I will have enough. I will let you know Mom. Don't worry; I think it will come together.'

The pace of the conversation lifted tempo. She became more and more frantic, until she threw in the towel on it all.

'Just leave the bikes, Marc. Just come home. Why are you doing this?' It was a hint of her disapproval of the trip, but I wasn't going to give up then.

'Mom, I will be fine. I have Rennie's number in Addis, and I will phone him. I am sure they sent Papa to either Austria or Addis. They couldn't send him to Yemen, because they declined his visa here. I don't know how deportation works; maybe he was allowed to choose where he wanted to go. I will call Rennie in the morning. You can check with *Tante* Inge in the meantime too.'

'Okay, let me see what I can find out. If you need money I will send it to you.'

'Thanks Mom, thank you.'

That seemed to reassure her. At least for a moment there was silence.

'I thought you might want to know Gregor has come home,' she said, less anxiously. 'It seems he just couldn't do it anymore.'

'Shame man, he had such dreams to make it work,' I said, genuinely concerned for him.

'It apparently just got worse and worse, and in the end, I think his parents gathered the money to pay for his flight and pay back the bursary.'

I was relieved to hear it.

'But he seems to be very depressed, and they are concerned about his mental health,' she added.

'I'm not surprised. He lived in such a terrible place, and it was very abusive. I will try to send him a postcard.'

Again there was a long silence. It felt like the conversation had come to an end, but I was enjoying the company, the familiarity and the care I heard from across the line. There was still one piece of news I wanted to share. It had been sitting at the back of my mind throughout but I was concerned about how to say it, and even whether I had the right to share it.

'Oh and Mom, there is something else. Sorry, I know this is a collect call ... is it okay if we chat a little longer?'

'Yes, sure, don't worry, what is it?' she said with trepidation.

'Actually, the reason they deported Papa is because he is sick,' I paused. 'When we had to apply for visas they needed us to do a medical, and the results that came back said Papa, well ... the blood tests came back positive for ... Aids, or HIV. It wasn't that clear.'

It went deathly silent on the other end of the line.

'Mom, are you still there?'

I could hear a break in her voice.

'What are you saying, Marc?' she whispered.

I shared the entire story again, and added in the traumatic sequence of events that had followed that day of the arrest. I began to feel a numbness as I told the story. I almost disbelieved myself, it all sounded outlandish, really. But my mom listened quietly.

'And what does Papa say? How did he react?' she asked tenderly.

'We haven't really spoken about it. Within a few hours of us finding out, he was imprisoned.'

'He didn't say anything at all? I mean, can it be true, really? Have you noticed any symptoms? Has he been sick at all, or weak, or losing weight?'

'No and no. He doesn't believe the results. He just denies it.'

'And the trip? What's going to happen to the trip? You can't continue, can you?'

'I suppose we will find out when I see him again,' I started to feel irritated by all the questions. Each question became harder to answer and exposed how little I actually knew, or even wanted to think about.

'Marc, it is a big responsibility to travel with someone who is that sick, especially with Aids.'

'I know, but maybe he doesn't have it, maybe they got it wrong. He thinks they definitely got it wrong,' I started to believe myself and the denial.

'Please come home,' were the last words I can remember of that conversation. I resisted the request.

I pushed the green phone into its berth and sat in silence while I looked at the floor. I removed all the uncertainty of the future weeks and months from my mind. I had to focus on the next day, the next 72 hours. I had to begin thinking of a plan. I had to make my way around the city and make the final crossing to Africa, to the home continent. That was it, it was all quite simple. To think about the trip, and whether it was over, was irrelevant. It was a nagging cycle of thoughts, but I needed to ignore that until a more appropriate time.

The following morning, I woke early and energised myself. I had rested my head on my situation, and had begun to percolate a plan there. I felt ready to make it all happen and was at action stations. I packed a small backpack with all the papers I needed, loaded my wallet with cash, and over breakfast rehearsed the plan. *Goal number one: find the bikes in cargo. Goal number two: get them released and then re-check in the bikes to Addis. Goal number three: pay for the transaction and get the hell out of hell.* Three simple steps and I couldn't see how that could take more than a day to organise.

I stepped onto the pavement, and breathed the cool, dry desert morning breeze. The air had a false dampness to it. It was already a busy start to the day, a Sunday, the first day of the work week, and people and vehicles were on the move. There were many yellow cabs already on the road, which reassured me. I looked across the skyline for the tallest building in the city centre. I had noticed it when I arrived and, most importantly, across its top story was a sign in bold red lettering – *'Yemeni Airways'*. That was my building, I needed to get there. It was the one common denominator on all the documents I did have. Sure, there was a shipping agent's name and address, but everything was handled by Yemeni Airways. My thinking was they would at least know where the bikes were, and could help me to find the agent. I began to wonder whether it would be more efficient to go straight to the airport where the bikes were likely to physically be, or to the actual head offices.

In my faltering state of confidence, I looked around and noticed the doors to an office opening. *What luck*, I thought, *how useful. I could do with some help.* The office looked smartly upmarket. I hoped they could speak English and would at least be able to point me in the right direction.

I stepped through the tinted glass front door and felt my shoes sink into a plush carpet. There was gold trim around everything and a large chandelier hung into the centre of the room. It looked like a hotel lobby. In front of me were four desks, all clean and each topped with a computer. A lone woman was booting them all up. She looked up at me with surprise.

'Excuse me, hello, good morning,' I said. I spoke very clearly and slowly. 'Do you speak English?'

'Yes. Good morning, mister, I can help you?'

'Yes please, I need to get to the Yemeni offices.'

'My friend, we can help you, for sure. Yes!' came a low, baritone voice from behind me. I turned towards the door and saw a dark-haired man stride through the entrance. His shirt was unbuttoned to the middle of his chest, he had a stubbly beard and was tall. In fact he was so tall he had to keep ducking beneath the chandelier. He had a smile that both endeared me to him, and made me wary of him. It was a syrupy salesman's kind of smile.

'Tea or coffee?' he asked, as he stretched out his hand to shake mine. He dragged the nearest chair with him and, as we met, hand to hand, I dropped into the seat.

'Tea, please,' I said, surprised and bemused by the familiarity. It was as if they'd been expecting me.

He greeted the woman and disappeared through a door at the back of the room. There were muffled greetings of '*salaam, salaam*' and then he burst back through the door, smiling and energetic.

'So Mr, why do you want to go to Yemeni Airways?' he asked, as he walked behind a screen where I presumed the tea was brewing.

'I arrived yesterday from Amman and have shipped some motorbikes that I need to now ship to Djibouti.'

'Motorbikes? What are you doing with the motorbikes? Where are you going?' he asked loudly and in perfect English. His accent was different to the others I had met in the Middle East. His face then peeked around the screen. 'Oh sorry, I am asking so many questions, but that is very rude of me. Let me introduce myself first. My name is Mustafa, and I am very pleased to meet you.'

'And I am Marc,' I said smiling.

'And where are you from, Mr Marc?' he asked, carrying the small cups on a tray.

'From South Africa. I live in Cape Town,' I said with pride. His eyes widened and he pulled an even bigger smile up his cheeks as I said that. 'We are riding on bikes from Austria to Cape Town, to celebrate the Millennium.'

'Oh, my African friend,' he sang with joy. 'I am from Kenya, we are African brothers, and I am honoured and privileged and actually so excited to be able to help you.'

He was the furthest from my stereotype of a Kenyan as one could imagine. I was surprised but rolled with it. He was such an upbeat and cheerful character I couldn't resist him. Besides, I really had nothing to lose at that point and desperately needed help.

'Isn't that amazing?' he continued. 'You walk into a travel agency and you meet a fellow African, here in Sanaa. It's amazing, isn't it? So I am going to help you my friend, I am going to help you with whatever you need.'

'A travel agency?' I asked, chuckling at the serendipity. 'Now that is very lucky indeed.'

It all started to make sense. I pulled together all the clues around me: the plush hotel setting, the walls filled with framed images of spectacular destinations, the English-speaking staff.

'Give me those papers and let's get started. It is really so good to meet you, Marc,' he said again, and put his hand on my shoulder to give it a tender squeeze. I think he would have preferred to hug me right then. He was thrilled.

I handed him the papers and sat quietly in the corner of the office on a tanned leather couch. Mustafa and his co-workers hurried about picking through the papers, asking for clarity on certain details and photocopying my passport multiple times. The tea was sweet and comforting, and kept being refilled. Mustafa's desk was filled with papers. He eventually beckoned me to look at something.

'This here,' he said, pointing to an invoice from the shipping company in Amman. 'Is this what you paid for all the shipping?'

'Yes, we were clear we needed the bikes shipped to Ethiopia. They mentioned a maximum of 2000 dollars for the entire trip, and we have already paid half of that.'

'Okay, this is not so clear on this here, but we will see. All I can see is 2000 is still due. Do you have any other invoices?'

'No, that is all the paperwork I have,' I replied, feeling the worry spread across my face. I had felt uneasy about the paper trail of commitments and payments around that freight company from the start. This was proof my suspicions had not been misplaced.

'Okay, before we go I will phone these guys and then let's see what we need to do.'

'Mustafa, I must also find out ...' – I looked for the right words – '...what will I owe you for all this help?'

'Well Marc, I haven't helped you yet, but don't worry, we will make a plan,' he said with his reassuring smile. He hadn't answered my question, and then was drawn into a phone conversation with the custodians of our bikes. He shook his head and scribbled notes as he listened.

'Are you ready?' he asked, dropping the phone into its cradle. 'Let's go and find your motorbikes. The man I just spoke to has a different story to your papers, but we will sort that out. This is Yemen. It may have impossible people, but it is a place where anything is possible. Chin up.'

We bundled into his large white 4x4 and inched through the busy Sanaa morning traffic. He entertained me with stories of his youth in Kenya, of his love of Africa and his longing to go back. He was genuinely homesick, but business was business and I was surprised to discover the links between east Africa and the Arabian Peninsula were significant. According to him, he was the only top-end tour operator, had excellent contacts in Kenya and Tanzania, and seemed to thoroughly enjoy sharing his motherland with the elite of Yemen. We had a lively conversation and he was fascinated by our trip. We were quickly becoming well acquainted and comfortable with each other. The drive took over an hour.

'Have you ever had *ghat*, Marc?' he asked on a totally different tangent to our prior conversation. We were jammed between two trucks for a long enough period of time to feel properly stuck.

'Sorry, I don't think so, what is that?'

'Aha, that will be our treat for later then. We can celebrate together,' he said with glee.

Everything around us was both frantic and in slow motion. It was surreal. Life teemed between the gridlocked vehicles, like water washing between rocks in a stream. People, animals, motorbikes and bicycles. And then there

I was with a stranger, in his car, driving towards a place I didn't know. I had lost my bearings and just had to succumb to faith. The outcome was not in my hands any longer. All I had was my charm to keep me in the game.

Predictably, by the time we finally reached the cargo hold at the airport, the papers we had were insufficient. In fact they were, according to those in charge, either all wrong or invalid, and even the word illegal was dropped in as a bargaining chip. The more the officialdom tried to speak to me, the more Mustafa physically blocked them. The haggling was fierce, with much spittle and flying of hands. They karate chopped the air and kept pointing at me, then slapped the papers against their legs. The act kept repeating itself and then, after about an hour, there was a handshake and a smile. It was done. I didn't see cash lube the exchange, but all parties seemed happy. I wondered whether asking to see the bikes might be pushing it. I decided to let it all be.

'Let's get out of here. We have a deal,' said Mustafa triumphantly. 'Let's get some lunch.'

'And what's the deal? It looked like everything was out of order?'

'No, your bikes will be on their way. I have the papers to sign and we will bring them back tomorrow, the deal is done. It's a very good thing you found me; I would say it was Allah's will.'

I couldn't believe my luck.

'So, Mr Marc, are you a Christian?' asked Mustafa.

That was a question that sent the rest of the day on an altogether different path. With the business of shipping done, Mustafa took the liberty to take the day off. It was an absorbing day of sharing, laughing, reminiscing and connecting. We had lunch in downtown Sanaa, discussed Africa, religion, war and history, and in the evening we celebrated with mouthfuls of *ghat*.

'It's very good for you, and makes you very awake,' said Mustafa. 'It's like coffee but a plant. You chew it and it makes you feel very strong.'

We sat there, delving into the edgy topics that plagued much of that part of the world. As I stripped leaves off a branch that was hidden in a brown paper bag, I found a rare sense of calm and assurance. The bikes were headed to Africa, and I was due in Djibouti within days. I still had not found my dad, but for a pause, for a reprieve, I ignored the ties to him, to the trip and to everything that had plagued my mind and my heart.

The Reluctant Trafficker

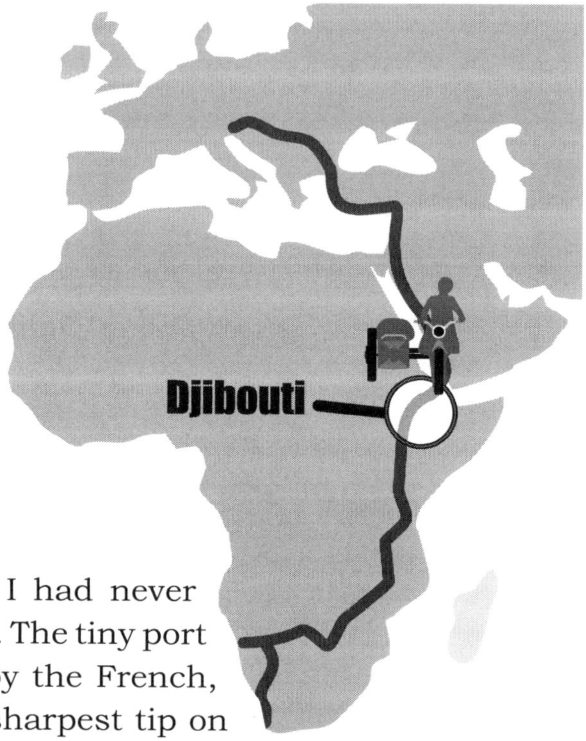

Just like Yemen, I had never heard of Djibouti. The tiny port country, colonised by the French, was pierced by the sharpest tip on the Horn of Africa. It was a typical mismatch of lifestyles and national dreams, and a clash of priorities that then rendered the country mostly forgotten or unknown. It was a piece of land that was chosen for reasons other than the people living there and so humanity became lost. Like so much of the continent, with its often geometrically-shaped countries, it was location and strategic value that mattered most.

I imagined colonialists leaning on maps of the continent draped over a billiards' table, their cognac glasses used as weights to steady the unfurled edges as they greedily scrambled and stretched for their land. I imagined the revelry as they shared the spoils in a game of continental poker, gambling on the fate of all Africans. What a devastating separation from reality that was. Unknowingly, or

– more chilling – with possible full intent, those colonisers divided entire nations into slivers and slices. They decreed and thrust new languages at them and embarked upon a systematic exploitation of the land and its people. The new countries made majorities in one place, minorities in another and, with lead and ink, disrupted the natural balance of the power vested in those places. In their wake they bred dependence and desperation, which in turn fuelled war and despair. They named the countries according to their European heroes, queens and myth. They used force and bludgeoned inferiority and pain into the African psyche. That vacuum of dignity crushed all that had value, and when the Europeans left, many Africans projected their anger, dispossession and hurt at each other.

I made contact with Papa again on my last day in Yemen. The Jordanians had thankfully deported him to Ethiopia. It was a short, matter-of-fact conversation. He focused on logistics, the bikes, the money, my Djibouti accommodation and transit to Addis Ababa in a truck. The outcome was a plan and not much else. I was relieved to hear his voice, but uncertain on what else to talk about, other than the plan. My mind was undeniably preoccupied with the state of his health. I wanted to ask him how he was feeling. I wanted to know if he had experienced any symptoms. But the timing continued to feel inappropriate. I thought that might change but I wasn't convinced I would ever get him to talk about it again. He sounded relieved to hear from me too.

The man I remember most from Djibouti was Selashi the trucker who, for some reason, I felt I had met before. He was a calm Ethiopian, strong in his silence and permanently smirking at the world. He had a raggedy beard, like a revolutionary, and a casual dress sense. Shorts and an unbuttoned, long-sleeved shirt were his trademark.

It was the glint in his eye that endeared him to me. It was naughty and adventurous. We shared many meals together in the compound, so by the time we set off on the long drive south, I felt comfortable in his company. Which was a good thing. I wasn't quite hitch-hiking with a stranger.

Djibouti is so small, just a city country, it took us only a couple of hours to trundle and belch out of the city limits and reach the Ethiopian border. Addis Ababa was an estimated three days away. I was quite excited at the prospect of being chauffeured, in an air-conditioned cabin, about three metres off the ground. That was easily twice the height of my seat on a bike. The views, oh the views. It was a holiday for me.

I had no reason to suspect anything as we neared the border, but Selashi suddenly stopped his truck. He left the engine running and gingerly hopped out of the cabin. We were surrounded by thickets and sand; there was not a person or a building in sight. The arid landscape stretched as far as we could see and then, from behind a large cluster of bushes, a young woman appeared. She walked confidently to the back of the truck as I watched her in the side mirror. She embraced Selashi. It was hard for me to tell her age. Her head scarf covered her face, and the slight figure gave nothing of her age away. They chatted and then she slipped her hand down her blouse and pulled out a small fold of notes. He snatched it, and expertly rolled it tightly into the shape of a pipe. It looked like it was a planned rendezvous and both parties seemed content with the outcome. Selashi pushed and prodded his stash deeply into his back pocket. They both walked behind the truck. I was distracted by a bug that flew at high speed straight into my ear. When I looked again, Selashi and the woman were gone. I leaned over to the driver's side to look down that end of the truck, and was startled by Selashi as he pulled open his door. He smiled at me, with an air of expectation, and then cleared his throat many times over.

'Okay, now we can go home!' he said, as he ground the gears back into first.

I chose not to ask any questions. I didn't have much time to try to piece together my assumptions against reality either. Within a few minutes, and after some sharp twists and rolls through soft bunkers of sand, we reached the border post. Or more accurately, we arrived at a gate. There was a lone rudimentary boom that stretched out from a small tin hut. The shack was covered in a colourful patchwork of discarded cloth and plastic. There was no fence on either side of the gate. The boom served only as a barrier that blocked the road. We could have driven about five metres to the left or right and tripped into Ethiopia by mistake. There were many foot traffic trails that had sidestepped the gate and the nearby paths were well worn. That was officially the Djibouti side of the border. I noticed Selashi straighten stiffly. He buttoned up his shirt and wiped his glistening forehead of sweat. He tried to pat the stray hairs on his beard flat. His usually calm demeanour turned to a busy and tidy tension. He gripped the steering wheel with both his hands, like a learner driver does, and checked his collar, not in an obvious way, but very deliberately.

A young French-speaking border guard kicked dust into the air as he shuffled over to us. He politely waved us towards the small patch of shade on the edge of his hut. The sweat was hiding beneath his arms, and the salt in his body drew white lines in the creases on the back of his shirt. It was stiflingly hot.

'That is good!' whispered Selashi, speaking to himself, 'I

am happy with that. Come, let's go.'

I listened and followed. We exchanged pleasantries with the armed official and smiled and nodded. After what looked like a mere visual inspection of ourselves and our truck, we secured a stamp in our passports.

I hopped back into the truck, expecting Selashi to be priming the diesel, but he wasn't there. I leaned across to spy in the side mirror and saw him duck to the back again. He walked with a hunched back and bent knees, talking to himself in a whispery shout. He was out of sight for just a few moments, and then, with vigour and energy, he was neatly seated next to me again.

'Just one more,' he said, clearly speaking only to himself, oblivious of me. He sighed for a long time through his clenched teeth, and stared ahead. 'Almost there, all is fine.'

'Yes,' I answered, not sure what else to say. 'Then we are there.'

There was an S-bend in the road that led to the Ethiopian border post where a single brick and mortar building stood guard. All around it were small wood, reed and tin structures. In comparison to these basic structures, the border post was a five-star building, complete with a national flag and a sign. It was comforting to see it. And I watched the flag lift and fall like a dancer doing a solo.

'Oh *shit*, oh *shit*,' snarled Selashi. 'Oh no, *shit* man!'

I saw three soldiers step out from a small hut in no man's land. They had a heat-stroked look and waved our truck off the road with limp gestures. We dared not ignore them. They stood blocking the road and then pointed to Selashi in a way that suggested they knew him. They had ominously wry smiles on their faces.

'Okay, you just stay here, it will all be fine, this is no problem, all will be fine,' he jabbered, scratching his nose and stretching out his neck in a rotation of all directions.

Selashi joined the soldiers on their walk to the hut. I had not been invited. I figured out it was a pre-customs stop, some kind of a sorting station. I had never seen it before. It was almost as if, in that no man's land, men with guns could have their own territory to taunt and terrorise. Selashi was jittery enough to make me believe that was the case. They walked slowly, with no one obviously leading, and stooped into the darkness of the little outpost. I waited and waited, watched and watched. The heat expanded the metal of the cabin and made it creak and clap. Midday was on its way.

A flurry of movement caught my attention. Small puffs of dust rose where he took his steps. He looked nervous and harassed and walked as fast as he could, without actually running. He didn't quite look panicked, but he was purposeful as he swung open my door.

'They want your passport and to search the truck,' he said, holding out his hand.

'What do they want?' I asked.

'I don't know, but it is a problem all of this. This is a problem,' he whispered, and then jog-walked back to the hut. I was basically a spectator, grasping snippets of the plot line to an action thriller. I had no idea what was going on, and before I could ask him, he would disappear again.

There is a cardinal rule of travelling that you should not give up your passport, no matter what. It is critical to keep your hands on it at all times, bartering any and all other valuables, if necessary. The passport is your freedom, and that should never be surrendered. That day, in the heat, we broke the rule, and it was too late to do anything about it. My passport was gone. The harsh desert sun pulsed bursts of heat through the cabin. A weak and inconsistent breeze was the only momentary reprieve. It was silent in no man's land. In all that time, we had not been passed by another vehicle or person. Up ahead, I could see the bustle of the border crossing, a typical sight of traders and travellers who bartered and socialised. The Ethiopian flag still danced with the breeze.

I couldn't hear him, but I saw Selashi come bursting out of the hut. I wasn't sure if he had been pushed out or hit on his way out. He stumbled, but didn't fall. I then watched him face away from the hut and slowly raise his arms either in defiance or deference. He just stood there. One of the soldiers moved into the white, midday light and placed the barrel of his gun between Selashi's shoulder blades. The guard pushed him once and then stood with his gun aimed at Selashi's head. Selashi stomped through the soft sand, cautiously but with haste. He didn't look back once.

'*Fuck*, we have a problem,' he said, the tension etched on his forehead in deep wrinkles. 'We need a plan fast or they will search the truck.'

I didn't see the problem with that; it seemed like the standard thing to be done at any border. He walked a circle into the sand and fretted with clenched teeth.

'Okay, so this is what we do. You must be the son of a very rich man, okay?' he demanded. I wasn't sharing his extreme edginess, but felt I was being lured into an underhanded game. I began to feel tense, as if I was wading into dark waters without knowing what might be lurking in the depths.

'What do you want me to say?' I asked nervously. 'What are we trying to achieve here?'

'Just pretend, I will speak, you just stand there and play along.'

'Okay, but pretend to do or be what? I am rich and then...?' I shut myself up as the soldiers beckoned to us from the gate.

'Just stand there and say nothing, nothing at all,' said Selashi. 'Just let your white skin do all the talking.'

There is a second rule of travel: At border crossings, never tell a lie.

Selashi darted to the back of the truck again. I could hear him pull and push the awning ropes that closed the back of the canopy with canvas. There was a loud clang as he slammed one side of the tailgate back into place and secured it. He hurried back and clapped dust and grease off his hands and onto his shorts.

We met the soldiers half way between the truck and their hut. Still in no man's land.

'Hello sir, how can I help you?' I asked, using a question to try and grasp what was going on. 'Is there anything you need from us?'

I'd broken our deal and Selashi gave a sharp nod of his head, like a dismissive parent. He disapproved, but the way I saw it, I had to act legitimately rich and be somewhat entitled. I had to take charge. So I did.

'Yes sir, we must keep your truck and search it,' said a young soldier, his fine black moustache shining with sweat. All three of them were chewing *ghat*.

'But you must tell them, Mr Marc, how we have no time,' interrupted Selashi. And with that, the lies became our single truth, unrehearsed and impromptu. We were reading every signal we could from each other to survive.

'No no, this is not possible, we must do a big search,' insisted the guard. He pointed at the truck, 'You must go to that hut and wait there.'

They marched past us and before we knew it, we were stranded between the guards and the hut, isolated from the truck. We had been outmanoeuvred. Our passports were gone, the lies had rolled out of our mouths and the inevitable search was about to begin. The heat became unbearable, both inside and out. Selashi just stood there and shook his head while he looked at the dirt between his toes.

'But Mr Marc, please explain how we must get home now,' he begged. He stared into my eyes, trying to give me a message, but whatever more he was trying to tell me was masked by evident panic. 'We cannot be here for long, we cannot, and we really cannot! Remember?'

'So you are very rich businessman?' interrupted the second soldier. As he asked the question I prepared for the bribe. To border officials, usually lowly paid and isolated, any trace of power emboldened them to covet and confiscate pretty much anything they fancied. That whole rich and important storyline was about to backfire.

'Well no, not really ... but I am actually the son of a very big businessman. That is his truck,' I said, trying to deflect attention away from myself. I lied so easily.

'But then we can search your truck, even if it is your father's truck. What is the problem? Do we have a problem?' asked the third soldier. His gun swung forward and almost right off his shoulder. He caught it with a raised elbow. He had done that many times. It felt like deliberate intimidation. Selashi shook his head again, more vigorously with each sentence, like a director unhappy his cast had gone off cue and script. Our skit had gone into no man's land.

'But Mr Marc, your father. It is very urgent, isn't it?'

I had no idea where he was going. Selashi had melted from a main player into a cameo as if he had forgotten his lines or something. So I rose to the role. It was clearly a deadlock and it was very distressing. Something was wrong and I had to lead them off a scent I was unaware of.

'But sir, my father is one of the richest men in Ethiopia,'

I said, playing my first move. I scanned my racing thoughts for a checkmate sequence. 'He is in government and a close friend of the president, but he is a sick man, a very very sick man.'

The men smirked back at me, but I pressed on. 'We need to get to him now,' I said, raising my voice and acting exasperated. 'Okay, just give me your names then.'

That was my final play, to write down their names and subtly threaten to report them. That trick had worked before in Bulgaria with a corrupt traffic official, but at that point, it was hard to tell which way it could have gone. They could have laughed back into their barrels and ignored us, or they could have been offended by my cheek and locked us up. There was a small chance their junior rank and profile would make them more gullible. The hope was they wouldn't feed off my urgency and block us, just because they could. Their sense of worth, after all, often came from holding people's movement at ransom.

The moustached soldier stepped forward. He almost touched my nose in an Eskimo greeting. I felt a prod into my gut. It was not the barrel of a gun, but rather the edge of our passports. He said nothing, and defeat glazed over his eyes. He prodded me again, and then looked away with contempt. His finger pointed an order for us to leave.

It was an abrupt end to the simmering altercation. I was suspicious of their about-turn and slowed my movements to a calm and controlled pace, so as to avoid attracting too much attention. I expected the unexpected and didn't quite believe we had free passage. Every step of the 100 yards to the real border gate was silenced with anticipation. Nothing happened and within minutes we were through the border and on Ethiopian soil.

Selashi was calm and composed again as he guided his truck towards a squat of street-side cafes. He didn't thank me. He didn't explain a thing, but I was on a buzz and curious to know: *What was that all about? What were we ferrying? What was he hiding? Was there contraband? Weapons? Shit, possibly even drugs?* To play games like that at a border post, in the middle of what seemed like nowhere, was daring and dangerous. Whatever it was, we'd acted our way out of it and I have to admit it was thrilling.

'Everything okay Selashi?' I felt compelled to ask.

'Yes yes, no problems. Come, we will have a coke now. It's very hot. Let's take a break, we don't have to rush too much today.'

'Are you sure? Maybe we should just keep going,' I suggested.

I had hoped we would drive all day. Sitting around at the border seemed a little aimless. We were also within rifle range of a disgruntled soldier we had bullied with false authority and veiled threats. It was too close for comfort, and a little too nonchalant, even brazen.

'No problems, we have to stay here, just for a coke to drink, and then when we are ready we will go,' he said firmly.

We pulled over. As I stepped out of the cabin I again heard Selashi speak loudly and with a cheerful lilt to his voice behind the truck. I headed for some shade; the heat had cooked my eyes and nostrils until they stung. I was craving that coke, or anything cold and fresh. I sat down on an old, weathered couch covered in corduroy that had become polished with years of weight. The backrest was broken, and had been replaced with a discarded, wooden pallet. I rubbed the sweat and dust from my ears to the back of my head. When I opened my eyes again, I looked out of the café and past our truck. I saw vegetable and snack sellers across the way, perched on old cooking-oil buckets. I watched young and old carrying baggage of all shapes and descriptions. Some bicycles were piled three metres high with boulder-sized bags. It was busy and commercial and gritty.

The young waiter placed the 500ml bottle at my foot, which rested on the edge of the low table. I opened it, vigorously wiped the mouth of the bottle, and tipped back a huge gulp of the good black stuff. As I lowered the bottle, I saw something that made me freeze. I dropped my drink onto my chest and into my lap while I watched a crowd of young people emerge from the back of our truck. They slipped around the front of the vehicle and melted quietly into the crowds of travellers mingling along the road. Within seconds I had lost track of all of them. *The conniving sneak!* I thought to myself. *Selashi was trafficking people. No wonder he was shitting in his pants.* Thank God I hadn't known, or I would most likely have vomited onto the fine moustache of that young soldier.

'After lunch, we head home,' said Selashi, with not a hint of guilt, just that smirk. 'It's been a good start to the day and to our trip.'

I laughed, lost for words. He was a finely-tuned opportunist and for most of the trip it was very useful to have him as my travel companion. But that episode had been sensationally close to having grave consequences. For the next two days, we trundled along through the sweeping escarpments of northern Ethiopia, and then spent a number of nights in quaint roadside villages. We ate pasta for every dinner – possibly the best in Africa. We chewed *ghat* and listened to local music every moment the engine was on. We always got the best rooms and most doting service. As we were about to enter Addis, Selashi pulled off into the thickets and onto a long dirt road. It wasn't the way home. In the twilight the truck bashed through the undergrowth.

He had been rushing all day and the trees and rough terrain didn't slow him down. We burst into a clearing where men were standing with forks, spades and pick axes. He reversed the truck and, without much chatter, the men began to fill the back of the truck with white sand. After an hour, the truck was full and we were off again.

'The sand is for my business,' he said with a grin. 'I will drop you off first and then deliver it, it's for a little extra money, you know.'

I admired the ease with which he did pretty much everything and anything, a born entrepreneur, and right then, a confirmed smuggler of all things valuable.

The Death Wish

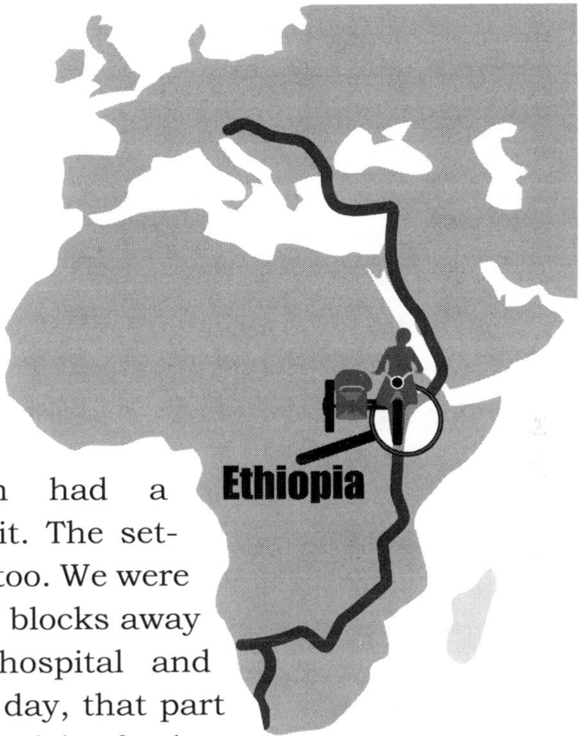

The conversation had a familiar tone to it. The setting was predictable too. We were in another bar, a few blocks away from the military hospital and abattoir. During the day, that part of town was shadowed by feathery clouds of vultures that circled the 15-metre high pile of animal bones and carcasses. The hospital was right next door. It was crowded by slow, hobbling lines of soldiers maimed and broken from the dirty war with the breakaway state of Eritrea. The air was pungent and putrid. In the evenings the vultures were gone, but death hung low in the cool, thin air. On that night, we had passed a hyena, skulking in the shadows, using broken street lights as its shelter.

'You know, they don't actually live here,' Papa said, as we stepped out of the car. He must have sensed my hyper vigilance. 'They come in from the rocky outcrops on the edge of the city. It's not a good idea to walk about here at night. But the bars are safe!'

We drank our first beer in silence. Papa scanned the

room for old faces, and nodded a quick hallo at people who looked familiar. Expat communities are small; everyone seemed to know everyone. Some didn't stay long, others came in for a chat. It was always the same: he shared a brief précis of our ambitions for the trip, then he would introduce me, sometimes in German, sometimes in English. All that time, the beer kept flowing.

A day had passed since we were reunited. I had clattered into the house late that night. With daybreak we again pressed play on the trip, and continued as if nothing had happened. Within me something had shifted, I could sense it. My independence over those weeks had boosted my confidence. I felt emotionally stronger too. It was strange to have these gaps in the story, but we did very little to bridge them. I enjoyed having a paragraph of a chapter all to myself.

'At least we have the bikes back,' Papa said.

'I know; what a relief. I really thought that one sidecar wouldn't make it.'

'That would have been interesting,' he chuckled. 'If they hadn't sent it, we would have to have done the trip on one bike. Now imagine that. It would have been very uncomfortable.'

As he said it, I realised I hadn't even thought of that option. I had assumed the trip would then be over, but maybe not. I had thought the trip was touch-and-go with the diagnosis, but that never seemed to come up again.

'Next, we need to make some modifications,' he said. 'I think we need to add some wind funnels, to make sure air gets onto our cylinders with more force. It's going to get hotter as we head further south. I know a guy who can do it for us.'

'Great idea. That means fewer of those one-hour bike breaks, right?'

'Yes, but it also means they will not over-heat as much and blow any more pistons or rubbers,' he said, stating the obvious. 'If all goes according to plan, it should take another week.'

'Perfect, then we will have the visas too, and we could be out of here by, say, next Friday?'

There was a long silence. We hadn't been on our bikes for close to four weeks, and yet so much had happened in that time. There had been a shift from bike-generated calamity to an altogether different kind of challenge. In the silence, I again mulled over his diagnosis and the deportation. It was impossible for me to ignore it. Every time I looked at him, it was like a label was stuck to his forehead saying, *'I am sick'*. I had begun to think more practically about safety and health facilities and symptoms and precautions. All those things made me feel out of my depth. If only I could have talked to him about it, about his illness.

'You know, those hyenas reminded me of a plan I have for one day,' he said.

I was curious. Unlike so many other stories, I actually hadn't heard that one before.

'When I was living here I used to tell everyone what the plan was,' he continued. This was even more interesting. Everyone else had heard it and now it was my turn. I leaned in, literally sitting on the edge of my seat.

'So my plan is to not get very old, you see. I don't want to end up like my father or my mother. They really suffered, you know. Getting old is like being a child. I don't want that, and I don't want people to have to look after me when I am like that.'

A frown deepened across my eyes. Wherever the story was heading, it sounded ominous.

'So, when I am about 70, or maybe 15 years from now...'

He paused and looked for a bottle behind the bar. He

scanned the shelf left to right, and right to left until he found what he was looking for.

'I will come here to Ethiopia and I will walk to the outside of the city where the veld begins. I will find a tree, one of those acacia trees, and I will sit under it and drink probably two bottles of whiskey,' he said, pointing to the Jameson's bottle he had been looking for. 'It will be Jameson's, neat out of the bottle in the bush!'

I was morbidly fascinated, and appalled too.

'And then I will cut my arms until I am bleeding,' he said with a wry smile, 'and I will wait for the hyenas to come. With a lot of blood, it would all be over very quickly; that way no one has to look after me. And besides, I have already had such a good life, no regrets, just a good life.'

I didn't know how to react. I was stunned by both the words and the tone of the delivery. There was a triumphant air about him. I wasn't sure what to say next. He had always been a maverick, and in truth, to die that way would be fitting for him, but I was still shocked, and had nothing to add. What surprised me the most was he had already told people of this plan, as if it was something to brag about. I couldn't understand that, but the unfazed approach to his Aids diagnosis made more sense after that. I shook my head, and faked a laugh to make light of this macabre plan. *Was that normal? Was he normal?* I had lost touch.

'Hey *fuckers*!' boomed the distinctive accent of Rennie coming out of nowhere. 'So when did you get here? Thanks for waiting for me. *Shit* man, you guys. What are you drinking?'

Rennie had burst his way into our chat just like he had always done in my dad's life. And with that, the opportunity passed again. He turned to clash glasses with Rennie. I looked at the bottle of Jameson's. It was a brutal suicide idea he really hadn't needed to share with me. In fact, it felt highly inappropriate. I mean, *who does that? Who tells his son about how he plans to kill himself? And sets the date?* I looked at him, he was more of a stranger than ever to me.

Road to Moyale

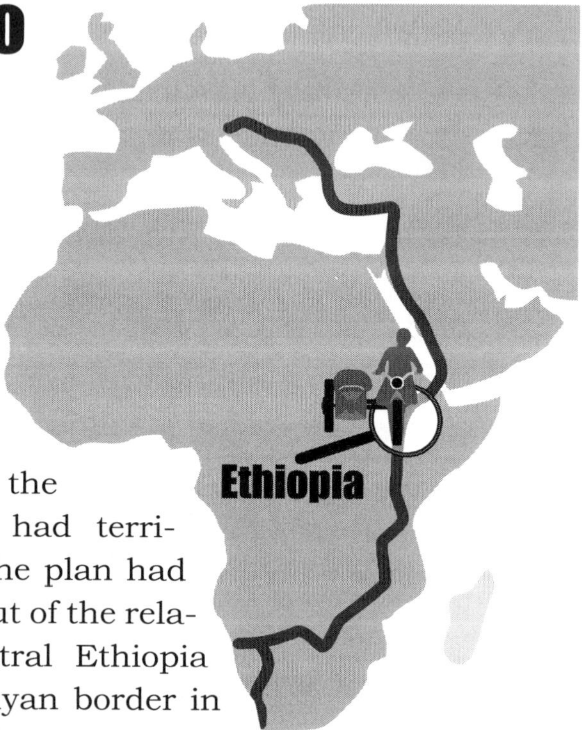

Thinking about the road to Moyale had terrified me for weeks. The plan had always been to slip out of the relative security of central Ethiopia and drive to the Kenyan border in one day. When the day came to get back on our bikes, we shared big gulps of schnapps at 5am. It was the first and only time I joined my dad in his daily ritual. We both felt uneasy and, with every kilometre we drove further south, my anxiety headed higher.

In our first hour, we slowly weaved up a hill bursting with wild woods. The tall trees cast motley shadows over the patchwork tar. We were focused on the quality of the road that day and had started perfecting our S-shaped approach to the bigger holes in the asphalt. The technique was simple; I would crouch into my seat and squeeze the ribbed rubber of my accelerator a little harder than usual. It seemed counter intuitive at first to push fuel to the engine, and speed faster and faster towards a gaping pothole, but with a quicker approach I could steer to the left of the hole and, at the last moment, turn right, neatly skimming the left edge of the hole with my front wheel. As the bike lurched left, the sidecar would crunch low into its suspension, and the quick turn to the right would force the sidecar to jump, thanks to the energy of its springs, just high enough over the holes. Explaining it like that makes it sounds effective, but in truth, every third manoeuvre failed and I would wince at the jarring clash of the rim against the crumbling tar.

As we turned east near the top of a hill, the sun flashed through a gap in the trees. We were both temporarily blinded and missed an eagle pecking away at roadkill in the centre of the road. It was just two metres ahead of my dad's bike when I saw it pull its body to the ground and, with a sharp push of its legs, try to scoop enough wind beneath its broad and elongated wings. It seemed startled by our sudden arrival. It pushed its wings down and then forward, banked to the left, and tried to avoid the bike. My dad reacted late and pulled left too, and the eagle struck his helmet, knocking him so hard one of his arms lost its grip on the steering wheel. He held onto his bike rodeo style while the bird flailed directly at me. Its wings were tangled like a rugby player's legs knotted by an ankle tap. I ducked, just as it found a strong wing compression and clumsily shot over my head. It was a close call. Getting knocked off our bikes, hundreds of kilometres from help, could have been lethal. My mind was flooded again with a sense of vulnerability. Travelling on motorbikes was an exposed and dangerous mode of transport. It was always risky, and any wandering of the mind could lead to an accident.

Once atop the hill, we looked down to a flattened horizon. The road was squeezed ever smaller by long road-side grasses, and it was easy to imagine the smudge of black far in the distance was Moyale, marking the border to Kenya. That was the stretch of road that agitated my adrenaline, sharpened my senses and gave life to a blood-smeared show reel in my imagination. The stories had been relentless about that place. In Addis Ababa, everyone had a real-life account of tragedy on that stretch, and each story came to life in my mind as we looked down that road.

'*Shit* man, they just pulled him from his truck,' the dishevelled drunk next to us had drawled. The beer had spilled into the ashtray as he pushed it back onto the bar.

'No one knows why, no one knows much really, but the buggers killed him … *and* they cut off his penis!' His Australian accent lingered in his ballooning beer breath, '*Bastards!* They are *fucking* dangerous cannibal-like *fuckers*, man!'

'Where did this happen?' I asked, but he wasn't listening. His face flinched as he processed the memory he had evoked.

I cleared my throat and asked again, a little louder and with a tap on his shoulder, 'So where did this happen?'

'Just near Moyale, mate, the *fuckers* there are wild. Even the government doesn't go there. There are tribes down there that eat people, like real *fucking* cannibals. *Fuck me* man, there was a guy, they stopped him. Yes, simple tribesman stopped an 18-wheeler truck …' he said, accentuating each word. He banged his hand for emphasis, but it seemed to be out of rhythm with the effect he was hoping to achieve. It took a while for his head to steady back to its pivot at the base of his neck.

'Down there they are all armed,' Rennie added. His raised eyebrows signalled disapproval.

Rennie had been telling us for weeks to take the bikes on a truck through the south. My dad felt that would be cheating and, with a flight already under our belts, there was no room to deviate off the seats of our bikes. I simply smiled at the thought, hiding my ever-growing levels of doubt and wondering whether a truck would have been safer anyway.

'Down there, there is a custom when you kill a man, you cut off his genitals, add them to your necklace and cut a short line across your chest. I have seen men down there with their entire torsos etched with knife wounds...' Rennie was reluctant to let the topic go, 'and they are all armed, with Kalashnikovs!'

He had downed his drink, dragged his keys across the bar and into his palms and left, shaking his head.

As I looked down that road, I imagined what I would see and hear, like a road I had travelled before. My imagination kept projecting my greatest fear the bikes would break down, that we'd be unable to go any further, and as night fell, they would attack us. That's how all those other people had died there. It felt as though we had driven through an invisible gate, behind which there was no law. It felt as if we had slipped back a number of centuries and were now at the mercy of a survival game, where the road was the target, and where we were being marked for an ambush.

After about a kilometre, I felt as if we were being watched. I kept thinking I saw people jogging through the trees alongside us. I was convinced I saw a man tapping the banana trees and pushing their leaves into motion. I peered into the green foliage beside the road and thought I saw shadows of tall people and the silver reflection of a well-used rifle barrel. Or maybe it was a knife, or a sword or a spear. I noticed the sweat making my palms slip on the handles. I struggled to keep my eyes on the road.

Suddenly, my left eye caught a sharp black object, tickling my leg as I passed it. I braked hard, and sucked on tyre smoke as it clouded my goggles. My helmet slipped forward over my sweaty shaved head and rested against the bridge of my nose. For a moment, I couldn't see anything and I panicked.

'Holy shit!' I shouted.

'*Jesus*, man, Watch what you are doing!' Papa scolded. 'Let's stop here for a cup of tea and a snack.'

I looked around nervously but saw nothing but the wind moving leaves and grasses, in a part of the world that seemed totally untouched and unspoiled by humankind. It was peaceful, quiet and felt comfortingly pure. My dark imagination retreated into its creepy hovel and I savoured tea on the African plains. *That was what it was all about,* I thought. The open road, in an isolated and untouched part of the world. And all the way to the border we were alone and never in any danger.

The CIA

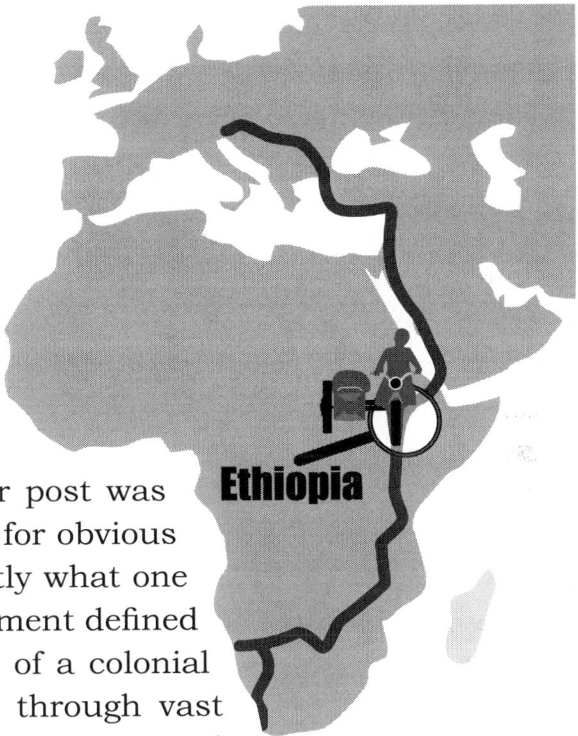

The Moyale border post was a welcome sight, for obvious reasons. It was exactly what one expects from a settlement defined purely by the stroke of a colonial pen. We had driven through vast plains of savannah, seen no people or vehicles, and very little to suggest humans lived there. Then, there was a border post. It was a scattering of official buildings, a small inn and a restaurant. All very simple, and with a view of another border hut on the Kenyan side of the fence.

Moyale was the mid-point of our danger zone. The south of Ethiopia was swollen with whispers and myth. It was apparently a place of death and lawlessness. Our road was the arterial line that was feared for its blood-spilling potential, and although it had felt as if we were being watched all the way in those final kilometres, we had made it. That exposed road, with no place to hide, gave way to the dangers of no road at all in our next dash with danger. It was Somali bandits who were ambush-ready on the next part of our journey. They were rumoured to race across the arid flats, mounted on 4x4s, to pursue any straggler vehicles that slowed or broke down. The route was cut by deep ravines and sharp cut-offs, devoid of direction signs and littered with debris and cargo, left behind where people were too scared to stop.

'*Oh my God* mister, there are very big lions down there, you know,' laughed a border guard whose teeth were a brilliant white. 'You will see them, maybe? You could be very lucky.'

He laughed a little longer as he reached for our passports and shared a smile with his colleagues behind the desk next to him.

'We haven't had motorbikes do this for a long time, mister. Are you sure you know what you are doing?' he asked more seriously.

It was the same story. Bandits were threat number one, but lions, apparently large prides of lions, were threat number two. Every expat in Addis could tell us about an unlucky traveller who had come short on that leg of the trip. No matter whether it was a mechanical breakdown, or a run in with gun-toting locals, lions were always the ominous prospect at the end of each tale or legend. It was hard to know what to believe.

'Misters, I need you to now empty your bikes. You must take everything out please,' commanded the man as he clipped the friendly banter and scowled into our passports.

'Um, really?' I asked. 'The whole bike?'

His change in mood was inexplicably sudden, as if he'd been reprimanded by the voice of his border-guard training manual. '*Do not be too friendly, or care*' it would have read; 'that is a sign of weakness, and border guards are strong, the protectors of our nation'. He crumpled his beret off his head, tucked it under an arm and cleared his throat.

'Yes everything. I can see you have come from Djibouti and near Eritrea. You must listen to me, this is very important. I have a lot of time, and I will wait until everything, absolutely everything, is lying on the ground here. I will need to do a full inspection.'

He couldn't have been clearer in his instruction, bar to explain the reason for it. We had travelled well over 9000 kilometres at that point, and there in a dusty, five-man town, we would for the first time have to empty our meticulously packed motorbikes completely. In Marmaris we had reorganised the big items, but not every single screw, tool and loose belonging.

We unlocked and unzipped every tie down, rope, fastener and lock, and were about to dive into action, like a dog searching for bones, when we were called off the bikes.

'Stop! That is enough,' said the official in charge. 'Stand there, we will do the rest.'

The inspection only began once we had retreated onto the low step of the passport office. We leaned back into the cool of the tin roof's shadow and watched them empty the bikes for us. Slowly a pile of our belongings grew on that dusty patch. I was impressed and astonished by how much kept coming from those sidecars. It was as if every item had been vacuum packed and then expanded as it was hit by sunlight. He was a meticulous man. He read the label on anything that had one. He squeezed the linings and ribbing of bags and clothes and spares. He eventually put his head right under the small compartment at the front of the side car, and emerged in a flap of dust. He kept shaking and slapping a large square piece of paper in the air, holding it with just the long, sharp ends of his finger nails. It was our map and he opened it, because he was a man of detail.

'Come here!' he shouted suddenly with a tremor in his

voice. Papa shot a glance my way. It was one of those, 'Oops, we are now in the *dwang*' kind of looks. He pushed himself forward off the cool concrete and peered down the guard's arm and finger to the bottom of the sidecar.

'Look what I found down there!' he said sternly. 'Yes, down there is where I found what you were hiding from us!'

He waved the map in my dad's face.

'It's our map,' said my dad, perplexed.

'No, noooooo, it's not just a map, mister, oh no!' he shouted imperiously. 'Where did you get this map? Who gave you this map? And what were you going to do with this map?' he bellowed.

Papa leaned into his sidecar, and through the red dust and fine shavings of spares and tools, he saw the clear outline of where the map had been lying. The entire sidecar was empty.

'Well, actually, I worked in Ethiopia for a long time. We built a sugar factory, you know it? It is a great thing for Ethiopia to have this sugar factory.' He was trying hard to find common ground. 'These were the only maps of that area. It's up north, do you know this place?' Papa pointed to the map and a scattering of town names on it.

'They gave these to us because we were engineers. I didn't take it, and I am doing nothing with it. It is just a map.'

'No!' said the soldier, looking away and squinting his eyes across the bridge towards Kenya. 'The only people who could give you this map is our military or the ...' he paused and stepped away from us. He scratched his head, and sucked lungs full of air through his nostrils.

'But look there,' said my dad, on the defensive, 'see there, that is the stamp of the company I worked for.' He pointed to a faded Deweto logo. 'You see it there? And what is that next to it? Can you read it? It looks like a signature, something official.'

'No, that is fake! This, my friend, is not any kind of ordinary map. This is a T.P.C., my friend. A Tactical Pilot's Chart. This is military map, and it is of Eritrea and the north. And we are at war with the north!'

The guard kept shaking his head. He would look at both of us intensely, stare at us, and then look away, clench his teeth and then shake his head again. Something unthinkable seemed to be unfolding in his mind. He was agitated and lost, as if he had no idea what to do or ask next.

'The only people who could have given this to you, who could have these kinds of maps, are our government, our military and…' he paused, seemingly mustering courage, 'and the CIA!'

Tremors shook his bony hands.

I knocked back my coke and watched, unmoved, from my reclined position.

'Mister, this is big trouble now,' said the soldier, waving his finger. 'Are you from the CIA?'

I sprayed a mouthful of cooldrink over my legs in an automatic reflex of disbelief. My dad laughed. We both enjoyed the break in tension, but with beret in his hand again, the soldier just scowled and stepped forward, placing his hand on the handle of his sidearm.

'You are from the CIA of America, aren't you?' he asked again, very seriously.

In those situations, there is never really a right answer. We were damned if we were and damned if we weren't. Either way, we would not be believed. We emphatically denied connections to any secret service and threw in references to the KGB for good measure. But that only made things worse. With our belongings strewn across the gravel, we were in *shit* and stuck. Going nowhere.

'Stay there,' said the guard. He called for his colleagues to join him. He shared the discovery, and their faces became as sullen and serious as grumpy matrons.

'This man will be with you,' said the guard, ushering forward a wiry, wily looking man with spectacles and the cleanest white shirt of the lot. 'Now pack up! You must, you absolutely must leave tomorrow first thing in the morning. And I will keep this map. You can consider yourselves deported!'

They were not interested in any other version of the map's source but their own. We were essentially assigned a shadow for the night. The man was a member of the police who kept an eye on us until we eventually left Ethiopia. He booked a room next to ours in the motel, he sat and smoked about five metres from us as we watched the sun set off our small veranda. He followed us to a roadside restaurant that night, and sat a couple of tables to our left. He cut short his meal when we had finished ours, and left his cold beer untouched on the table. He said goodnight and waited for us to lock our doors. We weren't sure if he kept watch all night, but he probably was ordered to. It was hard to tell if he was an aspirant spy or a bungling official who took his moustache and title a little too seriously.

The Somali Bandits

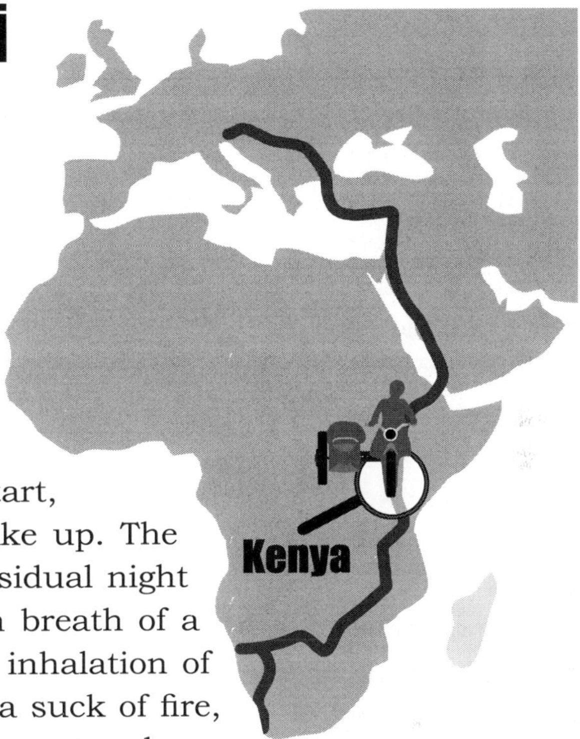

It was an early start, the usual 5am wake up. The air was a swirl of residual night smoke and the fresh breath of a rested veld. My first inhalation of this air though was a suck of fire, singed meat and the sweat and pungent smell of urine and faeces, both animal and human. It was a familiar smell we only escaped when we forced crisp and clean air into our nostrils on a moving bike.

The idea of bandits seemed fantastical at first. I always imagined them as tunic-wearing, toothless delinquents. Land pirates in turbans, slinging Kalashnikovs, didn't register as real to me. But then there was Robin Hood, and I believed in him. Throughout the trip I had underestimated the potentially fatal consequences of some of the risks we faced. I chose to approach them with ignorance and naivety. That morning was no different. We pulled our bikes to the border post where there was no another traveller in sight, and no convoy to join.

'How much sand are you taking, mister?' asked a young man, smiling as he twisted the spade that sat on his shoulder.

'Um, sand? For what?' I asked, 'Sorry. I think you have the wrong person.'

'No, you are the right person. You going to Kenya now, aren't you?'

He spoke to me but was staring at another man who was chatting to an officer at the gate.

'Just wait here,' he said, pointing to the ground between us. My dad followed him. When all four men were at the gate, Papa pulled out a roll of cash and handed it to the guard. He counted it slowly.

'Marc, they will put sand in that truck,' he yelled. 'It's to make sure the bikes don't move around too much. It's to keep the truck weighted down and less springy. We have to pay for that!'

Everyone had kept telling us the roads between Moyale and Marsabit were inaccessible without a truck. So we had found a truck and once the bikes were bedded and tied down with chains we buried their wheels and rims in two feet of river sand. The truck bellowed black diesel fumes and revved with a drummer's rhythm. We steadied ourselves against the cattle-guards at our backs. The border guard slipped our passports through the metal bars and waved us on. It felt like the starters line to the Paris Dakar rally. The trucker revved and rocked the truck as the gates slowly opened.

'*Jambo*!' greeted a young face which climbed past me up the outside of the cattle-guards. I almost jumped out of my skin with surprise. He scaled the top of the railings and perched himself against the floodlights on the cabin. He was then joined by another beret-wearing man in military fatigues. They were in fact not military, though, because they had no stripes or insignia, but they had guns, real Kalashnikovs. And knives. And they were in charge.

'For the price of the sand and an extra 10 dollars we get a guard, so I asked for two,' said my dad.

'Okay, so bandits I couldn't quite imagine, but an armed escort? Thank God Mom doesn't know about any of this.'

My dad smiled back and we both looked ahead across what seemed to be flat terrain. From our vantage point, we could see the landscape all the way to the horizon. The earth looked like it had been draped with a collection of interweaving threads, like a ball of tangled, oversized wool had been rolled into the distance. There were traces of tracks everywhere, and most of them disappeared into deep holes. Myriad random lines and so many places to hide and to lie in wait if you were a bandit. There was no road whatsoever. My knuckles turned white as I gripped the bars in anticipation. And then we took off.

At first, we followed a straight line through the bush, and the truck accelerated with relative ease. We rapidly pulled through the first three gear changes. The truck screamed into third gear, and then gave way to a burst of speed. It felt reckless and wild and insane. We had no choice but to hurtle at high velocity through a bush obstacle course. The first few turns were manageable, and even the odd hard bump was expected, but then we hit our first elevation.

'Holy crap!' I shouted, as the truck launched in flight through the air and landed deep into its suspension. We hurtled forward with momentum and hopped into a triple jump, out of control. We drove straight over a tree, stripping its branches and splitting its trunk into two. I looked back as the roots clung on and half the remaining pillar of wood bounced back. That explained why, along that corridor of mayhem, most of the trees had been violently dismembered.

I turned around and tried to see ahead of the truck, but

it swerved and banked. It was too late; we took off again, and gravity lost control of my body. My legs shot up and when the truck landed, my body followed. I held on for dear life, but my legs slammed down against the metal sidings. Within a second, we were up in the air again and I noticed out of the corner of my eye my bike had been released from the thick sand that had clogged its wheels. It was suspended and free, rising into the air next to me. It all happened in split frame, slow motion. The violent veering of the truck sent the bike into a mid-air spin. It spiralled a full 90 degrees. It hit the peak of its ascent and then all 650 kilograms of metal came crashing down. I pulled my legs in and narrowly missed being crushed between the boxer engines and ribbed metal wall of the truck.

'What the *fuck*!' I shouted. 'Are we seriously doing this for the next eight hours?'

'Yes, until it is dark,' yelled my dad, trying to crane his neck to see what was ahead. 'We will go as fast as possible and hope the truck doesn't fall apart.'

'This is insane! There is no way back from this, is there?"

'No, the best option is to get a view of the tracks ahead of us. Being blind like this doesn't help, I can't prepare myself for any of this!'

I truly felt at the mercy of menacing calamity. The variables were random and racing at my senses. My anxiety peaked as I realised we were willingly taunting death, at full speed, totally blind, armed to defend against arms, and in the middle of nowhere. I struggled to decide whether that or the bandits were more dangerous. It went on all day. We never stopped, not once. We didn't see another vehicle either. We saw some herders with their cattle, strolling through the undergrowth, calm and content. There were no wild animals. Yet we pushed on, at full diesel-gobbling pace.

Finally, we could see Marsabit in the distance and I felt the muscles in my neck, back and arms ease. The tension of that journey had many roots. We had been hyper vigilant all day, scanning the brush and sandy terrain for signs of life. The situation was unique. I had no reference against which to compare it. On the one hand, the armed guards and the tense, terse banter between them suggested extreme danger; on the other, my naivety and lack of any similar exposure masked an almost childish adventure lust. It all seemed quite cool, a bit like a boy's dream. Truck, dust, fast, guns. But, as we started to near the frontier town, I recognised the relief in my body as having been in danger's way. My eyes were dry, with sand scratching against my eyeballs. My nose was caked in the finest dust, my lips cracked from the heat and I had a barrel-clanging headache. I was dehydrated, which the guards had noticed. They had offered me water hours earlier, but my body was protesting with pain.

The dusty edges of the town were lined with misshapen shacks. The roads wound through piles of garbage, building materials, small stalls, stray dogs and children. There were many children. And seemingly in an instant, an invisible wall of security closed between us and the bandits, and I felt safe. It was like crossing a finish line, but there was no cheering. My ears woke up again as the truck engine that had been at full revs finally slowed down to a purr, and that was it. Within a few minutes, we felt secure again.

My dad and I never debriefed those kinds of experiences. His macho posture shrugged off danger. Whenever we were invited to flirt with harm, we simply never talked about it. I imagined the tribesmen of Ethiopia's south being much the same. They would escape the swinging knife of a dangerous foe, then dig their blades deep into his or her guts and walk away. No one would need to ask, because the drying blood and clean cut across the tribesman's chest marked the deed. No questions would be asked, no debriefs would occur. I was different. The anxiety would sit in me, finding no way out until I had spoken it through, but there was no one who would listen. I sometimes wrote it down, but the silence of an empty and unwilling audience was frustrating. My father would drink it out.

'One beer – a Tusker lager?' he asked. The slender waitress who stood to attention at our table nodded her head and looked at me.

'The same thanks.'

'We will stay here tonight, then,' Papa said, waving his hand around his head, pointing to the balcony that surrounded the courtyard we were in. 'I suppose we don't really have a choice.'

It was an interesting, bustling courtyard. The trucker hadn't asked us where we wanted to stay, he had just dropped us off there.

'What is this place?' I asked. 'It looks like a Shakespearian theatre. You know what I mean, those old theatres with the stage in the middle and the audience around the balcony?'

I noted the unmoved frown on my dad's brow. The Shakespearean reference was lost on him. It was another example of how little we had in common. My upbringing was an infusion of English tradition, values, history and living; entirely different to my dad's life, a motley mix of alpine joviality and post-colonial abandon. We had lived worlds apart, literally and figuratively, for most of our lives.

'You know, I think I know what this is!' he exclaimed, pushing his lips to the cold edge of his beer. He suddenly smiled, 'Yes, it's a whorehouse! I wonder how much sleep we will get tonight.'

He laughed, fixing his gaze on a gaggle of nubile, shiny, black-skinned beauties warming the walls with their exposed backs. They were staring at us. I had become accustomed to being stared at. For much of the past few weeks we had been the only white people around, and that night was no different. But now my stomach churned. I was scornful of Papa's apparent familiarity with such places. I was upset by his blatant interest in women. It had started in Ethiopia, with a woman he knew well. It hadn't gone unnoticed that he yearned for intimacy, and I was unsure of whether he had fulfilled his needs. It made me furious to think he may have lusted for her, and done so in full knowledge of his HIV status. Again that night, he expressed a hint of temptation, which to me seemed like an almost disrespectful act, like the evil beginnings of a psychopathic killing trend. Right there, in the middle of a brightly lit and busy travellers' inn/brothel, I faced the likely truth; those kinds of places and people were not new to my dad.

I have to admit, there were times when I didn't think about it, especially on those days when the events were dramatic and daring. Days would pass, scenes would race across my biker's goggles. Each moment would trigger benign memories, alert me to a fresh new view of the world or simply bounce with the light off the edges of the glass. I am not sure what the longest period of oblivion was. Maybe a day or two. Fact was, we never spoke about it again. Never. He had Aids, and since the long silent walk through the fir trees in Amman, we had never referred to it again. I didn't know how to ask. I was gripped with a sense of ominous truth each time I thought about it. The question that obscured all empathy, and at times reason, was *how did he get it?* I would have liked to think it was through a needle prick, like in a medical procedure. I knew in my bones though it was from between the sheets of an intimate affair. Most of my care faded in a flash when I pondered how it had all happened, and how he had behaved since then. By my count, he had in all likelihood passed the illness on already. That enraged me. So, to avoid what I predicted to be a descent into animosity, I chose to ignore it.

Every sneeze and sniffle made me wary and vigilant. I was informed enough to know he couldn't infect me, and that as his immune system dropped, he would become more susceptible to infection. The failure of each element of his health would be gradual, and then pretty swift. His brain would also start to degenerate, and within months, weeks, even days, he could be dead.

Those 48-hour escapes from mortal reality were helping to keep me numb to the truth. The fact we ignored it meant it wasn't real between us. But I often caught myself watching him. I would notice him breathing heavily as he reached for the tent pegs and stabbed them into the ground. He would kneel down as he drove them full length into the earth. He would often take a deep breath and use a silent countdown to snap his knees straight again and stand upright. Then he would pause, just long enough to fill his lungs. In those moments, I noticed his ageing, his clumsiness, his vulnerability. And then there was this virus that must have been pitching his body against itself. In that body, the degeneration would be fast.

It is amazing what sleep can do. I awoke in the brothel having reset my train of thought away from the seedy gutter and back to the incredible privilege of the adventure we were on. I couldn't shake the mix of emotions, but focused more on the remarkable experience I was having. The story wouldn't sound real to most people who heard it, but I was content with just waking up every day, safe and healthy. Whatever else would come my way, it would be easier to manage with those things in place. I was upbeat as we pushed our bikes through the gates of the compound. I sniffed the sour smell of breakfast burning in the stalls and huts around us. I savoured the uniqueness of that moment, and then reluctantly let it go.

'Are you going to take a picture of this one, Marc?' Papa asked as he began packing his man bag under the flap of the sidecar.

'Nope, it's all in here ... again,' I said with a smile and pointed to my eye. I pulled my goggles down and noticed how much smaller my view of the world became. The helmet drowned out the sound, and the goggles narrowed my sight. I had stopped taking as many photos and allowed myself to not be distracted by flashing a cut out of reality with a camera. I chose to rather be in it. I chose to leave each experience to burrow into my memory, either to die due to a lack of interest and care, or be snagged by a storyline that might reveal it all again. I was content with that approach then, but regretted it later. The visual feast each day was immense, and I could have plundered every hour of its views, people and places. But I was too lazy and left many memories hanging loosely in my head. Some were gone by the end of each day. Gone forever.

We slowly snaked our way between the potholes, stray dogs and smoky rubbish. I immediately felt something was wrong with my bike. At first it was a clanging sound that shook hard when I drove over any small bump or debris in the road. The bike also leaned permanently to the left, and made my knees seem perilously closer to the tar than usual. I slowed down, trying to work out what was wrong. It felt as though something had come loose, which wouldn't have surprised me after the beating the bike had taken on the back of that truck. My dad had already moved a good 30 metres ahead of me, and I tried to keep up, but eventually my seated gymnastics must have caught his attention.

'What's wrong?' he sounded irritated.

'Something's wrong, but I'm not sure what,' I was annoyed this bike was distracting me again from absorbing my surroundings. 'Can you see anything from where you are?'

'Yes. You are leaning to the side. Come on straighten it up, pull the bars up again.'

'I am trying, but it keeps leaning across and sinking down like this.'

'Sounds like a puncture. Do you have a puncture?'

'No, checked that all. It feels as if something is broken, or snapped. Every time I hit a bump, it's like there are no shocks, nothing to cushion me. It's a hard smack to the steering.'

'Oh *shit*,' he said, pulling his goggles down to allow for a clearer view. 'There is oil coming out of your shocks.'

'Oh *geez*, so what do we do now?'

'That means they are *fucked*. There is nothing we can do, just drive like that, and we will need to find new shocks in Nairobi. Wish we had taken from those bikes in Marmaris, don't you?'

The trip on the back of that truck had aged our bikes by years. Riding the bikes would have probably done less damage. They had survived though and, like a wounded boxer, kept punching forward. There were some newly raw and sensitive bits, and then some parts we instinctively knew would break in the near future. There was a rattle and clink that interspersed the drone of the engine.

Once we were on the main highway to Nairobi we hit

our straps and cruised. I readied my bones for a thorough jarring, because the higher the speed, the less time I would have to avoid bumps and holes. I was on full alert, but the roads were relatively good. The traffic around us posed more of a risk. It was on the descent down a long, gradual slope that my bike veered sharply to the right, into oncoming traffic. It jolted me awake as I narrowly missed the side mirror of a passing minibus. The black grill of a dump truck grimaced at me as we headed straight for each other. The more I turned the steering wheel, the less anything happened. The bike just kept following a path towards the edge of the road, on the wrong side. My steering was moving freely, left and right, but my wheels stayed straight and pure, heading diagonally across the highway. It felt as though I was boxing the air with my handlebars. The truck began flashing its lights, and so I leaned as far as I could to the left, pulling on the steering rack like an Apache riding a mustang's neck. I was using every ounce of my weight to try to displace the bike's direction. Then the wheels suddenly followed me and moved in a sharp snap back to my lane. It was, as with most such sudden unexpected events, a bewildering moment that distracted me enough to almost cause a fatal accident back in my lane. I swerved across the centre line and almost bumped a Peugeot station wagon. The steering began to respond again.

We were forced to pull over. Papa looked bewildered. Along with the shock absorbers, the steering column was broken. He guessed the bearings had been crushed by the pounding on the truck, and the steering rack was now jarring and jolting randomly, probably snapped. At times, the hairline crack would bite and hold a turn, at other times it separated and there was a break between the bars and the wheels. Again, there was nothing we could do about it there.

We crossed the equator and decided to stay the night, in an attempt to be as close to the sun as possible. The next day my wrestle with the bike continued, and by the time we arrived in Nairobi, I was drenched in sweat, had a pounding tension headache and struggled to pick up anything heavier than a fork. All the strain and hard work didn't really matter though. We were about to spend time living it up.

The Nairobi Mansion

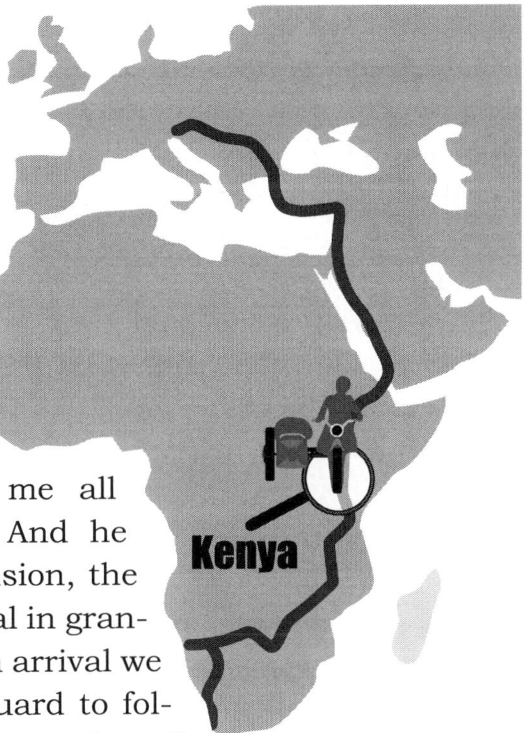

My dad had told me all about the place. And he was right; it was a mansion, the biggest and most colonial in grandeur I had ever seen. On arrival we had been told by the guard to follow the sandy path between the tall fir trees. With every turn, we were heading further away from the terraced lawns and slate-tiled roof of the grand old dame. The dirt track eventually stopped in front of a two-metre high, military-styled electric fence. I rattled the lock around the gate and tried to work out how to open it. Then out of the twilight I heard an ominous sound of scraping dirt and flying stones. Something was running at full speed towards us. I stepped away from the gate, and just as well, because tearing around the inner side of the fence were two of the largest Rottweilers I have ever seen. The low, almost bloodthirsty growls grew louder and heavier as they approached us. They slammed against the fence, contorting their snouts to fit as much of their teeth through the gaps as possible. They looked rabidly dangerous.

'They are killers,' said the estate manager. 'You must be Hans. Ah, yes, the old man told me you would be coming. Stay right where you are. I will throw the keys over to you and then join you once you get into the main house, okay? And whatever you do, do not get near these dogs. Ever! They once broke through our fence into the game park right here, right next door.'

'Wow, there is a game park right here?' I asked, pleasantly surprised.

'Yes, but those dogs broke through and hunted wild animals, even some big antelope. They are killers, so always stay away.'

It was definitely not what I had ever expected to experience. There I was, standing in a lounge on the second story of a Nairobi mansion that backed onto the Nairobi Game Park. When the buzz of electricity and chatter of the staff had died down, we could hear the lions and hyena calling in the night. We were staying in the lap of luxury, and on our first night I decided to explore the house and the pool. It was a warm and sticky evening. I wandered through room after room, and eventually found a small door leading onto a covered veranda next to a large square pool. I unlocked the door, and tried to recollect what the manager had said about the dogs. Apparently they were let loose to roam the property at 7pm each night, but could not get into the living areas, or the pool and sauna section. I nonetheless felt nervous as I stepped onto the first step. I stood there, listened and searched into the darkness. My only consolation was I would probably hear those monster dogs before I saw them.

'Good evening sir,' came a slow, deep voice just next to me. I jumped and screeched in fright like a girl, and stumbled off the steps in shock. There, two feet from me, totally unnoticed, was a tall man in the darkness. All I could see were his white teeth shaping a big and friendly smile. He stepped forwards into the light. He was easily 6ft 4, and wore the red robes of the Masai. He was armed with a bow and arrows slung over his shoulders.

'Sir, the dogs are in the garden, you must be careful.'

I was still stunned by how camouflaged he had been.

'I am your guard for the night. I am an Askari, a Masai warrior.'

'A warrior? Goodness that is, well, amazing. Hello! I was curious to see how close the perimeter wall was to game on the other side of it,' I said, feeling a little guilty for being such a snoop. So the dogs were dangerous after all.

On our first full day in Nairobi we decided to meet up with an old colleague of Papa's, to do the rounds, from pub to pub. We were astonished at being told about two bikes which, as he put it, were the spitting images of ours. Even down to the colour. They stood untouched but derelict in a friend's garden. Apparently, he'd bought the house and discovered the bikes completely hidden by nettles and undergrowth. It was an exceedingly odd discovery and so he had pursued the tale. It turned out two Englishmen had tried to make the same continental crossing 10 years earlier but, for unknown reasons, had thrown in the towel and abandoned their bikes. The story was intriguing, but we were more excited at the possibility of stripping the bikes for some spares. The thought of not having to rely on a DHL delivery for a new steering rack and shock absorbers was a relief. It was Marmaris, take two.

The next day we found the abandoned bikes, well camouflaged beneath thick swirls of brambles and long grasses. We salvaged a near-perfect-condition steering column and rack and pilfered a full set of shocks too. It felt weird dismembering evidence we were in fact not the first to have tried such a trip on those bikes. But it was also satisfying to imagine they probably hadn't had the guts or determination to keep going. Trying to think of a lame reason why they had given up suited us well. Either way, we were about to surpass whatever mantle of achievement they might have had, because within days, we would reach further south than they ever would have. That felt good.

That same day, I started to strip my bike to make the repairs. I worked alone in the open-air workshop out at the back of the estate. It was literally four skew poles with a roof of wood and tin, messily knocked together. In the centre was a workstation, and from that bench I looked straight into the Rottweiler compound. The dogs dozed against the fence but they had their lazy eyes trained on every move I made and craned their necks whenever I moved out of their range. I had always had an aversion to dogs. On two occasions as a young boy I had seen people being bitten, not quite mauled, but nonetheless attacked by dogs. I was forever wary, and as much as people told me to hide my fear and play it cool around dogs, I was *shit* scared. Apparently dogs could sniff the fear. Those Rottweilers must have been gorging on my caution that day.

The manual listed the instructions in eight steps. It looked simple enough, but removing my handlebars became a complex operation and I lost track of time. I was hunched over my bike when I heard a commotion at the fence. By the time I had stood upright again, I noticed the dogs had gone. It had suddenly become darker, and, as I searched in the twilight for the switch to the globe above my head, I froze. I looked at the compound, I looked at my watch, and then at the sky. *Oh shit,* I thought to myself, *it was twilight, it was killer-dog patrol time.*

When I saw them again, they were prowling towards

me, this time on the outside of the fence. Even from that distance, I could see them smiling through their salivary lips. I only had one escape route, a gate that was 40 metres behind me. It was an inter-leading, wrought-iron security gate to the main house. I slowly lowered my tools, and inched around the bike to give me a clear path. I thanked my lucky stars I hadn't found that light switch. I thought a bit of darkness might help, but then remembered they could probably smell my panic.

They must have sensed my imminent bolt for safety, and they made their move first. Barking loudly, growling, and whipping up dust on their sprint, they looked so fast. We were in a race. I skipped over tyres and a low bench and ran for my life. I didn't have to look back, I could feel they were close, and heard the air trumpeting from their nostrils. Their large paws sounded like horses' hooves cantering on my tail. I imagined they were crouched low to the ground, with no air resistance, ready to pounce, just as they must have done to kill that antelope. I was in serious trouble; they were so close and I thought I felt the slobber and spittle land on my calves. I tried to call for help, but between my deep breathing and frantic running style I couldn't make a sound. My lungs were just too busy. With just 10 metres to the gate, I vaulted straight over a medium-sized oil barrel. The dogs' legs were thankfully too short, and they had to run around it. That gave me just the time I needed, a few seconds advantage. By the time I slammed the door shut they were less than a metre from me. They pushed hard against the gate and thrust their noses as far as they could through the bars. I sweated through my nostrils. That was close. My adrenalin pumped and my shirt quickly bloomed with perspiration. I, for the first time on the trip, needed a drink.

The Brazilian

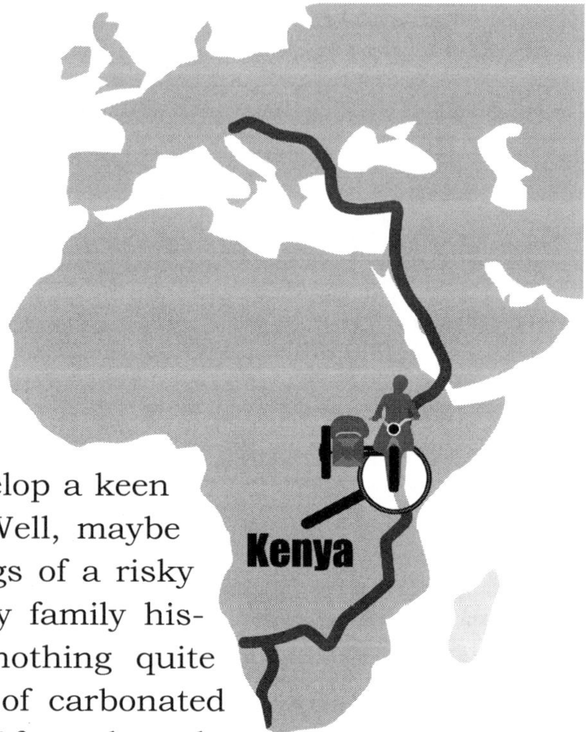

I had begun to develop a keen interest in beer. Well, maybe it was the beginnings of a risky habit, what with my family history and all. Yet nothing quite matched the tingle of carbonated beer on my tongue. After a long day of sucking in driving air, or sipping on diesel fumes, there really was not much that could knock a crispy beer off its flavour master peg. A cold coke came close, but a beer came with a tipped hat, and a medal of swag. In Africa, it completed the view, topped off the adventure, channelled the machismo and punctuated life with a popping tin lid. It became irresistible. But I dared to admit I wanted it, or even needed it. After all, it gave us a chance to savour local fare, to mark the map with a new brand of lager, and it helped us to fit in too.

So, like most days, we sought a new place to crack a cold one in Nairobi. It needed to be close, because driving at night was ill advised on our bikes. And I was riding shotgun while my bike was being guarded and scavenged by my hunters, those Rottweilers. I had left everything;

my tools, my keys and sunglasses on the work bench.

'Tuskers please, make that two,' I said, smiling at the barman as he cracked a bag of ice with a hammer. One hand wielded the tool, while the other dropped into the fridge beneath him to pull out a coke.

'Sure brother, you paying in shillings?' In one move, he flicked the ice out of the bag and into a glass perched on the edge of the bar. He allowed the force of the coke to spray out of his upturned can as he pushed it into the glass.

I smiled broadly. I was impressed and wanted him to know it. I loved that kind of moment. Almost Hollywood-esque. It captured my imagination and was notably novel too. I swivelled to look around the room, handed my dad a beer and just soaked it all in. I sat back to view the hodge-podge of people before us. Any pub on the road fitted the same genre, but with a diverse and fascinating script, and a motley band of players.

That night, it was the usual cast of businessmen, travellers and hangers-on. There were young travellers, both seasoned and virgin, drunks, whores and a smattering of locals, mainly tour guides and chancers. With that bunch, the money was always foreign, and predictably attractive to the locals. The dress codes were the give-away. The local businessmen were divided into two clear camps. On the one side, they were black and sharply dressed. Always suited and smart. They stood out and rubbed shoulders with a few others of their elite. Some endured the brawn and fashion failures of the white expats – they were the other business bunch. These European men shared a single commonality; the untucked shirt that hung off a yellowed collar. Two tone, three tone, patched and striped was the norm. The ties were always more noose-like than flattering and their beer bellies pushed through the buttons and folded over their mismatched belts, which often sported a few extra homemade holes to extend their lifespan.

Then there were the whores who were sometimes difficult to differentiate from the over-landers. There were oodles of eager, scantily dressed young women, allowing their legs and breasts to rub as much of each man as they could in passing. The more they all drank, the more they all behaved like seasoned ladies of the night. The wild side they unleashed was infamously recognisable and duly taken advantage of.

Finally there were the tough ones, sporting the 'don't-*fuck*-with-my-copper-bangles' look. They were men or women, either renegade professional hunters, rangers or over-land drivers. At times they could have been mercenaries too. They smirked at everyone and everything; they cultivated beards, and had vests of hair escaping from behind their beaded necklaces and rolled-up denim shirts. They drank quarts and smoked cigars, or self-rolled *tabak*.

I sipped at my beer, first sucking in the foam to cleanse my tongue before the wash of watery hops that followed. The music was loud and rocking, so we didn't chat much. It was a perfect night for watching the crowd. I kept checking the cash in my pockets, to make sure some wily pickpocket hadn't snuck a few from me. As I pulled my arm away from my pocket for the umpteenth time I planted my elbow into the bulging softness of a woman's chest. She was squeezing her way to the bar. The space was so crowded it took me a second longer than it should have to pull my arm away.

'Oops, so sorry,' I said, catching myself staring at her breasts. It took superhuman effort to divert my eyes. She looked down and adjusted them back into their formidable cleavage. My military discipline dissolved and I watched as she massaged her breasts, pulling at her nipples to put them into place. Nothing quite prepared me for that flurry of handling. I smiled at her sheepishly as she caught me gazing at her chest.

'Hey,' she said in a strong, yet untraceable accent, 'they are okay, I think? What do you think?'

She had dark, thick hair that smelled like honey. It hung over her tanned shoulders and neatly wrapped around her sharp features. Her green eyes were wide and locked with mine, and I swooned in a dance with her uncurled lips.

'So what do you think?' she asked again, giving her breasts another jiggle. 'You think they are okay?' She smiled in victory, as if she knew she had enslaved me.

'Um, I hope so. Should I check?' I said with brazen cheekiness. That was so unlike me, but I had a quick sip of my beer and gathered my wits for a bit of flirting.

'Depends,' she said, tilting her head to one side, 'depends if you are qualified.'

'Qualified? That's an interesting question, how would I know if I was qualified?'

'I can tell you if you are qualified if you know your way around a woman's breasts. Let me check.'

She lunged at me and grabbed my hands. Then placed one of them on her chest and forced my little finger to slip between her breasts. My chivalrous reflex was to pull back, but she had me handcuffed with both her hands.

'I like you, who are you? And what makes you so ... shy and interesting?' she asked with a laugh.

She let my hand go, but again, I took a moment too long to pull it away. Despite the brisk dialogue, I struggled to discern her accent. It had a curious cockney lilt that put me off. It was almost like the English language had butchered her Greek or Portuguese accent. I couldn't tell. I thought I'd try an attention-grabbing introduction.

'Well, I am from South Africa and I'm driving down Africa on a motorbike!'

She smiled, then frowned and rolled her eyes.

'Oh, not another one. This place is full of you. South Africans, Australians, and you are all the same. The motorbike thing is cool, but I need a little more.'

I looked for a twist in our adventure to make it more compelling. Some things would not be a good idea to share, but I settled on the side of history making.

'We are doing it on motorbikes with sidecars, and will be the first people ever to do it all the way down Africa on them.'

She leaned in, and her hair swarmed against my face. She came so close she touched my cheek with hers.

'Okay, that is interesting, I want to know more. How about you buy me a drink? That will be a great place to start.'

If that had been her angle all along, then *dammit*, she was a free-drinks hustler of note. The night was young, but it galloped into a very different direction from all other nights on that trip. She was a lawyer from Brazil, and yes, she had lived in England just long enough to confuse her pronunciation. She was crossing Africa too, but none of that was as alluring as her mesmerising Latin looks. She was tall, quite exotic, and she scared me a little. She used all manner of strengths to trap me for the night, and even my dad was pushed to the periphery of the conversation. She was not interested in him, only me. She had me cornered, both physically and with guile and panache. I happily surrendered.

'You are on motorbikes, but we are doing it on something just as cool, maybe even cooler,' she boasted proudly. 'We are driving on a bus down Africa. Yes, a real England bus.'

She banged her beer on the bar and gave a celebratory

whoop.

'A what?'

'An England bus. You know what that is – an English bus.'

'Um, hang on, I am not sure what you mean. Have you come from England on a bus, or am I missing something?'

The perfect timing and faultless execution of the script between us had developed speed wobbles. I was confused, but was trying to help her remain cool and in charge, and of course make sure neither one of us looked like fools.

'An England bus, you know? It's so famous, you don't know it? It's what everyone knows,' she lamented. She became frayed with annoyance, and was losing interest.

I stared at her, and for the first time saw a little hint of snake cross her eyes. I spotted a streak of something that made me hold my breath. She was mesmerising, but unnerving too. I was stumped. *That*, I thought, *would be the end of it all.* It had been a frivolous charge that would now fade into the tangle of my apparently poor common knowledge.

'Oh, sorry,' she laughed and blushed, 'I meant to say a London bus. You know, the red one with a double-decker; that is what we are travelling on.'

'Oh, now that is interesting, that is very very cool,' I said, playing it up a bit.

'But I want to come with you on your bike,' she said. 'I want to ride with you. What do you think? Can you take me on your bike?'

She wasn't joking, or trying to test me. She just meant it.

'Well, it is possible, but ...'

'Great, that is great. It really is no problem, I can make it work and meet the bus again. Yes, that really can work. I am heading all the way to Cape Town, and you too, so along the way we can always meet the bus again. It's perfect!'

I looked at my dad. His eyebrows were so high up his face they looked like wisps of a windblown wig. It turned out he was less interested in whether it was possible for her to join us or not, and more game to see how I handled that situation next.

'Oh God, they have left, there they go,' she said in a mild panic. 'I will have to find you, I need to get my things, so, well, I will find you somewhere, maybe here?'

In a swirl of hair and with a quick, wet kiss on the lips, she squeezed my leg and hurried off. In her mind it was a done deal. I watched her tight jeans weave through the crowds towards a haggle of her fellow travellers. She glanced back and waved. I knew she would find me again, and quite frankly, it terrified me.

'So what did you two arrange?' Papa was grinning.

'Nothing really.'

'Didn't she want to come with us on the bikes?'

'Yes, but we made no plans beyond that.'

'She's the kind of girl who gets what she wants,' he said. 'She will find you!'

I didn't believe that was possible and shrugged it off. Africa was big enough to get lost in, and that was exactly what I intended to do. Tanzania was next.

The Masai Kindness

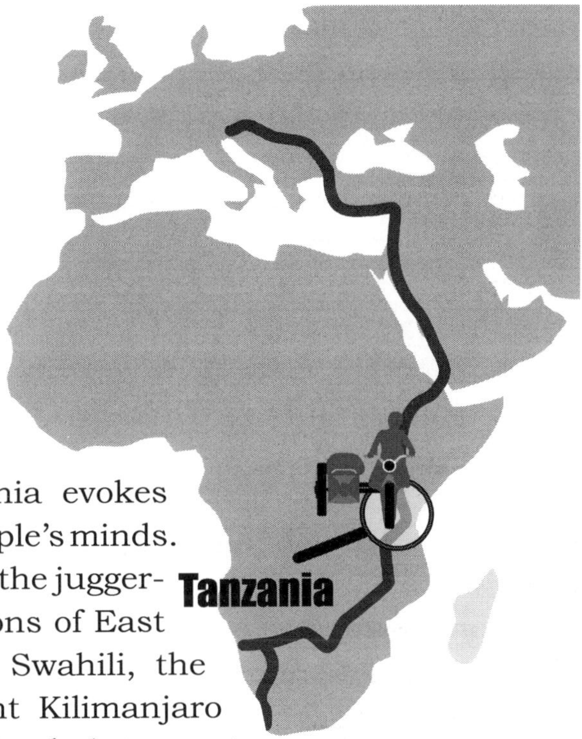

The name Tanzania evokes few images in people's minds. Kenya, however, has the juggernaut on all perceptions of East Africa. As a result, Swahili, the Serengeti and Mount Kilimanjaro seem to creep effortlessly into most people's minds as belonging to Kenya. While Swahili is predominant in both countries, Tanzanians insist they speak the purest version of it. Mount Kilimanjaro and the Serengeti are pure Tanzanian. As is Zanzibar. As far as tourist meccas go, the Kenyans bungle their way with random association into our minds. I have no idea how it happened, but I even hear the cadence of Attenborough's voice confirming this falsehood.

In my experience, Tanzania trumped itself. As is the case with most places, the people gave it stickiness and appeal. What was most noticeable was the exchange of greetings we invariably shared with locals every time we stopped our bikes. In Kenya, before the last puffs of exhaust fumes had evaporated, we would be engulfed by fiddling and groping locals, who touched and tinkered with our bikes and belongings. There would be the habitual appeal for money and food, and the obligatory parade of carved wooden curios. Summed up, it was unpleasant and an invasion of our personal space. I got into the childish habit of trying to count aloud the number of people who wanted a dollar and then would loudly work out how many dollars I would have needed to help them. It was pointless, really, and I am not sure why I did it, other than out of frustration.

In Tanzania, however, it was as if on arrival in a new place, someone stepped forward with a long, sharp stick and traced a line in the sand, dirt or grass. It was as if they created a large bubble within which only we were allowed. The crowds would gather and be curious, but always remained respectful of our space. No one would speak. There was no touching, and no gum-diseased breathing down our necks. It was orderly and remarkably polite. It was also surprising to see a hand held high in the air above the crowd, waiting for permission to speak. My dad often joked the behaviour of the people represented the difference between a German and British-run colony. The former remained civilised; the latter regressed. Above all, the ancient birthplace of man in the eastern and southern realms of Africa was beautiful. Green and lush with life, tropical and alive with heat and magnificent creatures. To drive through untouched savannah, pastoral lands and again into untouched havens of conservation, was a unique and liberating privilege. With the summer months approaching, we were witnesses to some dramatic weather too.

I was born in a thunderstorm in the summer of 1976. I gasped my first breath in Windhoek, the capital of Namibia. The colonisers pedantically called it South West Africa. With such a name there really was no doubt the scramble for Africa was a game. The spoils in the end were just compass markings and coordinates, almost as if they became bored. Namibia was almost the furthest from Europe, and most likely they had lost interest by that stage. We had lived in Klein Windhoek, a suburb that draped over acacia-speckled hills. On the afternoon of the ninth of February, the usually dry dongas had filled up quickly as the sky abandoned drums of rain. The water raced gravity to all the lowest points and within minutes, the dry gulleys became a muddied swirl of bubbling water, trees and branches. In the more violent storms, there would be livestock, cars and even people floating in the muck.

My heavily pregnant mother made it to the hospital just in time, and the rivers did flood. It was a memorable flash flood. I was born to the sound of rushing water and thundering skies, and, for the rest of my life I have loved water that rumbles and churns. I became addicted to the sea, and entranced by thunderstorms too. As we crossed the equator, we received the gifts of many passing storms. Some were spectacular and memorable, but it was in Tanzania they literally stopped us in our tracks.

We were driving south from Arusha in the early afternoon one day, when I began to celebrate what was forming in the sky ahead of us. Large unfurling explosions of vapour had begun stretching high above us. They were white and soft, and lined up against the horizon. Each seemed alike in shape. Their distinct silhouettes slowly disappeared and bled from their white cocoons. They absorbed the pigment of the sky and started to turn grey. The heat from the sun stoked their growth, and soon they enveloped the heavens in a watery barrier. The world went dark. In that moment, when the heat and rays of light suddenly disappeared, the sands, leaves and living things exhaled with relief at the cool moment of shade. Everything, it seemed, rested.

I could see the road bump over the hills, like a ripple of tar, for about two kilometres. It then disappeared behind a golden pile of granite rocks. The cloud-filtered light was gathering up the pink in each rock, and throwing it at my eyes. The greens began to pop and the sky became an ominous grey. It was a monochromatic wall of rising darkness, but not in the way night falls. It was the gloomiest the heavens could go with the sun still high in the sky.

I felt the sand and dust first. The wind swept and flicked red earth across the road. Leaves darted and jumped, and each failed take-off left them momentarily stunned, until the wind toyed with them again. The dry grit was sucked up my nostrils and swarmed into my goggles. We slowed down, because mayhem looked imminent and we needed to find shelter. There was a harried energy all around us, as any and all living things moved to find cover. We saw people rush around their huts, bent at their waists, covering their eyes as they battled the wind. Everyone was trying to anchor loose belongings, shut animal pens and close doors and windows that might be at the mercy of the coming deluge.

'I think we must stop soon,' shouted Papa, waving for me to come alongside him. I nodded my head and pointed to a blood-red Coca Cola sign across a building ahead of us.

It felt like we were in a race against the storm from that point. We were driving straight into a headwind and could see the showers drench the road ahead of us. The air began to smell wet, earthen and sticky. I guzzled it up, and filled my parched lungs with the taste of water. It looked like the rain was being hurled at the ground. Each drop exploded on impact, and then blasted across the savannah with the gale. We could no longer see the rocky hills, just a curtain of water that marched at us.

I skidded my bike in a sharp turn behind my dad in front of the building.

'Come next to me – we don't have time to wrap both bikes!' he yelled as my bike gurgled to a halt. 'Let's try and get one tarp over both!'

'Okay, but take your camera bag off first,' I shouted above the whistling winds. He had a tendency to leave his most valuable items as easy pickings. I turned the back of my bike against the wind.

'Get that tarp as low as possible beneath the back wheels; this is going to be a violent one,' he said, slinging a rubber belt beneath both bikes and hooking it into an eye at the other end of the tarp. We pulled it as tight as we could.

'I think we are still going to get wet, and the bikes will get soaked,' I said, looking at a distinct wall of mist and spray that galloped towards us. I felt the first drops on my head. Initially the drops allowed dust to escape where they landed, but within seconds a flash of lightning and an instantaneous clap of thunder forced us to run for cover. Sheets of water plunged around us.

We slipped onto the veranda of the café, and the world disappeared behind a wall of water. The tin roof exaggerated each drop, like thousands upon thousands of marbles that clattered down a wooden floor. It was impossible to hear anything else. We had to wait it out.

'I think we should eat, this could be a long one,' shouted my dad above the din.

We ordered some vegetables for lunch. We had been warned to avoid roadside meat and fish. It was common knowledge that for a weaker constitution, eating those foods could be deadly. We sat silently and watched the torrents reshape the road and buffet our bikes. Despite the chaos, the sound soothed my senses. The air and gusts of wind cooled us. It was so loud we just sat and listened.

Papa squinted into the rain, 'Hey, look – a bus is coming.'

'I hope it sees our bikes,' I said, half joking and half not. In our hurry, we had in fact parked in the approach area for any vehicles that might wish to stop.

The bus made a sharp, late swerve towards us. It missed our bikes, but not the deep hole bored by the waterfall running off the road's edge. Its front wheel dropped deep into it and, as the driver slammed on his squeaking brakes, brown, earthy water washed over our bikes. The windows were all misted up, which made it impossible to see who was inside the bus.

'There we go, our bikes are drenched,' I said.

'Ah wow, it's Masai people, and look, they are coming in here,' he grinned, 'this should be interesting.'

Fifteen people were the comfortable maximum that could fit around the four tables and benches in the small rest stop. We watched as, one by one, a bus load of 6ft tall men loped across the short, muddied lot and skipped in their sandals onto the veranda. I counted them as they just kept coming. Ten, 20 ... after 40 it was just a blur of red cloth. With every new arrival, they pushed each other deeper into the store. They squeezed and bulged into the open spaces and all fitted in, just. At final count, there must have been well over 60 men, and only men.

We moved ourselves into a corner and looked up at the lanky, red-robed bodies. They had polished black skins that shimmered over their chiselled features. They were all eerily quiet and stared out the small windows in anticipation.

'*Jambo*,' came a gentle voice from the man next to me, his head nodding in deference.

'*Jambo*,' we replied, sitting over our meals, conscious of the audience that watched us eat.

They were all staring at the vehicle. The bus driver emerged from the door. He walked in front, his grey uniform shirt untidily flapping outside his belt. His sandals were covered in mud and he carried a large umbrella with blue and red stripes. He held it with two hands, shielding an elderly man who walked with a slow, cautious gait.

I felt a nudge against my ribs. The first poke was polite, but the second dig came with force. I leaned slightly to the right but the pushing continued, until I eventually had to move. Instantly, four young men sat where I had been alone. I was surrounded on both sides, and sat square in the middle of the bench. My dad wasn't bothered by anyone, but he moved voluntarily as he saw the old man step through the door. My dad dragged his plate along with him, and another young man offered him his cutlery.

The old man walked along the back of the bench, passed my dad and instinctively bowed his head. He then lifted his slender left leg and placed it over the bench as he sat down. He swung his right leg over, more like a hurdler than an elder, and then greeted me with smiling eyes and pursed lips.

'*Jambo,*' he said, and then turned to the rest of the room.

He spoke in Swahili, and men switched and changed places until the youngest man among them stood behind him. I stared at the old man's ear lobes that hung low and snug against his jaw bone. The holes were large, where time had stretched out the flesh. He wore no adornments and looked like all of the others, but he was by far the oldest. We both sensed we were sitting with someone of stature.

'Shhhhh,' hissed the youngest, putting his finger against his lips. He waited until everyone was quiet. The old man began to speak, while the stern figure behind him translated.

'We have come from a market today,' he began, darting his eyes between mine and the elder. 'We have had a very good day today, and for that we are very grateful.'

As he said that, the old man sat back into his chair, and grinned. His wrinkled face cracked with his smile. He stared at me, then at the plate of vegetables and pap in front of me. With that, his smile quickly disappeared.

'We have had a very, very good day today. We are proud of our cattle, and today we sold them all. We finally sold them all. The ones we wanted to sell are all sold,' said the young translator, 'it was a day for making money!'

There was silence. The old man leaned towards me in concern, balling his hands into fists.

'The chief wants to know why you are not eating any meat with your meal,' he said.

As he posed the question, I sat upright. He was a chief and that meant something to me. He was the third traditional leader I had ever met. I can't remember much about the Zulu chief I had met in my teens while touring eastern South Africa, but he had been everything I'd expected. Short, rotund, swathed in leopard fleece and fawned upon. I had met the Himba chief while on a university holiday at Epupa falls, where that spectacular flurry of water cuts through the Makalane palms on the Cunene River between Angola and Namibia. We would never have known he was the chief. He had sat quietly in the shade, and watched the ritual slaughter of a cow beyond the palm trees. He was humble, and had beckoned us forward for a greeting. We obliged, and he gave us his hand. It was only when we had left his company that a trader nearby revealed his identity. The Masai chief was cut from the same cloth; he also personified humility.

From the tapered faces that stared at me, I realised the crowd was waiting for me to respond. All I could muster was an inappropriate laugh. 'Oh, I just didn't feel like eating meat today,' I said, nodding my head and smiling.

'But why not? Why are you not eating meat with your meal?'

'I don't want any today. I am not that hungry,' I replied, trying to blame it on a low appetite. In Addis I had eaten spiced, raw mince, but that had been prepared within 20 minutes of slaughtering. Those spices served to kill off any lurking germs. I didn't feel I could tell this audience that I feared the meat might make me sick.

The old man spoke again, persisting with the same question. 'Thank you for asking,' I said again, in my most diplomatic, charming way. 'We are travelling a long way, but it is late in the day and I have already eaten some food. So I am not that hungry, and didn't think I needed to eat any meat,' I was beginning to change my story.

Again, there were just blank stares and shuffling around the room. The old man shook his head. He stretched out his arm and shook my right hand. He then addressed all the men in the room who nodded in agreement with his words. They all began to smile and then revealed small pouches of coins and notes in their hands. The old man did the same and a collection began. Within a few minutes he was holding a palm full of coins and notes.

The young man smiled but didn't need to translate a word.

'My friend, we will buy you some meat,' said the chief. I started to respectfully protest, smiling and shaking my head, but he continued, 'If you cannot afford meat, then we are happy to buy the meat for you. It would be an important offer from us. Please accept our kindnesses.'

The old man looked at me with a fatherly smile. It was clearly his view no man in Africa on such a journey would not eat meat with his meal, unless he could not afford it.

Therefore, as a guest, and as a traveller, the elder chief wanted to spare me the embarrassment of admitting to this, and share his money with me.

The men ordered their meals and we all feasted jovially together, strangers at a road stop, but connected like ancient kinsmen. There was a sincerity and warmth to the unfolding events, and by the time the rain had stopped and washed the world clean again, I felt cleansed too, deeply humbled and in touch with something worth thinking about.

The Lions' Campsite

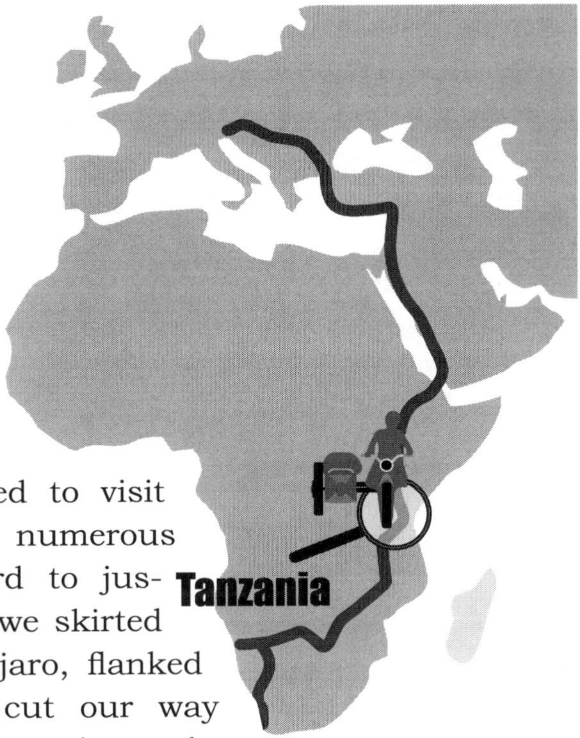

I had always wanted to visit Zanzibar, but our numerous delays made it hard to justify that detour. So we skirted the base of Kilimanjaro, flanked the Serengeti and cut our way south instead of east on the road to Mombasa. There was a stretch of road in the middle of Tanzania that had grabbed our attention. It was less the road, and more the small patch of conserved land that intrigued us. It would be the only time we actually got to drive through a nature reserve, filled with wild animals. According to the map, there was a campsite within its borders. We were assured by the legend on the map the area was predator free, but home to elephants. Either way, driving on our slow and exposed bikes past free roaming wild mammals was risky.

We entered the park's perimeter without a gate or fence to warn us. There was a tilted old sign with the words *'wild animals'* on it. I had expected a more official admission, but was more relieved than disappointed. I surmised the vacant entrance indicated the road was no different to the national road we had been on. Despite that, I still sat to attention. There was none of the usual scattering of huts, and no roadside fruit and vegetable sellers. The road edge was instead thick with trees and life. The place was emptied of humans.

Our bikes barely topped 60 km/h. Most of the bigger beasts could keep up with that, and they had the added advantage of off-road speed. Where we had to meander on the tar, any of the mega-ton grey animals could knock through forest, water and thick reeds and still take us out. There was nothing comforting about being on our machines. It was one of the downsides of travelling in Africa on bikes; they made the reserves off limits. But on that road, we had no choice. We got what we'd wanted but without the ability to escape or retreat. That was the only road.

After an incident-free 45 minutes, I was relieved to see my dad point at a sign with an image of a tent stuck on it. It was a campsite and time to stop. We made our way off the main road and trundled for a couple of hundred metres into a secluded encampment. It was beautiful, untouched and empty. All the sites were shaded by a variety of tall trees and the grass was long and lush.

'This looks good, doesn't it,' Papa said in surprise. 'It was on the map, but I wasn't sure if it actually existed.'

'So far so good, hey?' I sighed with relief.

'But no animals yet. Have you seen any? Even something small?'

'No, nothing. For which I am pretty grateful right now.'

'*Ag*, you worry too much. You know how many bikers and bicycles must have been through this road? I say a hundred. It's all fine; they would close the road if it was dangerous. I told you so,' he assured me.

I shrugged off his bravado, and tucked my gloomy

thoughts away. We hadn't seen a camp reception but slowly began emptying our bikes. The light was fading and these more remote spots usually had a caretaker living way off the property. He would come when he could. And he did. We saw the elderly man leaning heavily on his walking stick as he came through the trees. I stepped towards him, feeling the need to close the gap between us. He looked really old. We shook hands, his leathery fingers hung limply in my palm. He stared deep into my eyes, and smiled. It was odd, as if he was trying to say something, or had met me before.

'Mister it's no good to camp there,' he said slowly. 'You should camp there, instead.'

He pointed to a site about 50m away. That spot looked no different from the patch of balding grass on the flat ground we were on.

'Um, okay. Are there any other people here tonight?'

'No, no one else stays here,' he said, shaking his head.

We had the pick of the campsites and could choose wherever we wanted to sleep, so I struggled to work out why we would need to move so far away.

'No, we will camp here!' Papa's tone was belligerent and grumpy. He had already unstrapped most of his camping gear and let it all roll into the circle.

The old man smiled, his eyes disappearing between his wrinkled eyelids. Then he laughed as he leant on his walking stick.

'Okay, no problem mister, it is your choice,' he said, turning to walk back into the brush from where he had appeared. 'But just so you know, we have no fence in this camp and we have no guards.'

He took a few steps away from us and then stopped dead in his tracks and turned abruptly, 'And last night, 12 lions slept right here, just like they did the night before, and the night before that and every night last week. So, you can choose, no problem. But just so that you know, I have advised all campers to keep moving until they get outside the park to camp.'

That piece of information changed everything. It also raised some pertinent survival questions about the intelligence we had at our disposal. Firstly, there were not meant to be any lions in the park; secondly, if there were lions, they could be anywhere at any time, including on the road or near it. Finally, it was feasible that within the next 40 kilometres, I would be peeing down my pants if any tawny-coloured four legs came onto my radar. The light was fading too, and all that chit chat had delayed us even further. The happy hour of lion feeding, dusk, was upon us.

We had no choice; we had no gun, and nothing to protect us. We had to get out of the park, and we had to make a dash for it. We both decided to override all caution and forced ourselves to believe the bikes could handle a full-throttle race to the next village. There could be no more kid gloves. We had made small modifications to the cooling system and streamlined our packing. If the bikes weren't ready to race, then they never would be. They were well run in, with so many parts overhauled and renewed.

We lined ourselves up between the road markings.

'Forty kilometres, at close to top speed, means we will make it out of here in 45 minutes,' said my dad with a steely, racing stare.

'Okay, just in time for sunset then.'

We took off, Papa riding lead bike. Within minutes, my ears were ringing with the squeals and hisses of a cornered black sidecar. The power from the overheating engines came in pulses, and the smells of burning rubber and oil rose quickly off the bikes. Neither of us gave a *shit*, to be honest. I had seen many a dangerous animal from a car, but on a bike, and especially a loud, slow and now predictably faulty one, the idea of a lion on the tar terrified me.

We hurtled along. I looked left and right for any signs of life and after about 20 kilometres, I noticed something on the horizon. I squinted into the dusky light, and saw a large number of bumpy hills in the distance, like the bubbles on an aero bar. The knobbly bumps were however much smaller than the usual rounded hills we had been driving over and around.

Then, with enough time to register, we both worked out what they were. Within a few seconds of each other, we pulled off our throttles and the bikes ground to a rattling and veering stop in the middle of the road. Those knobs, those little bumps, were in fact elephants, and there were a lot of them. They stood on the road and wandered along both sides of the asphalt. There were 30 or more; it was hard to tell. As each one moved it revealed another behind it, and there were trees there too. There could have been 50. We sat and watched them, momentarily distracted from our lion obsession.

'They look pretty settled in, don't they?' I said. '*Shit* man, now we are sitting ducks! What do we do?'

'We wait,' he said. 'We just wait, but keep the engines running!'

It was a good call. Those engines sounded like a sabre-tooth tiger with a rotting canine and a hangover. It was a growling menace with more bite in its lungs than its jaws. A kick-start in a silent savannah usually alerted every living thing out there of our presence. We wanted to avoid doing that, and keeping the grumbling engines on meant we were somehow integrated into the wild. We sat there, helmets on and bikes running. On your mark, get set. And then over-heated.

'*Shit!* Stop, stop, stop!' Papa's bike began revving uncontrollably with the early signs of a fiery breakdown. 'Turn it off. These pieces of *shit* are going to blow a piston or gasket if we keep at it like this.'

'What now?' I said in a panic. 'We'd better get off the road. What if other cars come?'

The herd did not move at all, it was almost as if they were making camp for the night. And then, as if on cue, like Moses parting the seas, the entire grey mass split into two. Half of them began heading down the hill and the other half up it. They were all in some way or another moving away from the road. One would think that that was a good thing, but really, it wasn't. Trying to sneak between those two herds was very risky and, with our bikes and their clanging and blasting, we would definitely startle any young bull to run across the road and find his multi-ton Mom. Or it could be the other way around. Either way, it was pretty easy to see how we could be trampled from both sides. It was not ideal, but we also had no choice. It was literally our gap to take.

We both quickly skipped our bikes around, tightening any loose cables and ropes we saw. I twisted the petrol cap tighter and checked the seals on the jerry cans. My dad kicked his tyres, I am not sure why, but I presume to check they were still securely bolted to the axel. I pulled the helmet strap tighter than usual across my chin, and pushed my sunglasses flat against my eyelashes.

'Let's start the bikes at exactly the same time, and just go,' Papa said with a military tone to his voice. 'Don't hang around and let them heat up again. Just go! Okay?'

I was *shitting* myself. With a show of his fingers counting from three to one, we kicked like wild donkeys on those starters. Any other bike would have sent white smoke flaming off its tyres as it rocketed forward, but we doggedly built up speed, inch by slow inch.

The elephants hadn't noticed us from 200 metres away. We slowly accelerated closer to that 80km/h mark, our maximum speed. At about 100 metres, we forced the first of many floppy ears to turn our way. One by one, the entire herd lifted their heads and opened their ears towards us. There was a sense of agitation in their head tossing and tail swinging. It looked as if they were nudging each other closer and closer to the road, as if they were curious to see what was on its way. A couple of young bulls reared their heads and trundled in small circles. They were the closest to the road, and I watched them keenly. We were then about 40 metres away, walled in on both sides by massive grey bodies. Their eyes were fixed on us, just as ours were fixed on them. It looked like we were going to make it, and despite the edges of the crowd starting to show disturbance, we had passed that critical point where they could still reach the road to block us before we could pass them.

I breathed for the first time in at least 50 metres of driving. We had hit our table-topping highest speed of about 90km/h, and eclipsed our downhill top speed. The bikes were nailing it. It was beautiful. We were heading ever closer to freedom when, at the 10 metres-to-elephants mark, I spotted it. A bloody speed bump at ground zero. There was no way we could slow down in time. Those kinds of obstacles were motorbike Ebola, and there was usually very little chance of surviving such a high-speed impact. But we were committed, so, at full speed, and with every muscle in our arms pulling that throttle beyond an awkward wrist angle, we took flight. We launched over the bump and collapsed into our seats as we landed. We veered and clanged our exhausts against the tar, but held on with all we had to keep the pace and make it through.

We instantaneously moved our attention from the animals behind us to the bikes beneath us. I kept looking behind me, almost expecting large limbs of the bike to be breaking off and rolling down the road. Most of our packing had survived but was now badly mauled and moved. We pulled back on the throttle and reclined back on our seats. We had made it, there was not a single elephant on our trail, and it looked as if they'd never had an interest in us anyway. But it was one hell of a thrill to go so hard and not break down.

As we exited the park, we found a spectacular campsite all to ourselves again. It was nestled against a rocky outcrop, filled with broad shade-bearing trees. It had a fence and was well tended.

'*Jeez*,' Papa said. 'What a day, again!'

'Man, every day in Africa has been action-packed, just as I expected, I suppose,' I replied.

Behind us, the setting sun pasted a pyramid-shaped hill with a golden glow. We fell asleep beneath the stars in the open air.

The following morning, I decided to scale the small *kopje* behind us to greet the day. As I watched the sun rise, I had a moment of solitude. A brief escape from the bikes, my dad, my life on the road. The sun's rays were rousing the earth to life, but my thoughts went inwards. I couldn't have picked a more typical view of Africa and all its stereotypical images.

I looked down at the small figure of my dad. The past three weeks had more than fulfilled my expectations. There had been adventure, daring and wildly-close shaves. We had been physically challenged and tested by every possible thing. It had been gripping, and each experience catapulted up my very own bestseller list. I had imagined the entire trip being one high-paced page turner after the next. I had been living in a boy's fantasy and I loved it. But the glow didn't really last. The more I tried to cast a net over the details of each of those escapades, the more I was aware of how hard I was trying to stop the other stuff getting in the way. The sight of Papa, moving around below, kept wrenching me back from the superficial storyline, dropping me into the sobering reality. My dad and I were no closer than when we'd started. There was enough that had happened to make us inextricably linked through deep experiences, but we had been slowly drifting further apart. I didn't understand why I was surprised by that, but I was. He was sick, and probably dying, but even that didn't make a difference either. That admission scared me more than anything. We may have covered thousands of kilometres, but the journey within hadn't moved much at all. Like a yoyo is how I felt most of the time, swinging between anger and pity, between empathy and scorn. I hadn't worked out whether those emotions were directed at myself or at him. That journey was still a long way from even starting.

I just wanted more and more adventure. It was like a drug-fuelling self-medication, and the past few weeks had been an exciting binge. Facing all the other stuff was making me feel jaded and frustrated.

The Malawi Tears

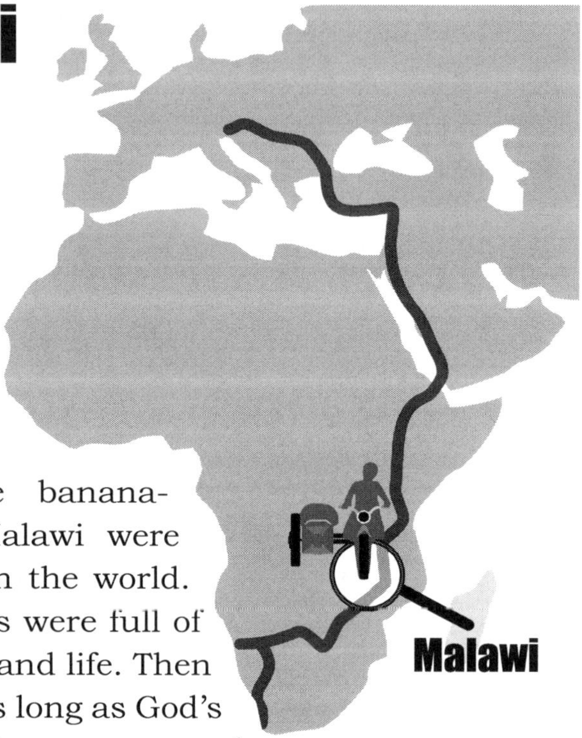

Legend goes the banana-treed hills of Malawi were once all there was in the world. Those hills and fields were full of animals and insects and life. Then people arrived. For as long as God's memory, there had been peace and balance. One day, there was a change, which started in the people's hearts. They became selfish and greedy. They stopped sharing and only wanted more of everything for themselves. They fought with each other, hurt and stole and even killed. Hatred enraged them, and the balance in the world was lost. They trampled the hills and chased the animals, and used fire and force against nature. They waged war over the lands, over the fruits and the trees, over all of God's gifts. They were about to destroy one another forever, when God began to cry, lamenting all of mans' failings. God had blessed them with more food than they could eat, and had led them to land that was abundant and free. But man was addicted to winning and the war kept on. In a flood of tears, God produced a powerful strike of lightning. It cracked open the land and all God's tears began to fill the deep rift that split the fertile soils and lush plains. For days and weeks and months, God washed the land with tears and created an apocalyptic flood. When the crying stopped, God had divided and even drowned the warring people. A long, inland sea remained, and it was a reminder forevermore to the people to be peaceful, to love their neighbour and love the earth. That sea would later be called Lake Malawi.

Driving through Malawi, there was no doubt God was having a good day when he made it. His tears had washed pure goodness and life across that scar-shaped country. The majestic trees were nut- and fruit-bearing tributes to Him and rose out of the thick, chocolate-coloured soil. Between the hills, mounds, trees and waterways was row upon meandering row of broad-leafed, long-stalked and rain-rinsed vegetables. Africa seemed at peace with herself there. The gods wailed and drowned the land with tears, but what was left behind was a people who sipped from the fountain of gratitude and hospitality. Visiting Malawi was like drinking warm milk. It comforted and soothed us.

Everywhere we drove, we were greeted with boisterous waves. We often joked that, while further north the adults ignored us and the children pelted stones, in Malawi our main concern was an over-active and fast-tiring waving arm. The roads were rarely straight, as if they had been overlaid on ancient footpaths rather than surveyed for their most efficient route. They wove between water, soft green hills and rocky, granite clusters. We edged along the shores of Lake Malawi from north to south. From Nkothakotha to Nkatha Bay, through the markets of Senga Bay and Cape Maclear, from Monkey Bay to Mangochi. The lake was a mid-continental mecca for sun-worshipping overlanders, backpackers, adventurers and sailors. We had been looking forward to our time on the lake. We had both been there before and knew the nature of the place would force us to slow down, take it easy and chill. Trips over land tend to be more arduous and stressful than most people think; they certainly don't feel like a holiday. We needed a break, our daily trips were shortened and we had more time to just be. We also met more fellow travellers than we had in the previous weeks.

'Hey man, are you a sailor man?' interrupted a young dreadlocked teen as we sipped at another ice-cold coke in the midday heat. 'Are you going to sail in the regatta?'

'No, sorry, not us,' I replied, looking away to swat his interest. I had no idea what he was talking about. I had become jaded by the persistent interjections from every vendor we had encountered. They tried to lure one into conversation and I had become weary and wary of this ploy.

'So where you from, my friend? UK? Sweden? America? Ah, Germany!' he said triumphantly, pointing at my Bavarian number plate. He thought he had a hook into this conversation, but I just nodded and remained seated on the crate I was resting on.

'Manchester!' he sang, stepping back and opening his hands in a Jesus pose. 'Yes, Manchester!'

'No, actually not Germany and not Manchester either. South Africa and Austria!' I said with irritation.

'Oh my God, a fellow African. What a pleasure, my friend,' he celebrated, pulling a reluctant looking passer-by into the conversation. 'My name is Manchester and this is my brother, Luton.'

He beamed. I gave them that on-the-edge-of-condescension look that basically said, 'who do you think I am? Some stupid tourist that might fall for false familiarity, so you can fleece me of my goodwill and cash?' And yet...

'Manchester and Luton,' I said, half surprised and half interested. In many parts of southern Africa it was common to hear such names. I had once met an entire family named after Shakespearean characters. I had also met men named Terror, Painter and Whiskey.

'Yes, those are our names,' he replied. 'You see over there, that guy with the pink hat, and the girl in the red dress? Those are Essex and Dover. They are my other brother and sister.'

He called them, and within seconds we were crowded by what could have been a map of England. They all jingled and clattered their portable display stands in our faces. They carried everything; hundreds of cheap sunglasses, lighters, knives, baseball caps, cigarettes sold in ones or packs.

'Our parents were English teachers,' explained Manchester.

'So how did you get the name Manchester? How did they choose?'

'That I don't know. I think my father liked football, but I don't really know,' he shrugged.

I then heard something that sent a chill down my body. It was a shrill female voice.

'Marcus! Marcus, is that you? Oh my God, it really is you!'

It didn't take me long to find her among the market crowds. She was standing with one hand pushed against her hip, and the other shielding the sun from her brow. Her shorts barely covered her bikini, and her ballooning tank top swung as she waved at us. She had gathered a smouldering tan with bleached lines over her shoulders and low across her cleavage. Her long legs looked smoother than an eggshell and the African waters had brought wildness to her hair. She looked irresponsibly devastating, and even more of a hunter than I remembered. That part made me nervous again.

'Hallo, my man,' she purred, and flung her breasts onto my chin, each fleshy mound pushed around the sides of my neck. She smelled of the wild. 'I told you I would find you. I have been searching and searching for you.'

She greeted my dad, who raised his coke in salute.

'Look, there it is,' she said, holding my neck in a wrestler's grip and swinging her other arm away. She pointed to a double-decker bus parked behind a large mango tree.

'*Holy mol*ey, you guys have made it all the way here!' I said, surprised. 'That is very cool, very impressive, I have to say.'

'And you too. Well done! So when did you get here? And where are you going next?'

'We've just arrived and are on our way to…' I stopped myself from giving too much away.

'We are going to Kande beach tonight. They say there is a big party there every night,' she said, swaying her hips and shoulders in a dance.

We had also planned to go to Kande beach, but I changed our plans then and there, on the fly.

'We aren't going as far as that today,' I said.

'Is that a UK bus?' Manchester asked excitedly. 'Is that really a UK bus? Do you know from where it has come? From which city? I have never seen one alive like this.'

Gaping in amazement, he crossed the busy street and began pacing alongside the tall red bus that towered over everything but that mango tree. There were buses everywhere in Malawi, but a red double-decker, London bus which looked more at home on a 1970s James Bond set, was a rare treat.

'So, I can come with you on your bike now, it's perfect isn't it!' she said with a sizzle in her smile. 'I will just ride the next few days with you. I want to spend some time with you, you know. Spend some time on the lake, in a tent with you. Today! Tonight!'

She bunched her hair above her head and posed in all her splendour, seductively tempting me. I was trapped and I knew it. It wasn't entirely terrible, but I wasn't used to that predatory style.

I had imagined how the scenario might pan out should she corner me at some point. Travelling down Africa was confined to a handful of well-trodden roads, and we often bumped into the same people many hundreds and thousands of kilometres apart. There were two versions to the sequence of events I imagined, should she find me. The first involved her wrapping her legs around my waist as we drove south, her toes neatly tucked into my shorts while her neck twisted around the back of my head. We would arrive at a quiet and secluded patch of lake, where the ripples of warm water tingled the white sands. We would then lie on a soft bank of grass, while dappled light peeked through the palm fronds, and she would reveal all of her Brazilian goddess.

Version two was entirely different. I imagined she would sit on the second seat behind me and would hold on for dear life while her head bobbed and crumpled under the weight of a heavy helmet. We would drive and drive and find no secluded beach, just crowds of locals, and eventually set up tent right next to my dad and spend an awkward afternoon and evening trying to make small talk. It was that latter scenario that was the more likely, and actually the more appealing right then.

'That's not from Manchester,' said Manchester, 'but it is from London. Those guys are in Malawi in a bus from London, and they met me, Manchester from Malawi. *Fucking* funny is what they said.'

He was aglow in his moment of fame.

'And they bought two Manchester United caps!'

'So what do you think?' she asked again, running a finger along my chin and cupping the back of my head in her palm.

'Well, look at the bikes; we don't have any space in the sidecars and the back seats are covered with our belongings,' I explained.

'Well, you can move them. We can make a plan? You can even put them on the bus, on my seat. There will be space,' she insisted.

'The main problem is we don't have another helmet, and you will need one.'

She stood silently, looking at the bike and thinking.

'Maybe we can buy one here, there are so many bikes in this country,' she suggested. She wasn't giving up.

It was now in the hands of the proverbial gods. She had an answer for everything. She had a lawyer's argument at hand, and the dice always seemed to fall her way. We both scanned the stalls looking for a motorbike helmet. I hoped we wouldn't find one.

'I can even buy one from a local; I can even buy a bicycle helmet,' she said, failing to spot the right thing in the nearby stalls.

What she had thankfully not noticed was no one in Malawi wore a helmet. Whether on a bike or bicycle, helmets were conspicuously uncommon. And then, with perfect timing, the bus began to hoot and a young Briton came over to call her. She kissed me with a protruding tongue and a pinch on my bum.

'You haven't escaped me yet,' she scowled, 'I will see you at Kande beach, then?'

'Um, yes, okay, I will see you there,' I lied.

She pushed her lips against mine once more, ran her

hand down my stomach, winked and pranced away.

'Mm, now what?' asked my dad, intrigued. 'Off to Kande beach, then?

'No, anywhere else but there, please.'

The Old Friend

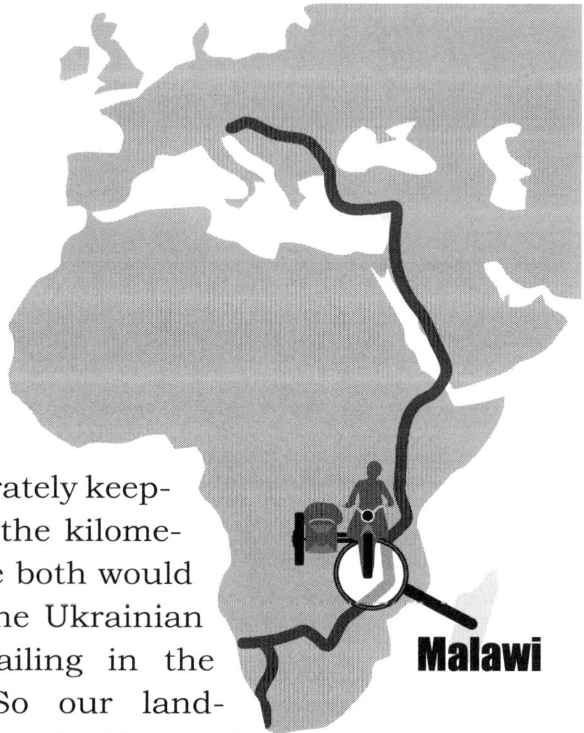

We weren't accurately keeping a track of the kilometres we travelled. We both would have liked to, but the Ukrainian odometers began failing in the early thousands. So our landmarks became more significant. I imagined if we had kept an exact reading, we might have celebrated every 1000 kilometres. We might have made a moment of it, and probably noted it on something; maybe even etched it on the bikes. My dad would have ceremonially logged the following: the place (with descriptions), total kilometres, time of day and date. I would have added 'what we did yesterday' and captured my mood. But in the end, we didn't have any of that and as the trip went on, my estimation of distance became more exaggerated, and my dad's seemed to become annoyingly stingy. What we did do however was celebrate border crossings and any sign that had Cape Town on it – and there are a surprising number out there in the middle of Africa. We celebrated the day we sat closest to the sun and sizzled in the midday heat on the equator. The tropics were moments too. We reluctantly remembered most places where we had broken down, although that list was becoming more muddled as we went along. It simply was too much to remember.

Crossing into Malawi was significant, but the moment we headed south of Nkothakhota, I became aware of something more noteworthy. My confidence seemed to be on the rise. I felt more at ease and comfortable. This was because I had been there before, all the way to Nkothakhota. On that maiden voyage in 1995, Malawi had been our final destination. We'd spent Christmas there and I had loved it. It felt familiar and home seemed within reach. I made a mental note to self that it was all downhill from that point on. In some ways it felt more like my turf than my dad's.

Mangochi was an idyllic fishing village that hugged the lake. It was often overshadowed by its more famous neighbours, the fantastically-named havens of Monkey Bay and Cape Maclear. The southern reaches of the lake were highlights for all travellers. The beaches were white and golden. The waters were clear and blue. A few hundred metres offshore, small islands and rock outcrops sheltered birds and tenacious trees and plants. Beneath its silky waters, thousands of fish kissed with the genes of rainbows darted about and drifted calmly into the deep. The water was warm, the people were kind and cheerful, and it was no wonder the lake was crowded with small camps and lodges.

Mangochi beach was a favourite for the over-landers and as we rattled our way past the small reed houses, we saw the thatched cap of the beach camp. It looked unkempt and Rastafarian and cool. I hoped we could stick around there for a few nights at least. Evidently my dad was lured by the soul of the place too. He kept himself busy with tools and things, while I found a spot on the beach or at the bar. The camp was empty and quiet. I read, wrote, drank cold beers, swam and rested. It was that quiet. It felt like the whole place was mine, and I lost myself in paradise for a while.

I had decided my bike needed a total repack again; the first time since our short stint as CIA operatives. It was a mess, and on closer inspection, much of the bike was beginning to rattle and tear apart. I tried to ignore the bumps and bruises all over the poor machine. My dad and I sat about six feet apart, quietly in our thoughts, and tinkered and tightened all we could. We heard the noise at the same time, and turned our ears in all directions to capture it.

'What's that sound?' I asked, as I tried to make out the direction of the noise and then what it might be.

'Sounds like a generator,' Papa said, 'or maybe a boat or ferry, or something like that.'

'I can't see anything anywhere, though. What a pity,' I lamented, 'it's been so calm and peaceful.'

The sound became louder and more abrasive, but we could still see nothing.

'There it is!' I said, pointing at the small village behind us. We could see the roof of a bright red vehicle peeking above the mango trees.

'Ah, it's the red bus!' smirked my dad. 'She's found you ... again!'

Oh *shit*, I thought. *Not the red bus, not the Brazilian. Not that all over again, and not at Mangochi.* We couldn't leave, so I would be cornered.

'Papa, the easiest story is we were on our way to Kande beach, but didn't get there in time. We broke down, and by the time we had fixed the bikes, they had gone, okay?'

He laughed and shrugged his shoulders, as if to suggest he might not play along with my plan.

'Maybe, maybe not; let's see what happens,' he teased.

'Please, just play along with me,' I pleaded.

As the vehicle meandered among the huts, we could hear the typical sound of a belching diesel engine. It moved closer, appearing and disappearing, but getting ever louder. There was no doubt it was heading towards Mangochi, and to us.

'Holy *shit*, it's not the bus,' I exclaimed as it rocked into view on the narrow potholed lane. It was a bright orange over-land truck. I'm not sure what they must have thought when they saw me, but I was beaming and big eyed with relief. Over-landers were often great fun to have around, and I was game for some of that. I leaned, bare chested against my bike, waiting for the truck to wheeze to a halt. Those trucks mainly overnighted for a single evening, but that bunch decided to do what we had done. So we spent a few days chilling with the crew of Australians, Greeks, Canadians, Poms, Americans and a couple of Mexicans. We played football, a lot. Drank and drank, a lot; and for a few days I was the most relaxed I had been all trip. And it felt good. I again noticed I was settled and just easy in my skin. Throughout our stay, the lake became a ritual. Every half an hour, we had an obligatory dip. Sometimes we lounged in the shallows and between the watery sheets all day. Small waves nudged us back and forth. The humidity and burning sun made it an essential daily practice. On the third day, the entire camp was silently wallowing, and floating in serenity when the driver of the truck asked me a question.

'Hey you, Marc, where are you from?'

Over-land truckers were rugged adventurers, part trucker and part explorer, and he fitted the mould perfectly. Unshaven, tanned, muscular and ever-so-camel cool.

'Cape Town, and you?'

'Cape Town too,' he said, with a short smile that rolled through his patchy beard. I couldn't hide my surprise. He had an accent, more British than South African.

'Oh, really? I thought you were a Brit. Sorry,' I apologised. 'Where in Cape Town?'

He ignored my question.

'And what is your mom's name?' he asked, pulling a beer bottle up from his lap. Its small top had been sitting just above the water's surface. He kept his eyes on me as he sipped. *Weird question,* I thought. *Creepy actually.*

'Um, Gabi ... Gabriela,' I said. 'Why do you ask?'

I half expected him to land a punchline to some dirty joke to please his fawning guests. But he didn't.

'I thought so. So you are Marc and you have a brother, right? What's his name again? Damian?'

'Daniel, actually,' I said, surprised.

I was floored. I looked back at my dad who was reading on a deck chair, oblivious to the conversation.

'How do you know that? Who are you? Do we know each other?' I quizzed him, and tried to find a match in my memory, but it came up blank.

'My mom's name is Deborah, and she was best friends with your mom,' he said. 'I'm Gavin. You went to that funny school, what was it called again? Oh yes, Waldorf.'

'What! *Holy mackerel,* I can't believe it. No ways, what are the chances?' Now I remembered exactly who he was.

'I know, I can't believe it either. You have looked so familiar for the past few days,' he said. 'Who is that?' he asked, pointing at Papa.

'That's my dad. You probably never met him. He left when I was pretty young.'

'So you guys are on a trip?'

'Yip, overland on bikes from Austria to Cape Town.'

I could see he was impressed. There we were in our own world surrounded by strangers. We knew each other, we had grown up together. He was a pretty wild guy and we had lost touch for many years. I think he just got a little too rough, and our moms' friendship slowly faded.

'On bikes across Africa. Respect man, is this your first time?'

'On bikes yes, but I've done two- and three-month trips around southern Africa, and you?'

'I've lost count, but this is my life now, and I love it.'

A deep breath filled my chest. Here was the first person who knew me on our entire trip, and I felt suddenly proud of my achievements. Telling the story to someone I knew made the epic trip come into perspective. Like punctuation in a sentence, by his mere presence and loose connection, he helped me give a different meaning to my trip. It became a boast-able thing. I had craved some recognition, maybe even admiration, and in one line he gave that to me. That feeling was stark, and I realised for months I had been starved of it. What we had already done was quite unbelievable.

'And your brother? What's he up to?' he asked.

'Not much, he's studying at the moment.'

'And he's not on this trip?'

'Nope, he decided not to do it.'

I could see the surprise in his face, but was grateful he didn't ask me for details. Being reminded of Daniel's refusal to do the trip made me confront what I had not wanted to face. It was clearer than ever that despite the thrill of that life-lasting adventure, the price I would pay was to actually get to know my dad. I had originally only seen this as a positive, but now understood the heartache it had brought to me. Those experiences, where I was reconnecting with my world, even with familiar geographical locations, were making me feel less and less dependent on my dad. That meant nothing to him, but nurtured something that grew in me. It was a turning point.

I never saw the Brazilian again.

The Canadian Pilot

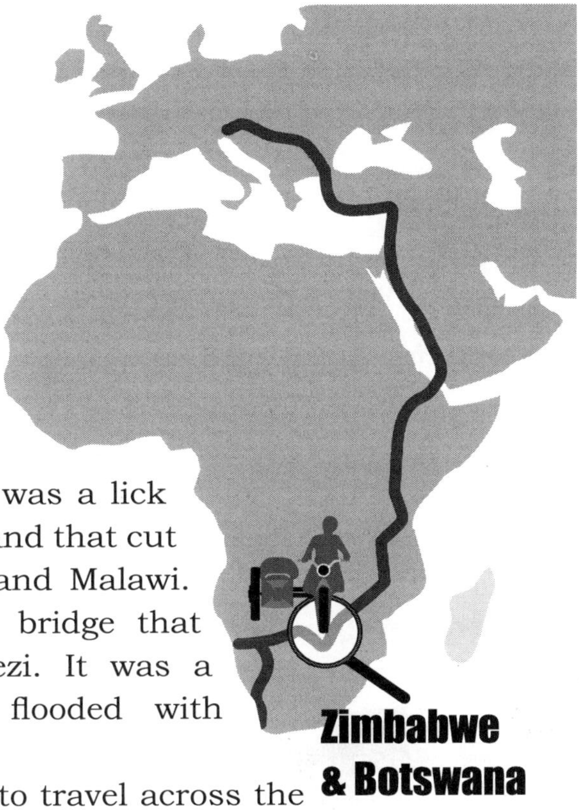

The Tete corridor was a lick of Mozambican land that cut between Zimbabwe and Malawi. There was a single bridge that spanned the Zambezi. It was a transit point and flooded with travellers.

'We have one day to travel across the Tete,' said my dad, peering over the crumpled map.

'Yes, we have the border crossing and then a dash across the Zambezi and then another border crossing. I remember it,' I said.

'It's about 300 kilometres we have to cover in a single day. You only get a one-day visa.'

'Back then it was the regular police stops that slowed us down, so let's hope we don't have too much of that.'

In the end, it was an easy day. Passport control went smoothly and we made the crossing with sunlight to spare. The bikes behaved and for the rest of the week we had a comfortable trip. Non-eventful, slow, and ordered. Everything went according to plan. We spent a few days with an old friend of my dad's in Harare, and then camped in Bulawayo.

It was the perfect time to broach the Aids diagnosis. With nothing else to bother or distract us, I felt it would be a good idea to discuss it. But Papa entirely dismissed it. He maintained they'd got it wrong, but he couldn't convince me he hadn't been at risk of contracting the disease. His refusal to go for another test was denial at its most blatant. The message was clear, then and on all previous occasions. Talking about Aids was a no-go topic. We may not have spoken about it, but it was always on my mind. Even more so as we headed into the rainy season when the malaria belt became its most lethal. The combination of any tropical disease and Aids meant certain death. So every night, as I rubbed on the insect repellent, or tucked my pants into my socks, I thought about how vulnerable we really were. But as before, every day and all day, those thoughts remained in my head, and were rarely spoken.

Before we knew it, Christmas was around the corner. Summer was in full heat. The days were long and sticky and each evening was greeted with refreshing showers and storms.

'I don't really want to say it,' I said as we sat at the border crossing into Botswana, 'but these have been such good days, haven't they?'

'Oh boy,' said my dad suspiciously. 'Now what's going to happen to us? Whenever we say things like that, something goes wrong.'

'Well, it just seems since our Malawian retreat we have been all good, been on a good run, don't you think?'

It was true, it was like we had been pulling goodwill and good fortune with us for the past few weeks. As if those happy tranquil shores had infected us with luck. As we crossed into Botswana and the dry edges of the Kalahari enticed us westward, we seemed to be sailing along. We had planned an L-shaped route through Botswana. We skirted the delta to the east and south with Maun being our one major stop along the way. They were long and straight roads, typical of a flat country. There was no need to have shaped the tar in any other way. Long straight roads made me think.

Roads are life, and they take on an altogether different meaning when one travels them for as long as we had. Each day, the crushed earth or tar lay still beneath us. It may have been broken, shattered or warped, but it was always the certainty on which we rested our wheels. Most people sit at their desks, learning or working, eating or meeting, and yet for months the various versions of road were as close to a routine as we got. Roads truly are the most free and accessible of all land on the planet.

In most places in the world, roads can be neither owned, nor bought nor sold. They allow all and any of us to traverse them. They have no opening and closing times and freely ferry kings, paupers, slaves, criminals, families and presidents. They are arterial routes that move the flow of ideas, money, resources and life. They connect us, free us, and at times can trap us. Roads also carry disease; they become borders between hope and despair. They bring death too.

I had travelled more than 40 000 kilometres in 4x4s before we took the bikes across Africa. The journeys were all similar. Firstly, we had many drivers, and would take turns to split the distances between us. We always had music, and democratically rotated the choice of tunes. A highlight was often to try and tune into a local radio station and get a glimpse of the language, or glean an insight into the national agenda through the sequence and quality of the news stories. And then, there was the sleeping. When the conversation lagged off, and the roadside events, meals and stops had been done, there was always time to catch a few winks and recover from the daily discomfort in a tented bed. In those dreamy naps, the hum of the road would soothe with white noise, and I'd see through some boredom, but I'd also miss chunks of the journey. The map of my trips would have a dark line chasing the roads we travelled and that I actually saw, and a dotted line – or a glaring gap where I was fast asleep. That reality was more poignant given my constant self-assurance that while I was a very poor capturer of these journeys through the eye of the camera, I had my memory and eyes as the markers of my adventures. In truth, those big gaps were opportunities lost – and even images from those who were awake to take them meant nothing to me.

On a motorbike, however, there were no dotted lines at all. Each centimetre of road was vividly consumed. Each moment was forced into our memories, sometimes obliging and sticking in storage, at other times deceiving the senses and allowing the images to escape from our awareness and disappear. On the bikes, for eight, sometimes 10, and even 16 hours a day, I was in silence. There was no conversation, no music, no debates and no naps. There was only a flow of thoughts, ideas, observations and emotions that were trapped into the muffled sounds of passing noise, above and below me. My senses were clumsily out of sync. My sight was blinkered by heavy, padded goggles, but not my nose or the tactile sensations on my skin. They were as alive and raw as could be.

I quickly learned that dipping into the lower altitude of a valley or trough in the road would be a scene change in my sensory experience. Sights and sounds remained constant, but in some hollows, the inversion effect of a micro-climate made it feel like I was diving into a cool pool of air. Crisp, clean and fresh, the air would be trapped and scented with the fragrances of the grasses and flowers on its dome. I would begin to shiver, and become aware again of my skin. The chill would fill the gap between my gloves and long sleeves, and would tickle into the tear on the inside of my shorts. Sometimes we would be suffocated by the particulate heavy coughs of diesel trucks, and I would suck in spoonfuls of grit and grime. At other times, the smell of wood fires would singe my nostrils. Whatever the place, it had both sight, and sounds, and then smells and a hug of sensations that no picture, image or movie could capture. I often consoled myself that to truly remember what it was all like, I would have to go back to those exact places, and breathe in and embrace the air.

What was quite a revelation was the number 200. That was my estimate of the number of hours I had spent on the bike in total silence. It was like a moving retreat, a silent isolation. I had always believed I could think any situation right. I had always believed no matter what happened to me, I always had the choice of who I wanted to become. As much as I began to face the reality my dad was dying, and we had not found any solace in our relationship, I was also beginning to admit I may have been better off without him in my life. I was even grateful. The Middle East had made me think of my faith and had created space for me to believe I still had choice in what I believed. And with so much shock and so many unexpected twists, I wondered endlessly just how much the fragility of life really was the new normal.

It was in Maun that the hopeful thread of a relationship finally broke between us. It was as if the ease and sanity of our preceding weeks had made it impossible to ignore any longer the real cracks and patchwork of our connection. It all happened because of a young Canadian pilot.

We arrived in Maun earlier than expected, and camped

behind one of the small hotels. Maun is the launch pad from which most people visit the Okavango Delta. It is a busy little town, filled with tour operators who either drive or fly their clientele into the various secluded and private camps within the delta. The receptionist made it clear the campsite was separate from the rest of the establishment, but we were allowed to use the pool, which was a welcome permission. It was easily in the low 40 degrees that day. Everything looked newly built, and the site, too, was filled with saplings. Only one tree right in the centre of the camp offered shade though. The entire place looked empty. It was midday by the time we had set up camp and I planned to spend the rest of the day next to the pool. When I arrived, there was one other person swimming laps. He noticed us and swam across to chat.

'Where are you from?' asked the tall, dark-haired man, the twang of a Canadian accent trailing off into his straw. He sucked the last few drops of his drink that was sitting on the edge of the pool.

'Cape Town, South Africa,' I replied, 'and Austria ... and you?'

'Actually, I am also from there,' he said, with a smile as he noticed my obvious surprise. 'Yes, I went to school there, but you know what it was like in the late 1980s. So my parents skipped the country and Apartheid and we moved to Canada. I basically grew up in Canada.'

'So what are you doing here?'

'I'm a pilot, and I am racking up my hours to eventually join a commercial airline. That is the apex of my profession, but I have to do my miles first and I figured this might be the best place to do that.'

'For sure, what a pleasure. So have you got back to Cape Town quite a bit while you have been here?'

'No, I haven't been able to get there on this trip. You

would think a pilot could get himself across the continent pretty easily, but I just haven't had a gap.' He pulled the straw out the can and gave it one last rattle above his lips, 'It's what? A two-hour flight?'

My dad was there, but not in the conversation. He had nothing to say, and I didn't feel like including him. There were times when he got lost in fast English banter, and I didn't have the energy that day to keep filling him in. But he just sat and listened. The young pilot was a typical expat character. He regaled us with colourful stories of near escapes, fussy clients and the reckless freedom of bush living. Within 30 minutes we discovered we in fact had a mutual acquaintance. I couldn't believe it. The world was so small, and it was as though, from that moment, with that connection, my dad became a lurker around us. He must have picked that up and very soon just walked away. He didn't acknowledge us, just disappeared. It took me a while to notice he had gone.

The pilot and I chatted and swam and had a few more drinks. We spent the next couple of hours just chilling, trying to escape the Kalahari heat that boiled the pool. There was nothing else to do. The sky began to fill with flocks of clouds as the afternoon wore on.

When I eventually walked back into the campsite, I was startled to see my dad had, for the first time in weeks, pitched his own stretcher and mosquito net. We had shared the tent on most occasions, and when we hadn't, it was to sleep in the open air. When we had arrived we had pitched a single tent, but since he had left the pool, he had very specifically set up camp a fair distance from where the tent was. As I walked through the gaps between our separated camps, he remained seated, staring into his map. He ignored me for the entire evening. We didn't share a meal together, we didn't talk to each other. He just sulked and cut me off, as if I was a stranger to him.

It was yet another awakening. For so long I had been scared of offending my dad. I had been cautious about pushing too hard against his views or commenting on his way of living. At times I had made a stand, but although the debate had been intense it had always been brief, sometimes terminated by his dismissive stance. But that evening, lying in my tent, I realised a deeper belief I held. There was an enduring set of assumptions that lay beneath my actions. I had been trying to put words to an experience that differed between my parents. The word was love, or more correctly, unconditional love. I wondered what that really meant. From my own experience love was shown through deed over time. And it bound us. It allowed us to challenge each other, disagree, even cross a line that was hurtful, or sometimes mean. One deep assumption remained; the love was enduring and healed many of the differences we may have had. And so, no matter how big the gaps of opinion or views, or how damaging the transgression, love was bound into the relationship. That was what I realised as I lay watching the sky, black and deep, connected around and between the stars. I admitted to myself; it was not a bond I had with my dad. In fact, I sat with a more troubling reality based on a more limiting assumption. I expected my dad to leave me, to leave me behind, to abandon me. It was the deep fear from so long ago that lingered. I expected if there was too much friction, disagreement or even just a heightened challenge to his authority, he would leave. I believed with nothing to bind us, with nothing as deep and real as felt love, he could walk away and never come back. It was an assumption that influenced so much of our relationship.

It was an admission so much of our relationship felt untrue and inauthentic. I had spent most of my time fooling myself to believe the contrary. And so, as a result I often spoke down to myself, didn't share the full extent of my views and succumbed to his rhetoric. It also meant I spent much of my time trying to please him, to placate him. It was an apologetic stance that made me spend more time trying to understand his view on his actions, rather than dealing with my reactions to his actions. And so there he was, sleeping far from me, having purposefully removed himself. It was the furthest he could get away from me. It was the ease of his snub that cut the deepest.

I had a revelation. At that point, just a few weeks away from celebrating the first of our goals, the Millennium, I realised I had not dealt with the abandonment and how that had impacted my life. On that day I began to think about the choices I might have to free myself from the burden.

It felt like the bond in our relationship was more about the fact he had left me, and we had so little time shared between us. It was less about finding each other, forgiving each other and making a choice to start the relationship again. I had believed the trip would solve it all. But it had, near its end, done nothing but reveal to me the true nature of the man, both in him and in me.

I felt like running away before he did, and cried myself to sleep that night. The boy, hurt and grasping for love and attention, fell asleep alone. I believe I was finally letting go.

The Almost Homecoming

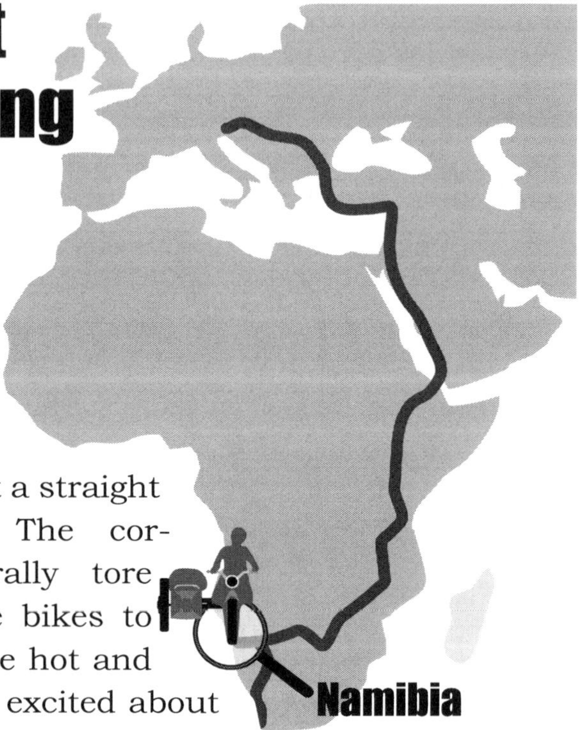

From Maun we cut a straight line westward. The corrugated roads literally tore the bodywork of the bikes to pieces. The days were hot and long and slow. I was excited about our entry into Namibia, my original homeland. It was the first time I had been there with my dad since I was six years old. I love sparsely populated land. It was rough, dry and very flat. It was all so familiar to me.

We entered the eastern border, a route I had never done before. On all my visits I had crossed the southern border. I had also dipped a toe into the slow-flowing Cunene that ran in the north-east with Angola, and dropped out the top of the Caprivi panhandle in the far east. It was a country of stark contrast. The south and entire western coast were desert, while the north-east teemed with life on subtropical terrain. I had come close to that eastern border before on an earlier trip with friends. We had come upon a dry pan, surrounded by acacia trees, and covered in knee-high grasses. It had been poignantly empty, probably because we could see so far and yet see nothing at all. We had decided to camp in the centre of the pan, where we thought was closest to the core of that natural drain. We had instantly made it a busy place. We lazed away our time in a series of tense and epic chess championships and made it through elaborate round robins and play-offs. Lost in our game, the grand finale, we hadn't noticed the slight figures of two San Bushmen strolling to our camp. One was dressed in traditional garb – a loin cloth and beads, the other in South African National Defence Force fatigues. The latter spoke Afrikaans and had carried the smaller of the bows.

'We are chasing a heard of kudu,' the man in military gear had said. 'They are about two days ahead of us. If we keep stopping like this, so slowly, then maybe three days ahead.'

'How long have you been on the hunt?' I asked in broken Afrikaans.

'Too long,' he replied with a laugh. 'It's been three nights already.'

They had asked us for water and we had offered them some left-over flapjacks. And then we had sat, sinking towards the end of our chairs, while they had rested on their haunches. We ate and they had seemed mindful of every bite. They then thanked us and left.

'Probably their first ever flapjacks,' my friend had commented.

My memories of Namibia were all nostalgic and good. I was excited at the prospect of spending a week in Swakopmund with my brother and mother and a host of other old family friends. It wasn't quite home, but it felt like a homecoming. We crossed into Namibia on Christmas Eve, 1999.

We initially thought we might make a dash from the

border to Windhoek, but we discovered a wildlife sanctuary along the main road. It was officially closed, but they let us set up camp. All my life we had celebrated Christmas on Christmas Eve. It was the German tradition. So we made a fire, cracked open a few beers and braaied. Our host came strolling over with a clutch of beers and a small basket of fruit in his hands.

'Happy Christmas,' he said cheerfully. 'Sorry to bother you, but could I chat to you for a short while?'

He carefully placed the beers and fruit on our camping table.

'It's not much,' he said, 'but we were kind of closed until you came along, so we really made no plans to have gifts and nice things around.'

He then reached behind his back and pulled out a paper bag with three long strips of biltong.

'Do you have this in Germany?' he asked innocently. 'It's called biltong, and this is from a Springbok.'

'Actually, they don't have this in Germany,' said my dad, 'but my son is South African and I lived here in South West Africa – sorry, Namibia – for many years. We know it well, and have really missed it.'

The man's smile broadened.

'Well then, welcome home!' He hung around for a moment longer, 'So now I have a favour to ask. Has anyone ever told you that you look like Father Christmas?'

My dad nodded.

'Anyway, we think you do, and tomorrow my grandson is coming here for Christmas lunch. Could I ask you to please come and give him his gifts?'

The next day my father made a little boy's day. It was a touching moment. The blonde farmer's son blinked and gasped repeatedly as he tested reality by pinching his mom. And every time he opened his eyes Father Christmas was still there and his smile became wider and wider. My dad was not the 'ho, ho, ho' kind of act, but awkwardly shook the little chap's hand and handed him a bag full of gifts. The room, filled with uncles, aunts, grandparents and friends, applauded and cheered. The boy ran to his mom and peered from under her sleeves. I almost expected we would be invited for lunch, or at least to stay for a drink, but my dad suddenly raised his voice.

'Well, we must go. We have a long way to go to Windhoek, and little Jannie is still waiting for me.' Calling on his inner Thespian, he skipped round the couch, deftly opened the sliding door and stepped out of view. I froze for a moment and then followed him out.

He was waiting for me at the side of the house.

'What took you so long?' He was irritated.

'That took me by surprise. I thought we might have stayed a little longer, maybe even had a bite to eat?'

'No man, Father Christmas can't stay to eat! It would ruin the little boy's day if we hung around.'

'*Geez*, okay, sorry. I didn't realise you were taking it all that seriously,' I said.

'Come on, just think a little. I was doing my job, okay?'

He huffed and shook his head and with that a dark cloud settled around his brow for the rest of Christmas day.

The following day we arrived in Windhoek and decided to stop at a pub before we found our campsite. It wasn't just any watering hole my dad was looking for. It was an old haunt, the regular pit stop he'd frequented over 30 years earlier. It had become a little more difficult to locate given the disorienting urban sprawl, but we eventually stepped inside. Within minutes an old man turned around with a draught in his hand and said, 'Rogatschnig, you pig. What are you having, a beer or a whisky?'

I felt warped in time. The old pub probably looked

exactly the same as it had done decades earlier. It had a dark, wood-panelled bar and beer-hall benches. It was a trippy experience. There was my dad, unannounced in Windhoek and, as if on cue, he was noticed. That was the start of an eight-hour revelry of reminiscing, romanticising and rinsing our gullets with beer. The entire experience was hard to recollect as a result. I also remember feeling as though I was in a time machine, looking through a window at the life my dad used to live. The scraps of stories they were feasting on usually involved too much alcohol, loose women, dangerous dares and the police. Each story had the same main characters, just different settings on different days and usually, with much hilarity, a different set of outcomes. It was an easy way to wind down. After two nights and a string of reunions with old colleagues and friends, we headed west for the last time. The 370 kilometre trek would take us to a small town stuck between the desert and the sea: Swakopmund.

In the end, we were early, and so we waited. That was in itself a first on the entire trip. Sweat layered salt on my arms. It left a sheen of stickiness against which a fine carpet of dust was glued. I slouched against my bike, one hand rested on the fuel tank and the other slipped into my pocket. I stared in reflection across the desert. The entrance to the golf course was behind us. The fairways were empty. A hot breeze rustled the palm trees that were clinging to life on each side of the gate.

We had estimated a wait of exactly 68 minutes. The straight desert road sloped gently towards the sea; we could see a mirage of buildings blur in the distance. Luckily, we were far enough out of town to not ruin the occasion. Of course, that would all have been unimportant, had it not been the first time in over 22 000 kilometres we had arrived in a place where someone expected us to be on time. We had left Windhoek at sunrise with a confirmed booking to meet my brother and mother in the centre of Swakopmund at 3.30pm. That made it the most predictable day of our journey.

We waited in silence. I looked down at my bike and listened to the stories it told me. The front mudguard wept with stitches of rivets and steel plates I'd hammered on after it had been shredded on the corrugated roads of the Kalahari. The faded surf stickers that randomly covered the sidecar were scratched and scuffed from months of bullying by the elements. I placed my foot on the back of the sidecar. The metal at its rear had been rammed flat in the chaotic, gun-toting dash through the Horn of Africa. I rattled the metal saddlebags that still hung firmly over the back wheel. They were filled with parts we had bought, made and even borrowed without permission. Each panel of black sheet metal was washed in dust, and in places re-blackened with dripping oil or water, or both. The indicator lights had been retrofitted with braces to stop them break-dancing off the front forks. I hopped onto the seat, and kicked my feet out against the aluminium wings we had custom designed after crossing the Red Sea. They were meant to channel air directly onto the overheated boxer engines, but they also gave the bikes some Harley swag. I gave the lamb's skin seat cover a final shake to plump out its thick, woolly padding.

The space around us was limitless. That vast, static simplicity of yellow, sandy swells was peaceful too. But the terrain around me embodied the very opposite of my inner turmoil. As I stood there, I played a memory reel across my mind. I had fleeting images of places, people, words and moments. It was however the rush of raw emotion that overwhelmed me. Entranced by the assault, I lost myself for a few moments in the golden blur between the land and sea out west. As I looked across the sandy ripples of Namib dunes, I was troubled by a feeling. It was an emotion, or awakening, that my sullen eyes and flat smile could not hide. I was inexplicably despondent and lame in my heart. It made me confused and inquisitive. *Would waiting for that staged entrance be the culmination of all we had been through? Would the sight of us, growling through those holiday streets, be the sum total of what we had done? What had we achieved anyway?* I felt as if I was about to be cheated. That it was all about to be boxed in a frame of us on that day, and only on that day.

It became as clear as the pristine desert sky that no one, other than myself, could ever know what it meant to have completed that trip. There was a deep echo of loneliness. I was sure many before me had felt it too. I realised, no matter how much I might try, no one would truly understand how that trip had shaped me. No one would ever know, and thus, even more devastatingly, few might care. I am unsure why that bothered me. I, of all people, know we are all shaped by our journeys. But to me, that passage, that exploration, that traverse was unique. To me it was a trial of kilometres and consciousness, of searching and staying, of choosing and letting go, and it *had* changed my life forever.

The final leg was in sight. We had pored over maps, traced lines along main roads, pushed our fingers against the highways and allowed our eyes to roam across countries and continents. At first we were always exploring our route going east, and then from Turkey, it was pretty much all south. From Zimbabwe it was towards the sunset of our trip, and we'd headed west. We'd plotted our stops, noted tricky routes such as mountain passes, desert tracks and geopolitical hotspots. We had used the range of our petrol tanks to estimate desirable town-to-town distances.

We had factored in rest days, usually near water and in well-known traveller nodes. We had thumb-sucked 'hassle points' such as borders and river crossings, trying to estimate how much time they might eat from our plans. From the outset, we had had a solid handle on our timing, but we had not factored in the lead times on the DHL deliveries we'd needed to wait for. In some places it had taken only a couple of days for the yellow lorries to reach us; in other locations weeks had gone by. It was this oversight in our planning that had significantly shifted our target dates and destinations. Arriving in Swakopmund was the completion of goal number one: to be as close as possible to the tip of Southern Africa to celebrate the Millennium. Of all the twists and turns, nothing could have prepared me for the way it ended when we had achieved the second goal: arriving in Cape Town, another 2000 kilometres away.

'We will celebrate the year 2000 and the end of the trip in Cape Town,' my dad had said. 'That will be the best way.'

At the time, I couldn't have agreed more. In fact, it had become the *raison d'etre* of the trip. At least that is what I had told people.

'We are doing this to celebrate the turn of the century,' was my PR line. And it worked. The millennium had been fraught with expectation and terror. The Y2K bug had threatened to render every digital gadget on earth impotent. We had imagined our personal computers smoking in confusion, all our bank accounts being either zeroed or topped up. Airlines, governments, and banks would face the risk of losing all date-bound data. In short, the new century would herald anarchy. Well, that is at least how the story had begun to mutate.

I could no longer ignore the growing pressure to acknowledge my life, too, was about to take a turn. Swakopmund was the new place to see in the Millennium and it was, in fact, quite fitting. The country of my birth, the place where I had first swum in the sea as a toddler, and the place where I had my first adventure behind the wheel of a Land Rover. It had shaped much of my masculinity, and continued to. Celebrating a new chapter there made sense.

After delaying our arrival, we finally drove slowly down the main road, heading straight towards the sea. There was a time when all the roads in that quaint seaside town were made of compressed salt, but while some of the secondary roads remained unchanged, the main road was now tar. We trundled along the bustling main drag, lined on either side by old family-owned German speciality stores, or the bigger, branded chains. The town was small enough to walk everywhere, and on that day, in the middle of its busiest season, the warm afternoon sun invited everyone to amble and browse. Most people didn't notice us drive past, though, not that it mattered.

As we neared the sea, we found my mother and brother sitting at a popular outdoor restaurant. I can't remember anything about that first meeting. I am not sure if it was a blur of chatter and hype, or just awkward, or both. All I recall is after about two hours we despatched my dad to a small apartment in the centre of town and headed to the home of old family friends, who we were staying with.

Over the next week, I only saw my dad a handful of times. He seemed content to while away his days at his own pace and in his own space. It worked for me too. I gallivanted, met up with old friends, made new ones, lazed on the beach, and drank with a wink of celebration permanently tagged to each draught beer. I had a short summer fling and for a brief time forgot where I had come from or where I was going. I was on holiday from my holiday.

I celebrated the Millennium at Vlotkasbaken, north of Swakopmund, painfully aware I was doing so without my father. In fact, for all the significance we had loaded into that date, we never did celebrate anything about the Millennium together. And as that date came and went, I realised I didn't care about the missed opportunity either. It was just another example of how, along the way, and through all of my life, he had never been there on the big occasions. It was recognition that, whatever the triumphs and trials of the journey, it was less about the date we were chasing and more about the reality we were facing.

With the explosion of fireworks and a descending moon heading into the Atlantic Ocean, I stood knee deep in the shallows, staring back at the dark silhouette of a flat desert covered in stars. I was overwhelmed by emotion, and smiled with tears wetting my cheeks. I knew then exactly what the New Year meant to me. It was to be the final letting go of the boyish aspirations to be fathered. It was the lungs bursting with freedom. The chance for me to choose a path for myself that didn't sit in the empty and desperate hopes of a final reconciliation. It was letting go of the myth that I would only find meaning through the relationship with my dad. It was also an admission I needed to grow up. I waited until the icy Atlantic had numbed my feet enough for me to feel real again.

With the collapse of the world into a technological typhoon avoided, we had no excuse but to start planning for our final descent. Within a few days we were on the road again. We toured with ease on the long, straight and horizon-grasping roads. The months of acrimony between bike and man had given way to months of harmony. Neither of us dared to appreciate it.

We took our time. It was a first to not be chasing a date. By the time we had crossed the Orange River into South Africa, we were just three days from Cape Town. The river bridge straddled two green banks. While we drove over it, technically in no man's land again, I watched the fast-flowing waters gurgle and roll on their way. The summer rains in the northern interior, thousands of kilometres away, were flushing the desert onto that western coast. I watched a branch, with an egret calmly perched on its starboard side. It was as if it was steering it down the waterway. It briefly disappeared under the bridge and then became trapped in an eddy, circling back from behind a clump of thick reeds. The bird just waited. It didn't work any harder, and didn't flap away to another piece of flotsam. With time, the eddy lost its grip. I saw it for a last time as it was about to bump down a rapid.

Passport control was calling, quite literally, and welcomed me home. As we searched for a campsite to spend the night on the river banks, I wondered if I was the egret, the log or the river. Maybe all of thcm, possibly none.

When we were finally within sight of Table Mountain, I became fidgety with fantasy. It should have been our penultimate day and then I would be home, but with the end in sight, it was our bikes that decided when we would finally arrive. Less than 400 kilometres from Cape Town, both of them packed up. Over a gruelling eight hours, we travelled no more than 40 kilometres. With a snapped accelerator cable, melted couplings and fuel blockages, we spent more time off and under the bikes than on them that day. They both danced a decrepit salute to their prior mishaps and topped them all off in grand style. We were agonisingly close as we spluttered and towed ourselves into the small town of Van Rhynsdorp.

We stared across the campsite. Small trees shaded a few patches of grass. In the centre of the grounds was a clubhouse. Each path and road was lined with small, white, painted rocks, poles and old tyres. It was neat and clean. We were baffled as to why anyone would need to camp there, though. Supposedly the crowds descended mainly in spring, when that part of the country would bloom in spectacular floral explosions.

'We had to fill it up,' said the old man in charge, when we asked if there was a pool. 'It was the only public pool in this town, you know. Well, kind of public.'

The sweat had glued my shorts to my legs. The air was still and fiery hot. We stood on the slate edging of a pool that was covered in lawn. My dry and dreary eyes were trying to will cool water from the grass.

'We just had too many people coming to use it; mostly the people we didn't want here. You know, the people who normally can't swim in this country,' he said, *with heavy innuendo.* There was a simmering, racist undertone to his comments.

'*Ya* well, at least we have peace now,' he said contentedly.

That DHL delivery was one of the longest on our trip: a full seven days of waiting. We just had to kill time. So we lounged in the games room and watched the Australian tennis open. It was sweltering hot and our tent was unbearable to be in during the day. Every time we stepped out onto the veranda we would begrudgingly walk across the pool and curse that logic on our way to having yet another shower to cool off.

The Last Day of That Life

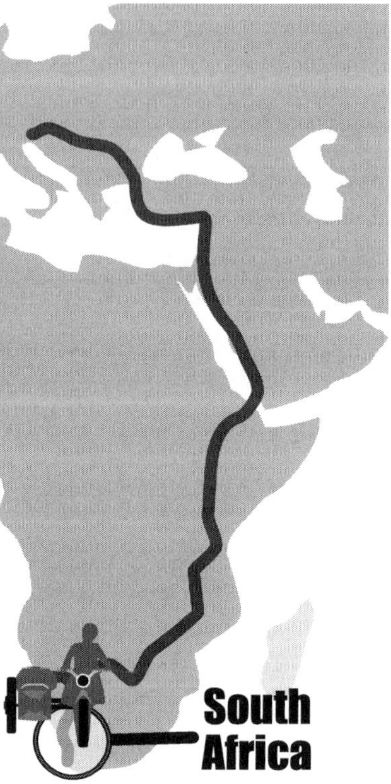

On our last day, we were in a hurry. Everything we did had become the new normal. Routine, habit and comfort were relative experiences. We had adapted, and would rise at 5am to pack and roll the tent. Coffee and breakfast would be served with about a quarter of a bike still to pack. Having spent a week idly waiting, we were faster and quieter than usual. I felt relief and excitement. I was done. It was a hot, mid-summer day. The wind usually blew from the south-east, fanning dry air from the interior before it was pushed over the ice-cold Atlantic Ocean in the west. That day it was breathless, and the conditions perfect for our Cape Town entry.

After winding south for three hours, we reached the outskirts of the city. I welled with an unmistakable pang of nostalgia. In that moment it was all over. I began fetching as many memories with my eyes as I could. I stared intently at my handlebars, trying to rub the dirt into my skin. I squeezed the petrol tank and puffed at the air. I knew it was so close. That was it. For the duration of the trip we had aimed to arrive in Cape Town, and that day had come. Well almost.

We came to a bend in the coastal road that runs north of the Blouberg beaches and I pulled off the road. The mountain view was unobstructed. The round-topped pinnacle of Lion's Head rose in the west. Kloof Nek's saddle linked it to the tall cliffs at the base of Table Mountain. The Table top was flattened to a shiny and sharp edge. It stretched across the full extent of the inner-city skyscrapers and then plunged down to Devil's Peak in the east. It was a perfect view. We stood there, white sand beneath our feet among small dunes. The cool sea seemed to reach all the way and touch the foundations of the inner-city buildings.

'Let's take a photo!' I said exuberantly.

'We made it! We made it, we did it!' My father placed his hand on my shoulder in a rare sign of tenderness. 'We did it Marc, well done!'

'Take a picture of me with my hands up, so it looks like I am leaning on the Table top!' I said.

I was so excited. Standing on top of my bike, with my home behind me, it felt like the perfect place to capture the very end. It was the last photo of our entire trip, and we made it count.

We drove on and had a beer at a rustic beach bar overlooking Table Bay. Our last meal on the road.

'I feel like we are sneaking into Cape Town,' I said, raising my glass to salute our adventure.

'Well, in that case, let's turn around and go back,' he replied with a naughty grin. 'Actually, that is my plan, but I will wait a few weeks before I do that.'

I couldn't hide my surprise.

'What?' I blurted out. 'Gee, we have just arrived and you are already thinking of leaving?'

'Yes, why not? I know what works, and what I can modify. I will make this bike a super-touring bike. And I will do it again. Alone the next time, from south to north, and probably only to Ethiopia.'

I was stunned. I nodded, struggling to find the words. We sat in silence, and again I felt the sadness of the end. I felt tears wanting to explode out of my face, but I held them back, not sure if they were prompted by joy or sadness. It was the end and I was not sure if I had really achieved what I had wanted to. I felt hollow and tired. Yes, we had covered the 22 000 kilometres, but there was more to it than that. *Had we done enough? Had I asked enough? Had I learned enough? Were the two of us any closer, or was the distance in our blood insurmountable? Despite our shared genes, were we destined to remain apart? To be men on bikes, covering the earth, as close as we could be, to go only as far as we could go?*

I watched from the corner of my eye, and felt a deep longing to love and be loved. I had anticipated the last day for weeks, but when it arrived I felt lost, as if I had not prepared myself at all for it. I was not ready for it to end. I wanted to begin from the very beginning. I wanted to share each story, recollect as many kilometres as possible, but then, for the last time, we strapped on our helmets and prepared our bikes for their final drive.

As we settled ourselves, I slowed down to soak it all up. After a few impatient kicks to the starter, the other bike was already rumbling to full throttle when an elderly man stepped in front of my bike and waved for my attention.

'Excuse me sir, can I ask you a question?' he asked.

'Sure, how can I help?'

Next to me, the bike started edging forward, slowly heading down the hill towards the main road.

'I want to know what kind of bike this is?' asked the

man.

'It's a Dnepr, a Ukrainian knock-off of the BMW boxer motor.'

'And what are you doing with them?'

'We have travelled from Europe on them, this is in fact our last day.'

The man struggled to hide his amazement. He smiled and shook his head.

'Hey! My bike is starting to overheat man, let's get moving,' Papa exclaimed.

He had reversed back up the hill to reprimand me and then rolled forward with gravity again. I could see he was pissed off and agitated.

'Sorry, I have to go,' I said apologetically.

'No problem, here is my card. I am with the Cape Classic Bike Society. Please call me, I would like you to come and speak at an event some time.'

I tried to start my bike and in haste, flooded it with fuel. Papa shook his head. He revved his bike and sat poised to leap into the main flow of traffic. It was already mid-afternoon and we had about 20 kilometres to go. I couldn't understand what the rush was. The more I rushed, the more the bike resisted. I could sense his fury.

It had become an unusually sultry Cape Town afternoon. There was no wind and the heat was slumbering close to the earth. The normally active southeaster had rested all day. As I drove deeper into the suburbs and away from the sea, the air filled with braai smoke, agitated insects, pollen and life. I smelled Cape Town, like the skin of a lover. The roads were empty as I finally drove into my street. There was no welcome party, no parade or banner as I turned into the driveway. It seemed the groan of the bike had not alerted anyone either. I slowly unbuckled my helmet for the last time. I paused and waited, the silence screaming in my head and all around me. Until I rang the doorbell. At first there was no answer. So I rang it again.

'Hello?' came my mom's voice across the intercom. She shrieked with excitement when I chuckled. She rushed out and we hugged months' worth of anguish and separation through each other.

'Where is Papa?' she asked, looking confused. She peered out the entrance to see where he might be hiding.

'I don't know,' I said, holding back the rage.

'What? What happened? Is he okay?'

'I don't know, actually. We arrived in Table View at about midday and went for a meal and a drink. I mean, what a beautiful day, it was stunning to see the mountain again, so we decided to celebrate.'

My mom hung on every word. She shuffled her feet back and forth in anticipation.

'We were getting ready to leave when a man came up to chat to me,' I said, placing the helmet on the kitchen table. It felt heavier than usual. 'Papa had already started his bike. We have had issues with the overheating of his engine for a while, so every time it overheats, the engine usually blows up.'

I paused. I realised my brother wasn't home. It was just my mom and me.

'Anyway, so this guy wanted to get my details, or he wanted to give me his and he took quite a while to get to the point. I mean, not too long, say five minutes. But Papa got irritated and started driving his bike around the parking lot to try and keep it cool.'

I felt the anger welling up as I got closer to the end of my story.

'You know ... this hasn't been easy, this whole trip,' I said slowly.

'I know Marc, I could see in Swakop,' she said tenderly.

'So anyway, then I tried to start my bike and it wouldn't start. In fact I kept flooding the engine because I was trying to rush it. He was shouting at me to stop playing games and basically told me I was doing it on purpose.'

'Doing what on purpose?' she asked.

'*Ag*, he said I was trying to get his bike to break down. I don't know what he was talking about, really, I don't. Anyway, without any warning, he rolled onto the main road and started driving away very fast.'

'What? Come on? So where was he going?' asked my mom, perplexed.

'I don't know. The plan was to come here, so I didn't think too much of it.'

'So where is he? I don't understand; is he still coming here?'

'I don't know Mom. I don't think so. I eventually got my bike going and followed the coastal road. There is just that one road you know, but I couldn't find him. He was gone,' I paused again and looked behind me down the road. 'I also had no money and was very low on fuel, so I decided I had to drive quite slowly to save on petrol.'

My mom stood in disbelief, stunned and mute, a mix of anger and concern on her brow.

'I thought he might be waiting just down the road, or would at least come back. So I waited at some of the main intersections, but he had just disappeared and gone on without me. So I came home.'

That was that. That was how it ended.

I arrived home on Sunday 21 January, 2000. On 25 February, over a month later, my dad made contact with me again. He had been in Cape Town all that time, living in the city Bowl. It was a day before his birthday and he wanted my brother and I to celebrate with him. There was no apology, no explanation, and no attempt to reconcile.

He had spent weeks purposefully avoiding me, hiding from us, escaping something I couldn't know or understand. In truth, I didn't want to know why he had done it.

On that final day of our epic adventure, he had left again. Since his disappearance when I was 11, I had spent all my adolescence waiting for him to find me and ignored my emerging self and identity. Then, in that short drive within my city, I recognised this time he had left me, not as a boy, but as a man.

I spent that month rooting myself back in the Cape, with a clear conscience that I had tried to make it work. I felt different. I felt more self-assured and less dependent. I admitted to myself and others that my father's frailties were now real to me and I shared a very clear formula for how I would engage in future. In my estimation, I had a good 20 years to cultivate a friendship with him. Fatherhood was a yoke over his neck, and I thought I would try a different way. I tried to see him not as my father, but as just a man, and a person I could choose to be in a relationship with. It was a recalibration of my ties with him. Daniel had discovered it long ago, but it was not something to share as an idea, it had to be felt deep in me. So deep it could turn the shape of my identity back towards myself. I don't know how Daniel had found it, or if indeed that was what he had unearthed, but despite the confusion around it all, I felt at peace with the unfolding of those final moments. A stranger tore through our cloudy bond and tested me. Arriving home alone was the choice I didn't know I had, but it was the most important experience of it all. He could have died, or I could have left, but he chose to leave me again.

And so it was only at the end I discovered the meaning of it all. I had spent the entire trip trying to find who my father was and, in the end, I stumbled upon myself.

I believe that is what all great journeys are about. There was no deep embrace, no tear-filled appreciation for each other. Not a single expectation of enduring closeness was realised. It ended as it had always been. I resigned myself to the truth that it was the only way it ever could have ended, to give me true healing. I was torn from the ballad of reunion and thrust out into life, more man than boy, and that was the gift he gave me. Through his absence and inability to choose a healing gesture, he forced me to face my own choices. That I only understood the day he died and left me behind forever.

Fifteen years and three months after completing the trip, I finally found the courage to start writing this book. After completing the manuscript, I reluctantly decided to send it to my father. Reliving every day of that journey had troubled me; it unsettled every relationship I was in with the ripple effect of an incomplete healing. Consequently, I avoided all contact with him for the fourteen months while I was writing. I also thought he would push my memories off course. Over the years, he would tell stories of our journey I could not remember, and would shake his head at versions of events I recalled. It was as if we had been on entirely different trips. I spent the 20th June 2015 editing a final version to print, bind and send via post. It was a Friday but after arriving at the courier desk in the print shop with the wrong version of the manuscript, I decided to wait until the following week. Two days later I was on a plane heading to Austria to prepare to bury my dad. On Saturday the 21 June 2015, just past 9am, he died of a massive heart attack. It was over quickly, just the way he would have wanted it to be.

In preparing for his funeral, I was forced to acknowledge that I had continued to yearn for his empathy and maybe even an apology for what he had done. This book was meant to be my version of the events in my life, and it was to have been delivered to him with as much expectation of reconnection as the trip itself. That was not to be.

Despite all my rationale and colourful interpretations of how the journey had healed me, I was still, on the day that he died, an 11-year-old boy, seeking redemption. In his death, that finally changed. A regrettable, final permission to move on.

Acknowledgements

I am forever indebted to my writers' group; a witty, warm and reassuring bond of writers who have supported my journey throughout. With their enthusiasm, energetic appreciation and sage advice, I endured the many periods of doubt and anguish.

Thank you to the leader of our group, Cathy Eden, and to my fellow wordsmiths: Rob Peters, Ellen Fitzpatrick, Jill Ritchie, Helen Faure, Jeanette Kroon and Sue Brown.

For fourteen years, my wife Shaune had nudged and prodded me towards writing this book. I offered countless excuses as to why I could not. In the end, at seemingly the most poignant time, she gently edged me forward onto a writing course, and I found a flicker of confidence to give this project the commitment it deserved. She has been by my side for most of my post-trip life and has witnessed the seen and unseen joys and wounds of my complex paternal bond. She is very much a partner in this book, from editing to designing, she has tirelessly offered her time and interest to every aspect of this journey. Above all, she has been there with grace and patience towards me when I swam in the murky confusion and sadness of an unfulfilled longing. She celebrates my emerging wholeness with me and I will be forever grateful for that safety and space to heal.

The neighbourhood Farewell, Villach Austria

Camping on the Hungarian Border

Austrian Autobahn

Marmaris, Turkey

My other
travelling partner

Breakdown,
Southern Turkey

Storm, Central Tanzania

River Crossing, Central Malawi

Maintenance, Monkey Bay, Malawi

Kalahari Highway,
Botswana

Christmas Meal,
1999,
Gobabis,
Namibia

Thunderstorm
Approaching,
Botswana

My Bike,
after 20 000km

Breakdown,
Northern Cape,
South Africa

Home,
Table Bay,
Cape Town